CAMBRIDGE STUDIES IN EARLY MODERN HISTORY

Editors

J. H. ELLIOTT AND H. G. KOENIGSBERGER

The Kingdom of Valencia in the Seventeenth Century

T0381677

CAMBRIDGE STUDIES IN EARLY
MODERN HISTORY

Edited by Professor J. H. Elliott, The Institute for Advanced Study, Princeton, and Professor H. G. Koenigsberger, King's College, University of London

The idea of an 'Early Modern' period of European history from the fifteenth to the late eighteenth century is now widely accepted among historians. The purpose of the Cambridge Studies in Early Modern History is to publish monographs and studies which will illuminate the character of the period as a whole, and in particular focus attention on a dominant theme within it, the interplay of continuity and change as they are represented by the continuity of medieval ideas, political and social organization, and by the impact of new ideas, new methods and new demands on the traditional structures.

The Kingdom of Valencia
in the Seventeenth Century

JAMES CASEY

Lecturer in History, University of East Anglia

CAMBRIDGE UNIVERSITY PRESS

CAMBRIDGE

LONDON   NEW YORK   MELBOURNE

CAMBRIDGE UNIVERSITY PRESS
Cambridge, New York, Melbourne, Madrid, Cape Town, Singapore, São Paulo, Delhi

Cambridge University Press
The Edinburgh Building, Cambridge CB2 8RU, UK

Published in the United States of America by Cambridge University Press, New York

www.cambridge.org
Information on this title: www.cambridge.org/9780521219396

First published 1979
This digitally printed version 2008

A catalogue record for this publication is available from the British Library

Library of Congress Cataloguing in Publication data
Casey, James, 1944–
The Kingdom of Valencia in the seventeenth century.
(Cambridge studies in early modern history)
Bibliography: p.
Includes index.
1. Valencia – History.   2. Valencia – Economic
conditions. I. Title.
DP302.V21C37   330.9′46′7605   77-88669

ISBN 978-0-521-21939-6 hardback
ISBN 978-0-521-08404-8 paperback

Contents

Illustrations

Preface

In this kind of study one is tied hand and foot without the help and guidance of the local people. My first and greatest debt is to the Valencians themselves, than whom no people could have been warmer, more open or more welcoming. In more senses than one this is their book. Sebastián García Martínez has been a much-needed friend over the years in which this study was in preparation. The late Joan Reglà, Peregrín Lloréns, Luis Cerveró and Thomas Glick helped open many doors for me, which would surely have stayed closed without their generous assistance. Jordi Nadal, Emili Giralt, Joan Fuster, Alvaro Castillo and José María López Piñero gave much time to discussing and focusing my early ideas on Valencian history. And more recently Dámaso de Lario, Pau Ferrer and Ricardo García Cárcel have done their best to keep me up to the mark in this respect. My debt to all those hard-working and hospitable archivists whom it has been my good fortune to come across in Valencia, Barcelona, Madrid and Seville is an outstanding one. Though it is invidious to single out names, I feel I should record the exceptional facilities for research which were given to me by José Sánchez Adell of Castellón, Joaquín González Moreno of Seville, Emilio Marín of Pedralba, Francisco Tormo of Orihuela and Rosa Rodríguez and her staff of Valencia. Henri Lapeyre and Tony Wrigley gave much needed advice on demographic questions, Richard Ling argued with me about Valencian economic development, and Helmut Koenigsberger forced me to remember that Valencia is, after all, part of Europe. To John Elliott, who supervised the original research for this study, and who has been a good friend and guide over the years, goes a very special vote of thanks.

The fieldwork in Spain was financed by a postgraduate studentship from the Ministry of Education for Northern Ireland, by the Research Funds of the Universities of Sheffield and East Anglia, and by a Vicente Cañada Blanch Senior Fellowship.

For Josyane, Manuel and Nicolas

Abbreviations

ACA CA	Archivo de la Corona de Aragón, Consejo de Aragón
ACV	Archivo de la Catedral de Valencia
ADM	Archivo de los Duques de Medinaceli
AHN	Archivo Histórico Nacional
AMA	Archivo Municipal de Alcira
AMC	Archivo Municipal de Castellón de la Plana
AMG	Archivo Municipal de Gandía
AMO	Archivo Municipal de Orihuela
AMS	Archivo Municipal de Sevilla
AMV	Archivo Municipal de Valencia
CM	Cartas Misivas
MC	Manuals de Consells
APQL	Archivos Parroquiales, Quinque Libri
APV	Archivo de Protocolos de Valencia
ARV	Archivo del Reino de Valencia
B	Bailía
G	Generalidad
MR	Maestre Racional
R	Real
BL	British Library
BN	Biblioteca Nacional
BUV	Biblioteca de la Universidad de Valencia
RAH	Real Academia de Historia

A note on measures

Coinage: 12 *diners* = 1 *sou*, 20 *sous* = 1 *lliura*
For most of our period the Castilian ducat was reckoned at about 21 *sous*.

Volume: 4 *almuts* = 1 *barchilla*, 12 *barchillas* = 1 *cahiz*
Though the equivalents vary slightly from one part of Valencia to another, a *cahiz* is roughly equal to 2 hectolitres.

Surface area: 6 *fanegadas* = 1 *cahizada*
A *cahizada* is very roughly equivalent to half an hectare.

Authorities
Earl J. Hamilton, *American Treasure and the Price Revolution in Spain 1501–1650* (Cambridge, Mass. 1934).
José Manuel Casas Torres, introduction to Antonio Joseph Cavanilles, *Observaciones sobre la Historia Natural, Geografía, Agricultura, población y frutos del Reyno de Valencia,* 2nd edn (2 vols., Zaragoza 1958).

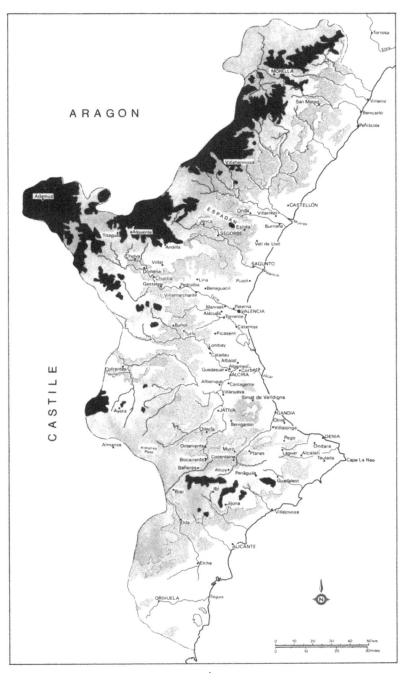

ARAGON

CASTILE

MORELLA

Tortosa

EBRO

Vinaroz

Benicarló

Peñíscola

San Mateo

Villahermosa

ESPADÁN

Onda

Villarreal

CASTELLÓN

Jerica

Eslida

Burriana

Mijares

Titaguas

Alpuente

SEGORBE

Vall de Uxó

Andilla

Chelva

Villar

Domeño

Chulilla

Gestalgar

Liria

Puzol

Pedralba

Benaguacil

Villamarchante

Turia

Sagunto

Valencia

Manises

Paterna

Alacuás

VALENCIA

Buñol

Torrente

Turís

Picasent

Catarroja

Lombay

Cataldau

Albalat

Cofrentes

Guadasuar

Algemesí

Corbera

Alberique

ALCIRA

Jucar

Ayora

Carcagente

Villanueva

Almansa

Almansa
Pass

Onteniente

Ontenente

JÁTIVA

Simat de Valldigna

GANDIA

Oliva

Villalonga

Benigánim

Pego

DENIA

Muro

Planes

Ondara

Bocairente

Cocentaina

Laguar

Alcalalí

Teulada

Cape La Nao

Bañeres

Alcoy

Peñáguila

Guadalest

Biar

Ibi

Jijona

Eda

Villajoyosa

ALICANTE

Elche

ORIHUELA

Segura

N

0   10   20   30   40   50 km

0   10   20   30 miles

xi

Introduction

The Kingdom of Valencia is a narrow strip of rugged territory, roughly half-way down the Mediterranean coast of Spain, and encompassing the modern provinces of Castellón, Valencia and Alicante. The region has a fairly distinctive geographical personality; it consists of a series of small coastal plains ringed by mountains – the Iberian chain to the north, the Sub-Baetic to the south, and between them the foothills of the Castilian plateau. It also, at one time, had a political life of its own – marked by an official birthday in 1238 when Jaime the Conqueror seized the city of Valencia from the Moors, and an official death in 1707 when another, less benign conqueror, Philip V, abolished its autonomy after it had backed the wrong candidate in a disputed succession to the Spanish throne.[1] These 500 years of independence have left the Valencians with a split personality and with the problem of coming to terms with their own history. Are they a nation as their political past would suggest, or a part of a greater Catalonia as the language (at least of the coastal zone) and the culture would imply, or just an extension of Castile to which their economy has always been tightly linked (Valencia is, after all, the nearest seaport by rail from Madrid)?[2]

Invertebrate Spain has been a medley of autonomous and conflicting cultures – Jewish, Moorish, Catalan and Basque – and the relationship between centre and periphery is one of

---

[1] There is a fine introduction to the early days of Valencian history in Robert Ignatius Burns, S.J., *The Crusader Kingdom of Valencia: Reconstruction on a Thirteenth Century Frontier* (Cambridge, Mass. 1967), and other works by the same author. On the kingdom's demise, see H. Kamen, *The War of Succession in Spain 1700–15* (London 1969).

[2] A classic treatment of the Valencian 'predicament' – it is also without question the best short history of Valencia – is Joan Fuster, *Nosaltres els Valencians* (Barcelona 1962).

the enduring problems of Spanish history. When Spain had an empire, the revolts of the Catalans and Portuguese against Castilian hegemony were among the clearest distress signals announcing the end of a Golden Age of imperial greatness.[1] J. H. Elliott's exploration of the Revolt of the Catalans in 1640 was at the origin of my own initial interest in that other peripheral province, Valencia. But since there was no 'revolt of the Valencians', my task – of explaining why something which might have happened did not in fact materialize – always remained a rather nebulous one. The political life of seventeenth-century Valencia proved particularly hard to grasp and seemed singularly lacking in historical relief. Yet the very monotony of the political records carried with it its own fascination. Valencia was an autonomous province, like Catalonia, and subject to the same pressures in the 1620s and 1630s, when Philip IV and his favourite, Olivares, began working for the greater fiscal and military integration of the various parts of Spain. If the economic decline of the empire was a prime factor throughout – spurring both the government's search for fresh sources of revenue and the people's determination to resist – then Valencia seemed poised to go the way of Catalonia. For no other Spanish region had a worse record of demographic collapse, none had been hit so badly by that major upheaval in Spanish history, the expulsion of the Moriscos. In 1609 roughly one Valencian in three still obeyed in secret the law of Islam. The embarkation of these 'other Valencians' for North Africa, begun that autumn and virtually completed by the beginning of 1610, left the region stripped of manpower and economically exhausted.[2] Yet Valencia went on to shoulder a military burden which Catalonia, Naples, Sicily and Portugal tried to throw off.

In trying to explore the roots of Valencian stability (or passivity), I was led into an analysis of the whole social and political structure of the province. Was the Valencian economy really as weak after the expulsion of the Moriscos as historians

[1] J. H. Elliott, *The Revolt of the Catalans: A Study in the Decline of Spain* (1598–1640) (Cambridge 1963).
[2] There is no good study of the expulsion, but Henri Lapeyre, *Géographie de l'Espagne morisque* (Paris 1959) provides a first-rate coverage of the demographic background. The best survey of the problem is Juan Reglá, *Estudios sobre los moriscos* (Valencia 1971).

– with the notable exception of Hamilton – tended to assume?[1] Who held the reins of power in the eastern kingdom, and what did they do with that power? These are the twin themes running through the present book: the nature of the much-debated 'decline' from which Valencia and all Spain seemed to be suffering, and the way in which a relatively stable political structure could be built on such apparently shifting sands.

[1] Earl J. Hamilton, *American Treasure and the Price Revolution in Spain 1501–1650* (Cambridge, Mass. 1934), 304–6, where evidence of price and wage stability after 1609 provided – and still provides – some of the few hard facts in the discussion.

1

A long depopulation

The survival of an Islamic culture despite the Catalan–Aragonese conquest of the early thirteenth century was one of the most decisive elements in the shaping of modern Valencia. To the south of the mountainous territory known as the Maestrazgo which lies along the frontier with Catalonia, the sierras were largely peopled by Moorish peasants working the land of their ancestors. The limits of the Christian Reconquest had been reached within about a century of the formal political take-over. Aragonese settlers had penetrated south and east along the Turia River as far as Chelva, occupying some difficult hill country, but failing to pierce the solid phalanx of Moorish communities which lay in a crescent-like formation around the central lowlands. These lowlands themselves had been taken from another direction, from the north by the Catalans.[1] Although after 1525 the mosques were all closed down – and largely knocked down as well after about 1574 – and Christianity was proclaimed the only lawful faith, an African culture continued to survive despite the efforts of preachers and inquisitors to root it out.[2] To ride up into the hills from the Valencian plain was to enter another world. The sierras always fell still by day and resounded with feasting by night during the traditional fast of Ramadan; ritual washing and circumcision appear to have been common enough even when the doctrinal content was missing;[3] but beyond the question of belief and

[1] A basic approach to the question is José Mª Font y Rius, 'La reconquista y repoblación de Levante y Murcia', in *La reconquista española y la repoblación del país* (Zaragoza 1951), 85–107.

[2] The incipient parish organization of the sixteenth century is exhaustively covered by José Sanchis Sivera, *Nomenclátor geográfico-eclesiástico de los pueblos de la diócesis de Valencia* (Valencia 1922).

[3] Peter Dressendorfer, *Islam unter der Inquisition: die Morisco Prozesse in Toledo 1575–1610* (Wiesbaden 1971), esp. chapter IV, 'Themen der Anklage'.

Table 1. *The population of the kingdom of Valencia in households* (*vecinos*)

	1565/72	1609	1642	1646	1692	1712/13
Moriscos	18,683	31,715				
Old Christians	44,894	65,016	63,548	61,324	(66,712)	62,852

SOURCES: 1565/72 and 1609: Lapeyre, *Géographie de l'Espagne morisque*, 18–47; 1642: ARV R 535 fols. 190 ff.; 1646: Pedro Pérez Puchal, 'La población del País Valenciano hasta la época estadística', Cuadernos de Geografía, 10 (1972), 23–30; 1692: AMV Churat 1636, document 146. The total here is actually only 49,545 households, because the city of Valencia and the coastal towns are omitted. I have added 7,167 households to cover the missing coastal communities and 10,000 for the capital city, which were the population figures for these areas in 1642; 1712/13: Gonzalo Anes, *El Antiguo Régimen: Los Borbones*, Historia de España Alfaguara IV (Madrid 1975), 35. For a criticism of the reliability of the census of 1609, Pablo Ferrer, 'Los moriscos de la Corona de Aragón a través de las listas de embarque' (Tesina de Licenciatura, Universidad Autónoma de Barcelona, Facultad de Filosofía y Letras 1973–4).

ritual there was the strangeness of the environment itself. Fonseca exaggerated when he spoke of 'huts of thatch'.[1] In the more prosperous communities – Benaguacil within a few hours' ride of the metropolis, or Alberique in the fertile Júcar valley – there stood the solid stone houses of the Abenamirs and other Moorish leaders.[2] But up in the sierras the descriptions which have come down to us recall the typical clay and thatch *gourbis* of North Africa. In Cofrentes after the expulsion, the Morisco dwellings were found to be 'mostly poor affairs...all made of clay and plaster with no brick or stone'. Further north in the Vall de Uxó the Old Christian settlers protested they could not possibly live in the thatched houses of the Moriscos: 'these must be changed to brick and tile at once'.[3] Valencia of the sierras must have resembled inland Tunisia at the present day, with the quiet villages of earth walls and straw roofs fading into the brown of the landscape.

The end of a traditional Valencia which had survived from the fourteenth century with little basic change came on 22 September 1609. The proclamation of Philip III expelling the Moriscos from this part of the peninsula – a prelude to the

[1] Damián de Fonseca, *Justa expulsión de los moriscos de España* (Rome 1612), 170.
[2] ADM Segorbe leg. 61 n. 9, 'capitulació fermada de Benaguacil', 9 Oct. 1611; AHN Osuna leg. 1926 n. 2, *carta puebla* of Alberique, 14 March 1612.
[3] AHN Osuna leg. 562 n. 33, *carta puebla* of Cofrentes, 1611; ADM Segorbe leg. 62 n. 5, 'memorial de lo que dizen los pobladores de la Vall de Uxó'.

general expulsion from the rest of Spain the following year – created an upheaval of colossal dimensions. With the removal of the Moriscos – 'this most barbarous act in the annals of mankind', as Richelieu termed it – Valencia lost nearly a third of its manpower (see table 1). Above all, the ring of Morisco hills from Cape La Nao inland and north to the Sierra de Espadán lay empty. In Cofrentes the handful of Christian settlers were allowed to hunt the 'partridges, rabbits and hares', now too numerous for the seigneurial guns; in Chiva, so Cavanilles tells us, the whole territory lapsed for a century or more 'into rustic woodland, prowled only by the wild beasts'.[1] As late as 1691 the Marquis of Castel Rodrigo, accustomed to depopulation in his native Castile, had to use the superlative *despobladísimo* to convey adequately his impression of Valencia.[2]

But to blame all the kingdom's troubles on the fact that it was bled of manpower in 1609 is to forget that the old communities actually had a fairly respectable rate of recovery. The Morisco villages (omitting here the ghettos of large Christian towns which were swallowed up after the expulsion) boasted something like 23,045 families in 1609; they had been repopulated by 8,344 Christian families by 1646 and by 13,044 by the time of the census of 1692. In other words, by the end of the Habsburg period about one in two of the old thatched *gourbis* were actually occupied. Some of this recovery was due to immigration. A few Castilians and Aragonese made the trip across the frontier and settled in and along the route down from their highland homes to the Mediterranean; a few Majorcans and even some Genoese (brought in by the seventh Duke of Gandía, brother-in-law to Prince Doria) made the trip in the opposite direction, from the sea up into the coastal foothills behind Cape La Nao. And there were the French – 'those flocks of transhumants who would exchange the rigours of their own land for the peace and plenty of Christian Spain', in the words of the chronicler Escolano.[3] There were 14,000 or 15,000 of them

---

[1] AHN Osuna leg. 562 n. 33, *carta puebla* of Cofrentes, 1611; Antonio Joseph Cavanilles, *Observaciones sobre la Historia Natural, Geografía, Agricultura, población y frutos del Reyno de Valencia*, 1795–7, 2nd edn (2 vols., Zaragoza 1958), II, 42.

[2] ARV R 593 fols. 342 ff., to the king, 1691.

[3] Gaspar Escolano, *Décadas de la Historia de la Insigne y Coronada Ciudad y Reyno de Valencia*, 1610–11, 2nd edn by J. B. Perales (3 vols., Valencia 1878–80), I, 100.

in Valencia around 1600, equivalent to about one in twenty of the Old Christian population at the time.[1] But immigration from France was declining rapidly in the seventeenth century as population pressure slackened on the other side of the Pyrenees. At the declaration of war on Richelieu's regime in 1635, there appear to have been about 10,000 recent French immigrants in Valencia (equivalent then to one in thirty of the population); and by 1691, at the beginning of the war of the League of Augsburg, the viceroy assured Madrid that there were only 2,000 people of French origin in the eastern kingdom.[2] The story of French immigration into Valencia has really still to be written. But it appears that they were never a major element in the resettlement of the Morisco villages as such. They would have fitted rather awkwardly into these closed little communities had they come to take land. In fact, of the nine French who were found in Valldigna in 1635, six were lackeys of the lord abbot, and one 'a poor beggar lad'.[3] Most tended to hang around the cities and big towns as coachmen or domestic servants, while those who handled a spade were frequently agricultural labourers.[4]

The resettlement of the old communities was done over-whelmingly on a local basis. To replace the 130 Morisco families of the hill village of Catadau there arrived 46 settlers, of whom only 7 were from outside the kingdom (3 from Aragon, 3 from Galicia and 1 from Ibiza). Of the 46 families settling in Pedralba and Bugarra, 14 came from beyond the frontiers (6 from Aragon, 4 from Castile, 1 from the Basque Country and 3 from the Languedoc). More significantly, 17 of the 46 came from the local *comarca* – from the towns and villages of Chulilla, Titaguas, Chelva, Andilla, Liria and Villar which lie within a 40 kilometre radius to the north-west. It was as if the spearhead of the old Aragonese advance of the fourteenth century, halted by the Morisco phalanx half-way down the Turia, had resumed its

[1] Jordi Nadal and Emili Giralt, *La population catalane de 1553 à 1717* (Paris 1960), 165.
[2] Calculations based on ACA CA legs. 589 and 716, documents of 4 June 1637, and 15 Jan. to 20 Oct. 1639, ARV MR 9338 (licences to French residents), and ARV R 593 fols. 342 ff., Castel Rodrigo to king, 1691.
[3] ARV Clero leg. 770, residence permits in Valldigna, 5 Jan. 1639.
[4] See the fascinating article by Abel Poitrineau, 'La inmigración francesa en el reino de Valencia: siglos XVI a XIX', *Moneda y Crédito*, 137 (June 1976), 103–33, which was kindly shown to me by Alfonso de Otazu while still in proof.

secular march to link up with the Catalans on the plain. In the ghetto of Oliva, down on that plain, a massive two-thirds of the new families were from just across the wall in the old town.[1] There is nothing very surprising in all this. Structurally the eastern provinces are not zones of high immigration.[2] The region is mostly mountainous, and its small oases of intensive cultivation tend to recruit their manpower from these native hills even at the present day. Anyway there was not a great deal of rich land in Valencia after the expulsion, and certainly no El Dorado of the kind which would have justified the sheer cost of planned immigration. The Moorish communities had often been situated, as Fonseca noted, 'in rough and mountainous places, where these savages chose to live the better to flee the company of Catholics'.[3] The people who would replace this expelled race were their immediate neighbours, local mountain men who knew the sierras, though by the accident of ancestry they happened to be Old Christians.

This limited redistribution of population was accomplished in roughly three stages, if we may judge from the specific example of the parish registers of Pedralba: a massive influx of settlers in 1610–11, on the morrow of the expulsion; a very high turnover in the first generation until about 1630, with more new people arriving and others moving out; and finally a period of stability and internal growth after about 1630–40, with those families already there staying put and only a very limited immigration from outside. These successive phases are reflected in the baptismal curves of three selected resettlements, Pedralba, Domeño and Ondara (see figure 1).[4] The instability which characterizes these and the other new communities in the first generation was to some extent due to the unsatisfactory arrangements for paying off mortgages and debts inherited

[1] AHN Osuna leg. 722 n. 6, *carta puebla* of Catadau, 1611; APQL Pedralba and Bugarra 1610–1714; Antonio Mestre, 'Estudio de la demografía de Oliva a través de los archivos parroquiales después de la expulsión de los moriscos', *Estudis*, I (1972), 180. And cf. J. R. Torres Morera, *Repoblación del Reino de Valencia después de la expulsión de los moriscos* (Valencia 1969), 73.
[2] Jordi Nadal, *La población española: siglos XVI a XX* (Barcelona 1966), 190–9.
[3] *Justa expulsión*, 170.
[4] The figures for Ondara were collected by a member of Professor Jordi Nadal's seminar group in Valencia. I am grateful to Professor Nadal and the Departament d'Història Econòmica, Universitat Autònoma de Barcelona, for permission to reproduce them here.

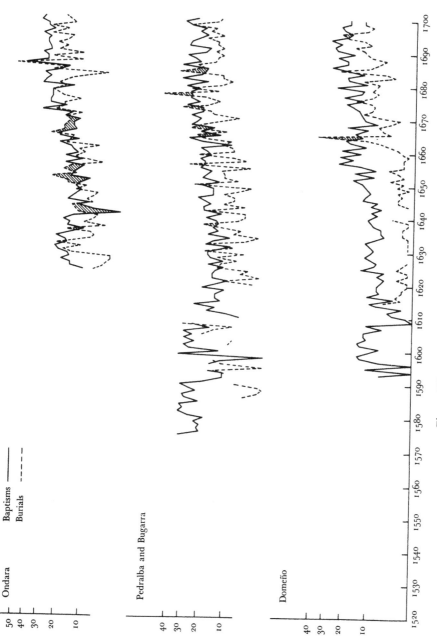

Fig. 1. The growth of the resettlements

from Morisco times. The Crown inexcusably held up a proper resettlement of the Moorish quarter of Játiva until 1623, for example, because it could not agree with prospective immigrants about who should pay these old obligations. In the meantime people from the old town entered the ghetto to strip off 'tiles, bricks, doors, windows and wood' from the Morisco houses.[1] More generally it was the barons who were saddled with the responsibility for Morisco debts, but they took their revenge by keeping the resettlements as dilapidated as possible, so as to force their creditors to come to reasonable terms – 'which is why...the villages are going to rack and ruin', as one disconsolate observer noted in 1624.[2] With the gradual solution of this problem of Morisco and seigneurial debts during the 1620s and 1630s the resettlements could at last begin to breathe.

Their subsequent, relatively fortunate history went against the demographic trend within the kingdom as a whole. The non-resettlement areas actually dropped from 73,686 households on the eve of the expulsion to 52,980 by 1646. Part of the loss was due to the exodus of 8,670 Moors from the ghettos of the big Old Christian towns – but only part. Nor did these communities recover so decisively in the later seventeenth century, having only about 53,668 families by the time of the census of 1692. Their demographic history is that of so many other areas of the Iberian Peninsula – a halting of the upward trend of expansion which had characterized the age of Charles V and the young Philip II by about 1580, and then a sharp decline in the seventeenth century. We can give slightly greater precision to this picture of ebb and flow by focusing on a specific series of Valencian communities, almost all Old Christian, which paid certain ancient poll taxes to the crown, and for which there exists a splendidly full run of censuses (see table 2).

So it would appear that for Valencia, as for Castile, there was something of a golden age around the middle of the sixteenth century. As the commissioners for the census of 1561 commented: 'by the grace of the Lord in the present time this

[1] ACA CA leg. 640 n. 4/71, Julián Gil Polo to king, 29 Jan. 1619.
[2] ACA CA leg. 869, petition of don Francisco Roca, ambassador of the Estates, 23 Oct. 1624.

Table 2. *Households in the taxed communities*

Date	Number of households	Date	Number of households
1505	13,022	1602	23,830
1561	17,871 (nobles and clergy missing)	1608	24,766
1565/72	19,121	1617	23,195
1571	23,206	1632	22,568
1584	24,029	1638	22,962
1589	24,787	1646	19,893

SOURCES: ARV MR 10405–6, 10413, 10881, 10894, 10897, 10899, 10903–5. For a discussion of these censuses, see James Casey, 'Moriscos and the Depopulation of Valencia', *Past and Present*, 50 (1971), 20–1. These sources have also been exploited by Alvaro Castillo, 'La coyuntura de la economía valenciana en los siglos XVI y XVII', *Anuario de Historia Económica y Social*, II.2 (1969), 4–13.

kingdom of Valencia enjoys very great prosperity and abundance'. Such optimism dissolved within about a decade, leaving only the bitter taste of disappointment in the mouths of every subsequent writer. One can see the reason for the stagnation of population in the censuses after 1570–80 by consulting the records of vital events in the Valencian parishes. The curve of baptisms had virtually reached its peak by 1585, if not before, in nearly all the agrarian towns. The three which appear on figure 2, Pego, Algemesí and Santa María de Cocentaina, are typical of the general trend. In the seaports, with their independence of the agricultural environment, growth may have continued longer, to 1607 in Alicante, to 1630 in Denia – though in the case of the latter the picture is complicated by the exceptional favours which this town received at the hands of its master, the great Duke of Lerma, who kept the customs artificially low after 1604 when he was handed them as a present by his doting sovereign, Philip III (see figure 3).[1] To the stagnation which sooner or later overtook all the Old Christian towns, there succeeded a phase of decline, from 1610 in Pego and Cocentaina (no doubt due to the exodus of part of their inhabitants to populate the empty Morisco villages which lay

[1] In general growth may have continued longer in the more southerly parts of Valencia; cf. Vicente Gozálvez Pérez, 'Notas sobre demografía de la provincia de Alicante', *Saitabi*, XXII (1972), 149–99.

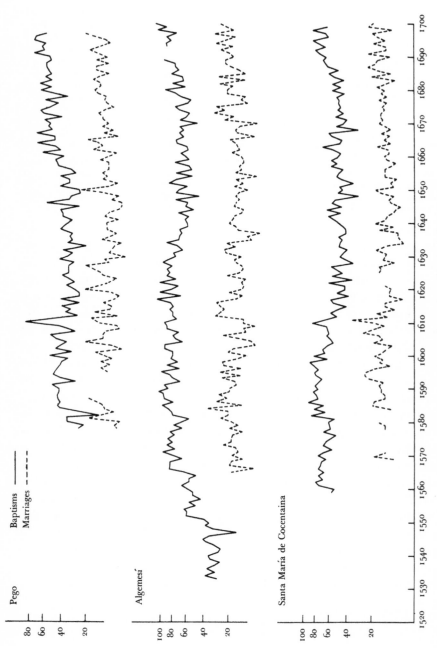

Fig. 2. Baptisms and marriages in Old Christian towns

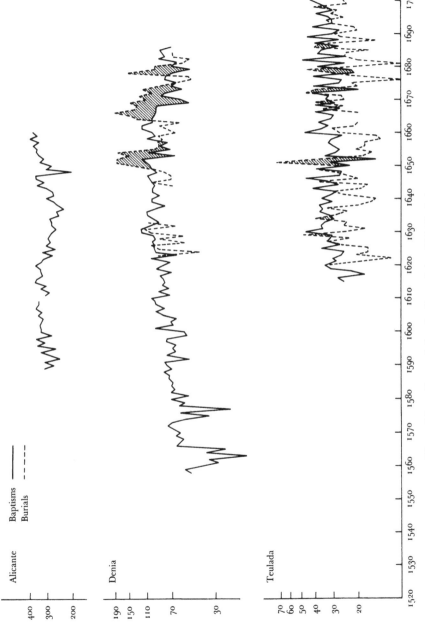

Fig. 3. Mortality and the decline of the Old Christian towns

all around them), from 1620 in Alicante (coinciding with the down-swing in the Seville trades and the onset of depression in the international economy). Denia continued to mark time after 1630, relatively strong still as a semi-free port, but then entered upon its period of crisis after 1649 with the resumption of the Lerma concession by the Crown, and particularly after 1674 when the customs were put under the general administration of the Valencian tax-farmers who were resolved to tighten up any loopholes.[1]

So, balancing the gains of the resettlements against the losses of the older populated areas, Valencia struggled through the seventeenth century with only about two-thirds of her old manpower. Why did the resettlements not do better? Why did the 'very great prosperity and abundance' of 1561 turn to ashes elsewhere? These were the great questions which contemporaries, like later historians, found themselves asking. Many studies tend to stress the growing toll taken by high mortality in the seventeenth century.[2] The black century of Spain's decline was punctuated by plague (the main outbreaks to affect the eastern provinces were those of 1647–52 and 1676–8; that of 1599–1600 which ravaged Castile had only a slight impact here, mostly along the trade route used by the Valencian silk merchants going to Toledo).[3] The great plague of 1647–52 killed something like 16,789 people in the city of Valencia (perhaps one in five of the citizen body), and 30,000 in the kingdom (perhaps one in seven or eight of the population).[4] On top of sickness came war, particularly after 1635 when with the all-out struggle against Richelieu's France Valencia lost for a couple of decades its traditional immunity from conscription. The Marquis of Castle Rodrigo was sure that Valencia's problems stemmed to a large extent from 'this old war in Catalonia', and from the continual Berber raids along the exposed south-east coastline; he also blamed the losses which the vendetta-prone

[1] ARV B 132, Farm of the Peatge and Quema, 1649.
[2] Most recently María del Carmen González Muñoz, *La población de Talavera de la Reina (Siglos XVI-XX)* (Toledo 1975), 228–35.
[3] AMV MC 126, acts of the *jurats*, May 1599 to April 1600.
[4] Francisco Gavaldá, *Memoria de los sucesos particulares de Valencia y su Reino en los años 1647 y 1648, tiempo de peste* (Valencia 1651), para. 33. On the plague in Alicante and Orihuela, ACA CA leg. 727, petition, 1 Aug. 1648, and AMO III/1/5.

Valencians inflicted on themselves, given 'the high incidence of murder and of condign chastisement for the same' in what was by general consensus the most bandit-ridden area of the peninsula.[1] Certainly the burial registers of the Valencian parishes have a grim enough tale to tell: 'a poor destitute, found in the river with no clothes on, with signs of having been struck on the head with a spade or a rock', Inés Vela, childless wife of Blas Martínez, done to death in the house of Jaime Rodrigo (who may have been her lover), the student Francisco Rosete shot down the same day as the woman he may have been paying too much attention to, the widow Villanueva. These are all examples from the quiet little hill village of Pedralba. In the seaport of Denia the record, as one might expect, is even more lurid, with an average of a murder a year for just under 500 families.

Apart from violence, Castel Rodrigo invoked an agent of depopulation dear to the hearts of Spanish economic writers of the Golden Age – celibacy. 'If you look in the parish registers for 1617 and 1618', suggested the *arbitrista* Sancho de Moncada, 'you will find there have not been half the marriages there used to be, and this is causing population to wither.'[2] The same message was being hammered home, meanwhile, in a slightly different way by the anti-Morisco lobby, who warned that this minority was in danger of outbreeding the Old Christians because they married so young and did not practise celibacy. 'They all used to get married', grumbled the Aragonese Aznar Cardona. 'They did not share the attitude of a Christian father of a family who would only marry off the heir and the eldest girl from among his five or six children, and get the others to become priests, nuns, friars or soldiers, or just stay chaste like a pious old maid.'[3] Part of the trouble afflicting the Spanish population, then, was held to be lack of marriage among the young.

Wishing to test out some of these hypotheses, I decided to do a reconstitution study of the families of one Valencian parish.

[1] ARV R 593 fols. 320 ff. and 342 ff., Castel Rodrigo to king, 1691.
[2] Sancho de Moncada, *Restauración política de España* (Madrid 1619), fol.20.
[3] Pedro Aznar Cardona, *Expulsión justificada de los moriscos españoles* (Huesca 1612), fols. 36–36v.

From among the 15 whose registers I had had the chance to examine, I picked out Pedralba with its annex Bugarra, villages which lie in a rugged and predominantly arid territory of grain and vine some 40 kilometres upstream on the Turia from Valencia, just below the point where the river emerges from the mountain gorges which straddle the frontier with Aragon. I was impressed initially here with the extreme care with which infant burials were recorded, usually the big omission in Valencian parish registers of the seventeenth century, which rule out so many of them for reconstitution studies. But in Pedralba, for example, one comes across entries like the following: baptism of 'Juan or Juana' Andrés, 19 March 1663 – 'the birth was a dangerous one, and the infant had to be snatched from the womb, which caused his death. He had been baptized three hours earlier.'

Pedralba and Bugarra were small communities, whose demographic history broadly follows that of the other resettlements. They had a maximum of 230 Morisco families on the eve of the expulsion in 1609, some 82 Old Christian by about 1646, and at least 121 by 1692, but more likely 145 according to the Rosary Guild ecclesiastical census of the year before. The occupational structure was relatively simple, the overwhelming majority of the inhabitants both before and after the expulsion being plain peasants. Both communities, however, supported a miller, a tailor, a weaver (the main garments seem to have been made out of canvas), a surgeon barber, a midwife (always an Old Christian), the priest and the seigneurial agent who was generally the notary. The Moriscos typically enough had a potter, who disappeared after the expulsion, whereas the Old Christians found it necessary to hire a couple of masons and a carpenter to attend to their more elaborate dwellings, and even by the early 1700s a resident doctor of medicine. There were probably no large fortunes in the parish. Felix Badal, son or brother of the seigneurial agent, rose to be a *ciutadà* (that is, a 'citizen' enjoying rentier status) by 1616, but the family then promptly disappeared from the village. Catalina Ortiz married Miguel Muedra, the chief magistrate in the 1640s and a leading member of one of the very old families, already established before the expulsion. When he died she married Juan Jixón, who died penniless and had to be interred as a pauper. Given the prevalence of partible inheritance among all the children (a subject to which I shall return), there seems to have been a fairly rapid rise and fall of certain families within the space of a generation. Those who were likely to keep big properties together were the *ciutadans*, one of the marks of whose status was precisely the entailing of land on the head of the eldest son; but those who achieved that status tended to leave the village.

One major surprise: men and women married very young in seventeenth-century Pedralba, notwithstanding the impression to the contrary left by the anti-Morisco lobby. Of 196 brides whose date of birth could be traced after the expulsion, the average age was 20 years 7 months, with the modal or most common real age actually as low as 19. Only 16 girls got married at the age of 25 or over, which was the typical age among the peasantry of England and France at this period. By contrast 87 girls, or nearly half the total, married while still in their teens, the youngest aged only 14. The 165 men tended to wait rather longer, marrying on average at 24 years 7 months, with 24 also the most common real age. These youthful brides seem to have been a peculiar feature of Habsburg Spain, for round Valladolid too girls were marrying at 20 years 2 months, and even younger – at 19½ – in Zaragoza.[1] On Hajnal's classic scale, Spain falls very definitely into the category of a traditional society, separated from the economically progressive countries of north-west Europe which were all moving by 1600 towards a marriage age somewhere in the middle or late twenties.[2] The Iberian matrimonial structure remained medieval, more like that of fifteenth-century Tuscany, where three-quarters of the girls were married by the age of 20, than that of contemporary western Europe.[3]

[1] Bartolomé Bennassar, *Valladolid au siècle d'or* (Paris/The Hague 1967), 197; María del Carmen Ansón Calvo, 'Un estudio demográfico con ordenadores: la parroquia de San Pablo de Zaragoza de 1600 a 1660', *Estudios del Departamento de Historia Moderna* (Zaragoza 1976), 225–45. The later ages found in eighteenth-century Galicia by Baudilio Barreiro Mallón, 'Interior y Costa: dos muestras de una estructura demográfica antigua en la Galicia rural', *Actas de las I Jornadas de Metodología Aplicada de las Ciencias Históricas* (Santiago 1975), 387–411 have to be handled with caution since they appear to include ages at second marriage.
[2] J. Hajnal, 'European Marriage Patterns in Perspective', in D. V. Glass and D. E. C. Eversley, ed., *Population in History* (London 1965), 101–43.
[3] Christiane Klapisch, 'Fiscalité et démographie en Toscane 1427–30', *Annales ESC* 24 (1969), 1313–37.

Africa begins at the Pyrenees, so the old legend runs. Certainly one Spaniard of the time, the anti-Morisco propagandist Jaime Bleda (a native of Algemesí), would have pointed out that the Moors married even younger – they were an idle, improvident race which 'held girls of 11 and boys of 12 quite old enough to wed'.[1] The records for Pedralba from before the expulsion, like those of most Morisco parishes, are unfortunately too short and poorly kept for us to prove the point. In Pedralba's near neighbour, the mixed parish of Turís, I was however able to trace the date of birth of 6 Christian and 22 Moslem brides in the early 1600s. The Old Christians were marrying, true to form, at the age of 20, the Moriscos slightly earlier at 18 years 1 month. It is interesting to note that Vincent found a very similar age, 18 years 7 months, for the Morisco women of Extremadura in the late sixteenth century.[2] So it seems reasonably certain that the followers of Islam had a start of two years or so on their Catholic compatriots, who themselves married young by the standards of the European peasantry.

Describing the peculiarity of marriage habits south of the Pyrenees is perhaps easier than trying to explain them. Bleda had his own explanation for the Moors: 'they did not worry about a dowry for their daughters; instead it was the husband who endowed his wife with half his property'. This practice is laid down in Islamic law, and it does indeed appear to have been observed among the Valencian Moriscos. Three marriage contracts preserved in the Pedralba archive from before the expulsion show the bride's parents in each case giving a small sum of 40 to 60 *lliures* worth of jewels, clothes or money, while the groom turned over to his bride all or part of the house and land which he had just received from his own father. In this sort of situation one can see why girls might have married young, even if their husbands would tend to be correspondingly much older.[3] The youthful marriage characteristic of much of eastern Europe until recent times has also been attributed to a relative abundance of land, the equal rights of the male

[1] *Crónica de los moros de España* (Valencia 1618), 1024.
[2] Bernard Vincent, 'Les morisques d'Estrémadure au XVIᵉ siècle', *Annales de Démographie Historique* (1974), 431–48.
[3] APQL Pedralba 1594–6. Cf. R. Levy, *The Social Structure of Islam* (Cambridge 1957), 95–7.

children to inheritance, and above all perhaps the fact that they continued to live at home under their father's roof after marriage.[1]

The favourable land–labour ratio may explain early marriage in Pedralba and the other resettlements; but it is obviously inadequate to cover the heavily settled areas of the peninsula where the pattern seems to have been just the same. Nor could Valencian children count on living under the paternal roof after marriage. There were 623 men, women and children in Pedralba and Bugarra in 1691, divided up among 145 separate establishments.[2] In only one household is it likely that three generations were living together, including a married grandson. In fact it is clear from the evidence that as elder brothers married they left home and set up for themselves elsewhere, leaving the youngest son to inherit the family homestead – and the household lares, for it was the youngest who kept alive the memory of his dead parents by inscribing their names in the community-wide pool of spiritual favours, the Rosary Guild. From all that we know of the traditions and domestic architecture of peasant Valencia, any other conclusion would have been surprising. The average house of the medium Valencian peasantry of the seventeenth century was a small affair – one room on the ground floor (the *entrada*), a yard for cooking at the back, and at best a room with a mattress (rarely a bed) on the first storey.[3] Certainly it was physically possible to split this sort of accommodation, and we know that the Moriscos did so – one reason perhaps for their lower age at marriage. Women were frequently endowed under Islamic custom, as we have seen, with half the man's house, and often enough that half passed back to their own family when the husband died. For example, in Valldigna in 1606 we find a widow selling her half of a small peasant dwelling to two friends, who were to share it with the mother of one of them. The other half of the house,

[1] Helena Chojnacka, 'Nuptiality Patterns in an Agrarian Society', *Population Studies*, xxx, 2 (1976), 203–26.
[2] APQL Pedralba, 'Cofradía de Nuestra Señora del Rosario', 7 May 1691.
[3] See, for example, ARV Cleo leg. 770, inventory of Julià Moreno, 14 Jan. 1630. A good introduction to the Valencian rural habitat (though it deals mostly with the *barraca*, the typical eastern barn-shaped hut, which is actually a nineteenth-century development) is J. M. Casas Torres, *La Vivienda y los núcleos de población rurales de la huerta de Valencia* (Madrid 1944).

meanwhile, had been left by the dead husband to his own son
and heir.[1] Three separate families were now crowded into what
had been a one-family shack. But this sort of arrangement was
unknown among the Old Christians, and the cramped living
conditions it implied would have appalled them.

Actually the more one looks at individual case histories, the
more it appears that marriage at an early age in Old Christian
Pedralba reflected simply precocious independence. A lot of
the teenage brides, in fact, seem to come from homes where
one parent had died. Francisco Juste and Ana Maria Rodrigo
married in 1652. Their daughter Antonia Maria was born in
1655, a couple of months before her father's death; her
despairing mother married her off in 1670 when she had turned
15. Josep Navarro died in 1686 when his youngest daughter
was aged only five, and poor little Isabel was married off ten
years later when she had reached puberty. One notes the
matrimonial strategy of the widowed mother, who quickly got
rid of Isabel's elder sisters after their father's death, aged 17
and 20, keeping back her son Miguel, the support of the family,
to the end. Miguel was only allowed to bring a woman into the
house in 1702, at the age of 24, after his sisters were all settled.
As in most poor societies the world over, children were expected
to stand on their own feet early in life. Pere Ferrando had been
digging maize as a hired hand in Valldigna at 14 when he was
called to testify in a court case; and a fellow witness was a
whipper-snapper of 10.[2] When little Gregori Calvet died in
Denia in 1649, aged 10, the priest thought fit to note: 'he made
no will, for he was *sub potestate paterna*'.[3] The *pícaro* was no doubt
the product in part of these unstable families.

Widows and step-fathers and unwanted children were a
fundamental feature of Habsburg Spain – and not only of
Spain, of course. Micheline Baulant, in her fascinating study
of 'the family in smithereens' in the Ile-de-France, noted that
something like one marriage in three around 1700 was actually
a remarriage for one or both of the partners.[4] The proportions
are exactly the same for seventeenth-century Pedralba: one

[1] ARV Clero leg. 772, 'Llibre dels lluïsmes de la Foya Baixa', 12 Jan. 1606.
[2] ARV Clero leg. 770, Lloís Ripoll v. Joan Pío, 27 July 1641.
[3] APQL Denia, 16 Nov. 1649.
[4] 'La famille en miettes: sur un aspect de la démographie du xviie siècle', *Annales ESC*, 27 (1972), 959–63.

marriage in three. I focused for the purposes of reconstitution on 118 marriages contracted in the parish between 1623 and 1675. Of these, 77 were first-time unions, which lasted on average 19.7 years. In other words, a bride of 20 could expect to find herself a widow at around the age of 40. In fact, 50 men who were left widowers, and whose ages we know, were aged 43 on average when their first wives died; 52 women were left as widows at the age of 40. The medians here are the same as the arithmetical averages. As regards actual age at death (and given the smallness of our sample it seems just as well to view the situation from all angles) the picture is not quite so dramatic: 46 adult males whose ages could be traced died at 51, and 43 women at 47.[1]

The growth of Pedralba depended on youthful and universal marriage. Widowers generally took a new wife, having waited on average 16.5 months after the death of the old; widows too usually tried to find another husband, and remarried on average after 44.5 months. Several men and women in seventeenth-century Pedralba had been married three or four times, retaining (interestingly enough) a certain attachment to their earlier dead spouses, since these were always correctly listed after their name in the Rosary Guild. Just as people rarely stayed in the state of widowhood, so there were very few peasant bachelors or spinsters. Weisser in his study of the villages round Toledo remarked on the great prejudice against the single man who was only admitted to full membership of the community on marriage.[2] There were only 3 women listed in Pedralba and Bugarra in 1691 who were aged 35 or more and still unmarried, and no men. No doubt the inheritance customs of Valencia, which emphasize equal division of the land among the children, favoured universal marriage – unlike the situation in Catalonia or the Basque Country, where one might expect to find younger sons or daughters condemned to life-long celibacy because property always passed to a single heir.[3]

On the other hand there was never enough land in seven-

[1] The corresponding age at death for adults in the Beauvaisis at this time was 42 years; see P. Goubert, 'En Beauvaisis: problèmes démographiques du XVIIᵉ siècle', in *Clio parmi les hommes* (Paris/The Hague 1976), 143–4.
[2] Michael Weisser, *The Peasants of the Montes* (Chicago 1976), 81.
[3] See the details of peasant wills in seventeenth-century Valldigna in ARV Clero legs. 728, 730, 764 and 770. And cf. the pertinent remarks in Fuster, *Nosaltres els Valencians*, 191–2. On the Basques see Julio Caro Baroja, *Estudios sobre la vida*

teenth-century Valencia to meet all needs, and the bad agricultural conditions of the age fostered emigration. I followed the careers of the 110 daughters and 109 sons born to the couples who married in Pedralba before 1650. A third (76) died young before the age of 20. Probably another 9 should be added to this total since they escaped confirmation, which was administered to any living child at the time the bishop made one of his too-rare pastoral visits. That leaves 68 girls and 66 boys, of whom we know that 53 and 51 respectively eventually got married, most of them within the parish but some as emigrants; their names can be traced because the banns were called for them in Pedralba prior to the issue of a licence by the bishop to the officiating priest in their new place of residence. Thus 15 girls and 15 boys make no appearance at all in the register of either marriages or banns. It is therefore possible – though it is always dangerous to argue from the silence of the records – that as many as one in five men and women over the age of 20 never married. This finding does not contradict what I said earlier about the absence of celibates within the village: only 5 of the girls and 2 of the boys figure later in the registers of mortality as bachelors or spinsters, and none of that generation of 1623–50 was left as a celibate in the parish at the time of the Rosary count of 1691. What then happened to the others?

It is no doubt tempting to look to the cities with their swollen Counter-Reformation clerical body. Lapeyre suggests that there were 1,500 monks and priests in the 50,000 strong population of the metropolis – 'equivalent, perhaps, to one out of eight adults of the male sex'; but the assembly of the nobility gave an even higher figure around the time of the expulsion of the Moriscos – 150 rectors and vicars in the 12 city parishes, over 1,200 chantry priests (some of course in minor orders only, but all celibate), 1,250 monks and friars divided among 25 monasteries, 850 nuns in 17 convents, plus an unspecified number of canons in the cathedral. This is a total of at least 3,450 adult men and women, or, on Lapeyre's estimate, one in seven of the total adult population.[1] One wonders, though, how

tradicional española (Barcelona 1968), 154. On the Catalans see Elliott, *Revolt of the Catalans*, 28–32 and 36–9.
[1] Lapeyre, *Géographie*, 31; ARV R 527 fol. 403.

many of these could have been refugees from the countryside. When the nunnery of Santa Tecla listed its income for the royal commission on mortmain in 1617, it furnished a record of the dowries from new entrants; these ranged from 300 to 700 *lliures*. In addition to the dowry there was the expense of clothes, the furnishing of the cell and candles for the entrance ceremony, all of which had to be borne by the postulant's family and which could amount to another 200 *lliures*. A nun would, therefore, have to find anything from 500 to 1,000 *lliures* to subsidize her vocation – no mean sum when one considers that the lower figure represents a year's income for a wealthy peasant farmer and the higher the annual salary of a judge of the supreme court.[1] The Spanish clergy as a whole seems, in fact, to have been a much smaller body than has sometimes been assumed – perhaps 100,000 men and women all told, around 1600, in a population of 8,500,000, though the proportion was to grow in the seventeenth century.[2] What tended to happen was that it was concentrated thickly in the major urban centres like Valencia, though recruited very thinly from the topmost ranks of the rural bourgeoisie. The ordinary hill peasant of Pedralba would hardly have been able to penetrate this sanctuary, unless as a lackey to a canon, or a maid in a nunnery. It is probable that the missing emigrants from Pedralba, those who did not marry, sank into domestic service or into the urban underworld. The urban demography of Spain is little known, but one may assume on the analogy of French studies that such rural immigrants would have had a naturally long, hard road ahead of them before they could even contemplate matrimony.[3]

By way of summary, one may conclude that there seems to be some evidence from Pedralba to bear out the *arbitristas* when they complained about the flight from marriage in seventeenth-century Spain. This flight may have taken the form of a rural exodus, not into the convents but onto the highways to swell the bandit gangs which roamed Valencia, or into the towns to

[1] ARV MR 7935 and ARV Clero leg. 739. I am grateful to my colleague Morley Cooper for a discussion of these points.
[2] Antonio Domínguez Ortiz, *La sociedad española en el siglo XVII: el Estamento Eclesiástico* (Madrid 1970), 7.
[3] M. Garden, *Lyon et les lyonnais au XVIIIe siècle* abridged edn, Science-Flammarion (Paris 1975), esp. 115–16.

serve counts and canons (whose need for domestic servants was precisely one of the greatest forces pulling French immigrants into the kingdom).

The slow growth of the rural population seems to have been due to the lack of opportunity for marriage in the countryside, thanks to the low level of economic development. The actual living standards of the people are difficult to assess in our present state of knowledge, but there are a couple of demographic clues which may point to nutritional deficiencies. For example, fertility in Pedralba was surprisingly low for a re-settlement. Our 118 reconstituted marriages produced just 504 offspring, a ratio of 4.27 per couple, close to the 4.2 found by Bennassar round Valladolid but some way below the 4.6 of Goubert's Beauvaisis.[1] It is true that some other French ratios are as low as the Spanish, but then none of the French villages had the advantages of low population-density characteristic of seventeenth-century Pedralba. The early death of husband or wife was mostly to blame for these small families on both sides of the Pyrenees. But even in the case of the so-called 'completed' families of Pedralba, where a bride marrying for the first time was still in partnership with her husband at the end of her fecund period (reckoned here at age 50, although only 12 couples managed this!), the ratio is still just 7.5 children per couple, rather below the 8 which Goubert found for the Beauvaisis. If we look at birth intervals, we notice that the women of Pedralba waited rather longer than those of the Beauvaisis before having their first child – 20 months as against a little over 16 on average. This was partly (paradoxically enough) because the Spanish girls married so very young. Teenagers did not have a child until two full years after their marriage; where the bride was in her twenties, by contrast, this protogenesic interval fell to 17.3 months – indeed to only 15.9 months (close to the French figure) if we exclude one aberrant case of a 64-month interval, which weighs too heavily in our small sample.

Subsequent intergenesic intervals also tended to be rather longer in Pedralba than in the Beauvaisis – 32 as against just

[1] *Valladolid,* 197; Pierre Goubert, *Cent Mille Provinciaux au XVIIᵉ siècle* (Paris 1968), 58–9.

Table 3. *Age-specific fertility in Pedralba and Bugarra: marriages*
contracted 1623–75

Mother's age group (years of age)	Births per year of marriage per 100 women
15–19	28
20–24	40
25–29	36
30–34	36
35–39	27
40–44	11

under 29 months. The Pedralba rates are reassuringly close to those found by Bennassar for Valladolid, where the interval was again just over 33 months. In fact, this rather low fertility appears to have been a long-standing feature of Spanish society, which still in the nineteenth century (when more reliable information becomes available) had one of the poorest rates in Europe.[1] It is particularly surprising, no doubt, to find this wide spacing of births in a resettlement like Pedralba. The 32 months here have to be set against the 23 months characteristic of French settler families in Louis XIV's Canada.[2] Nor does it seem likely that voluntary contraception is to blame in seventeenth-century Spain – the birth intervals are too regular throughout the woman's life for that to be a serious possibility (see table 3).

If Spanish fertility was low, the explanation must lie in natural causes. This suspicion is confirmed by what we know of the Moriscos. Among contemporary observers, this race had the reputation of being extremely prolific. Fonseca, for example, described the Morisco women trooping forth to the ships for North Africa in 1609, clutching three or four infant *criaturas* to their breast 'like gypsies'.[3] While it is unfortunately impossible to reconstitute the marriages of Pedralba before the expulsion, something can be learned from observing the intervals between random births to the same couple. In this way

[1] M. Livi Bacci, 'Fertility and Population Growth in Spain in the 18th and 19th centuries', in D. V. Glass and R. Revelle, ed., *Population and Social Change* (London 1972), 182.
[2] Quoted in E. A. Wrigley, *Population and History* (London 1959), 94.
[3] *Justa expulsión*, 58.

118 likely birth intervals could be calculated for the period 1575–1608. The average works out at 29.3 months, somewhat lower than the figure for the Old Christians, but certainly not low enough to confirm Fonseca's impression that the Moriscos were breeding like rabbits. Behind the dry statistics, one senses the fatigue of a peasant population battling with the harsh Mediterranean environment. And this factor held good into the age of depopulation and land abundance after 1609. The settlers of Pedralba, we may recall, did not have as many children as the French settlers along the Saint Lawrence – there was no new world to be won in seventeenth-century Valencia.

Nor was there much in the way of illegitimacy. Bennassar has painted a picture of a Spain whose sexual mores were more irregular than those of northern Europe – as seems fitting in the homeland of Don Juan.[1] Certainly one finds Don Juans at the level of the Valencian aristocracy – at least 65 of the 600 or so nobles in the kingdom had one or more illegitimate offspring.[2] But they did not exist at the level of the peasantry – at least not in seventeenth-century Pedralba, where only 8 of the 2,116 baptisms occurring between 1610 and 1714 can be classed as either those of foundlings or of illegitimate children, a rate of 0.4 per cent which is close to that of old rural France. Pre-marital sex was slightly more common; of the 96 couples in our reconstitution sample who actually had any children, 7 produced their first child within 7 months of going to the altar. It is perhaps interesting to note that 4 of the 7 were widows. Morisco illegitimacy was considerably higher than this, though – 3.2 per cent of children were born out of wedlock in Pedralba before the expulsion, 1.8 per cent in Turís. And, for another thing, in the big towns bastards and foundlings were more common than in the countryside (1.8 per cent of births in Denia, for example). In general, the Valencian rates seem to correspond to the picture we have of western Europe as a whole; during the seventeenth century illegitimacy fell to quite low levels among the peasantry, probably because of the greater control exercised by a reformed Catholic and Protestant clergy

---

[1] Bartolomé Bennassar, *L'Homme espagnol: attitudes et mentalités du xvie au xixe siècle* (Paris 1975), 149–62.
[2] ACA CA leg.1372, fols.221–5v, 'legitimaciones por fueros', 1626.

Table 4. *The mortality of the young in Pedralba: offspring of marriages 1623–75*

Years of age	Deaths	Percentage of births
0–1	79	15.7
1–4	71	14.1
5–9	14	2.8
10–19	27	5.4
Total	191	38.0

over its flock.[1] In Valencia there was one further control – the vendetta, which was particularly prevalent in this area of the peninsula. Illegitimate children were actually often entered in the parish registers here simply as foundlings, though the mother was known. The practice reflects a conscious decision by the priests not to record the name of either parent 'for fear this would lead to trouble'.[2]

Despite the lowish rate of reproduction, Pedralba like the other resettlements did increase in population during the seventeenth century, and part of the reason is obviously the overall surplus of births over deaths (see figure 1). The rate of infant and child mortality suggests that, though the margin of survival was always precarious enough, yet some growth was assured. The figures in table 4 seem rather on the low side for pre-industrial Europe. And unfortunately checks with the confirmation records (which list even toddlers) confirmed my worst suspicions that there was some under-registration of infant deaths before 1650. To be absolutely on the safe side, we have little alternative but to confine our analysis to the children born to couples who married after that date. In this case 119 of the 285 offspring falling within this category died before the age of 20, a rate of 41.9 per cent – which is interestingly close to the figure of 43.51 per cent which characterized nineteenth-century Spain.[3] Thus, taking the most extreme case,

[1] Pierre Chaunu, *La civilisation de l'Europe classique* (Paris 1970), 196–7. And cf. González Muñoz, *Talavera de la Reina*, 195–6.
[2] *Coses evengudes en la ciutat y regne de Valencia: Dietario de Mosén Juan Porcar, capellán de San Martín (1589–1629)*, ed. Vicente Castañeda Alcover (2 vols., Madrid 1934), I, cap. 1710.
[3] Nadal, *Población española*, 178 and 181.

something like two out of every five children born in seven-teenth-century Pedralba could expect to die in childhood or adolescence.

How typical are the Pedralba rates? In two other Valencian parishes that I have studied – Denia and Teulada – the burial registers regularly include the *albats*, children who died before reaching the age of reason fixed by canon law, which works out (in most observable cases) at 7 years. By comparing the total of births with the total of *albats* over the century as a whole one can get a rough idea of mortality in the 0–7 years age group. This method gives a figure of 31 per cent in Pedralba itself, which is close enough to the true rate derived from family reconstitution. In Teulada, an Old Christian parish perched on the rocky coast near Cape La Nao, the rate is also 31 per cent. In the big seaport of Denia, 15 kilometres to the north of Teulada, it is a lot higher, at 43 per cent (see figure 3). But then Denia was a major urban centre, with the overcrowding and lack of hygiene characteristic of its kind. Possibly the same factors explain the relatively high mortality among the Moriscos of Pedralba before the expulsion. From the few fragments surviving of a burial record for this period, which belong to the years 1575–85, the Moriscos were losing 22.8 per cent of their new born children within their first year of life, and another 14 per cent before the age of 5.

The Morisco and Denia rates, of course, will be thought to be more in line with the classic picture which Pierre Goubert has sketched for the Beauvaisis, where infant mortality before the age of 1 was 28.8 per cent, and where only one child in two could expect to survive to adulthood.[1] But the French demographers have been making us aware in recent years of how extremely varied the experience of their countrymen actually was. In the Bas-Quercy in south-west France, for example, infant mortality was only 19.1 per cent, which is close to the Pedralba rate.[2] Indeed research on this region generally is revealing a family structure rather more like that of Pedralba than the Beauvaisis – girls commonly married at 21, and had rather few babies. In trying to explain the peculiarity of the

[1] *Cent Mille Provinciaux*, 62.
[2] P. Valmary, *Familles paysannes au xviiiᵉ siècle en Bas-Quercy* (Paris 1965), 145–54.

south-west, with its combination of low fertility and low child mortality, the French historians have possibly hit on part of the explanation for Valencia, too. The argument runs that low fertility contributes to a higher standard of infant care, as the mother finds more time to devote to the welfare of her baby, unencumbered by new pregnancies. And the operation works in reverse, for the longer-surviving infants of the south-west stay longer at their mother's breast, perhaps thereby impeding ovulation, or at the very least discouraging sexual intercourse between their parents.[1]

Goubert has spoken of the 'fragile demographic equilibrium' of the Ancien Régime, and the phrase will no doubt serve for Valencia too, if we accept that the balance was struck slightly differently. A higher survival rate, at least in the resettlements, had to be offset against lower fertility and fewer marriages. It has been said, of course, that the demography of the Ancien Régime follows a pattern of periodic crises of subsistence which checked the growth in numbers. The mechanism by which recurring harvest failure, accompanied from time to time by outbreaks of plague, wiped out population gains has been well described for France north of the Loire.[2] But it is doubtful how far this model is applicable to seventeenth-century Pedralba. The most serious blow which the resettlement had to face was the crisis of 1677, when plague and bad harvests struck Valencia. But in Pedralba deaths were most numerous in the first quarter of 1677, before the bad harvest of that year had a chance to bite (see figure 4). No doubt the wretched weather which was destroying the crops that spring accounted for most of the deaths – possibly assisted by plague. Despite the sharp rise in mortality there was no corresponding fall in conceptions; this suggests that whatever else was happening, the settlers of Pedralba were not victims of amenorrhea brought on by hunger.

It could hardly have been otherwise. After all, 40 kilometres downstream from Pedralba lay the great city of Valencia, into which poured the grain of Sicily and North Africa. At no time in the seventeenth century did the price of wheat there even

[1] Jean-Louis Flandrin, *Familles: parenté, maison, sexualité dans l'ancienne société* (Paris, 1976), 193–4.
[2] Goubert, *Cent Mille Provinciaux*, 68–82.

Fig. 4. Repopulated Pedralba: absence of the classic crisis of subsistence
(4-month intervals)

double from one year to the next.[1] The contrast could hardly
be greater with the violent oscillations characteristic of conti-
nental France, where famine could and did wreak havoc.
Valencia was a small maritime kingdom, and no part of it was
too far from the coast. In the terrible famine year of 1606, 'when
all over Spain people had to eat grass', Valencia (as her
chronicler Escolano proudly informs us) ate the wheat of Sicily.[2]
Paradoxically, it seems to have been because the kingdom was
so notoriously short of bread in normal years – the price level
was always the highest in Europe[3] – that harvest failures had
only a limited impact. Landlocked Bocairente, near the frontier
with Castile, was about as cut off from the sea as any part of
Valencia; yet in the early spring of 1617 local grain prices began
to fall, partly in anticipation of a good harvest, partly because
of 'the wheat arriving in Alicante day after day by sea'.[4] The

[1] Hamilton, *American Treasure*, appendixes III, IV and v.
[2] Escolano, *Décadas*, I, 368.
[3] Fernand Braudel and Frank Spooner, 'Prices in Europe from 1450 to 1750',
Cambridge Economic History of Europe, IV (1967), 395.
[4] ARV MR 5576, bailiff to Junta Patrimonial, 16 Feb. 1617.

is not to deny the essentially self-sufficient nature of the local economies of the interior, which was inevitable given the poor communications of the day, nor the great disparity in bread prices even within the limits of the kingdom from one *comarca* to the next, a disparity which survived even in the nineteenth century.[1] But it would seem that the classic crisis of subsistence has less relevance to the demographic history of Valencia than, say, to that of Castile.

That still leaves the great killer, bubonic plague, as a possible factor in the long depopulation of Valencia. Gavaldá estimated the losses from the epidemic of 1647–52 at 46,789 persons – say 17 per cent, or one in six of the total population. The figure seems enormous. But the epidemic of 1557–9 was alleged to have killed 30,000 men, women and children, which is equivalent to about 10 per cent of the population of the time.[2] Yet 1561 was to go down in the records as Valencia's time of 'very great abundance and prosperity', while the population continued to expand unchecked for another decade. René Baehrel has tried to demonstrate that plague had little impact on the movement of the population of Provence in the seventeenth and eighteenth centuries.[3] His argument may appear to go too far. Anyone looking at the curve of baptisms and burials in Denia (figure 3) cannot fail to be impressed with the savagely high mortality in this seaport and seek to relate it to the catastrophic decline of the town from 492 households in 1646 to 257 by about 1735. On the other hand the burial records begin too late, unfortunately, for us to be sure how exceptional late seventeenth-century mortality really was. Another of the extremely rare good series of death registers is that for Teulada, a victim of the plague of 1647–52, yet a town which was able to hold her population constant at 192 households in 1646 and 186 in 1735. It is tempting to think, just looking at the curves of births and deaths here, that Teulada had simply reached her natural limits of expansion under the old conditions of a subsistence economy.

[1] Cf. Josep Fontana, *Cambio económico y actitudes políticas en la España del siglo XIX* 2nd edn (Barcelona 1975), 24.
[2] *Libre de Memòries de diversos sucesos e fets memorables de coses senyalades de la ciutat e regne de València*, ed. S. Carreres Zacarés (2 vols., Valencia 1935), II, 869.
[3] *Une croissance: la basse Provence rurale (fin du XVIᵉ siècle – 1789)* (2 vols., Paris 1961), I, 247–50, 267–9, and 271. His thesis denies generally that rising mortality checked population growth.

Teulada was a poor hill village, with little but her barley and her almonds (in lieu of bread) to keep her people supplied with calories. Weisser has noted that it was the smaller, more cut-off communities like this which first experienced the onset of demographic stagnation in the late sixteenth century in the area he studied round Toledo.[1] A good *prima facie* case could equally well be made out for saying that what destroyed Denia was not high mortality (for that had been a constant feature of life in this unhealthy, crowded seaport) but the closure of economic opportunities for her population with the forfeiture of her status as a semi-free port.

The 'catastrophe' factor has its limits in explaining Valencia's decline. This is equally apparent if we examine the impact of war. For all the travails of the Spanish monarchy in the seventeenth century, it has to be remembered that Valencia was never invaded (though there were occasional French forays south from occupied Catalonia in the 1640s and pirate raids from Algiers were a continual irritation). Valencia did not support a big army on its own territory, and military recruitment was never a really significant factor. The official figure put forward by the ambassador of the kingdom at court in 1637 was 12,000 men taken for the Spanish armies over the past decade.[2] But there must have been around 65,000 young adult males in Valencia in any one year in the 1630s.[3] The loss of approximately 1,000 of these every year – say 2 per cent of the active male population – was hardly a very dramatic one.

There is perhaps a lot to be said for Baehrel's dictum on

---

[1] Michael Weisser, 'The Decline of Castile Revisited: The Case of Toledo', *Journal of European Economic History* 2.3 (Winter 1973), 627–8.

[2] ACA CA leg.715, memorial of Canon Verdalet, 1637. However the Estament Militar in a separate memorandum spoke of 30,000 over the last 7 years (*ibid.*). But the lower estimate is closer to the viceroy's figure of 14,000, ACA CA leg. 712, to king, 8 Aug. 1636.

[3] The calculation is as follows. The 10,000 households of the city of Valencia probably contained 50,000 persons, and the 53,548 households in the rest of the kingdom (figures as of 1642) some 240,966 persons, using a multiplier here of 4.5. About half of this total would have been males, say 145,483 individuals. The mortality rate in the 0–20 year age group in Pedralba was 41.9 per cent. We can go with this information to Ansley J. Coale and Paul Demeny, *Regional Model Life Tables and Stable Populations* (Princeton 1966), 791, Model South, Males, where Mortality Level 8 fits – very roughly – the Valencian case. There would have been about 44.75 per cent, according to this model, of the Valencian male population aged between 15 and 44 years of age, say 65,103 individuals.

seventeenth-century Provence: the movement of population was directly conditioned by the number of people getting married, and that was influenced by economic opportunity.[1] For example, in Algemesí, which lived by its silk trade with Toledo, the bad harvests, high cost of wage-labour after the expulsion, and the decline of Toledo itself, reduced local production by two-thirds in the early seventeenth century.[2] The result was a fall in marriages and baptisms, and ultimately in the number of people (figure 2). In Cocentaina it was the same story. The whole of the territory surrounding this big southern town, 50 or 60 kilometres inland from Alicante, had been dominated by a Moorish peasantry. This was authentic colonial country, where the Old Christians held a skeletal network of urban centres – Alcoy, Jijona, Penáguila, Cocentaina itself – which linked Alicante to Játiva and the north. The relay of goods along these roads was assured in part by Morisco muleteers, so that 'with the expulsion of the Moriscos...all trade came to a halt or at least the greater part of it'.[3] The disruption could have been overcome, but Cocentaina's financial position was already so precarious that any loss of footing was fatal. Like other seigneurial towns, it had saddled itself with debts on behalf of its feudal lord long before the expulsion. With the loss of his Morisco vassals, the feudal lord claimed he was bankrupt, with the result that his creditors seized the ploughs, beds and furniture of the people of Cocentaina, who were nominally responsible for the loans. 'The trade of this land is wool dressing', noted one observer, 'but with the distraints it has all ground to a halt.'[4] The collapse of the Cocentaina economy led inevitably to a fall in marriages and baptisms (figure 2).

'Our species', declared the great geographer Cavanilles towards the end of the eighteenth century, 'always rises or falls according to the abundance of the fruits of the earth.[5] This comment serves as an apt reminder of how difficult it is to separate the demographic troubles of Habsburg Valencia from the general context of the country's economic decline. The case

---

[1] Baehrel, *La basse Provence rurale*, 292.
[2] ARV Comunes 1060, viceregal mandate, 21 Oct. 1639.
[3] ACA CA leg. 869, 'información de testigos de la necessidad en que se halla la villa de Cocentaina', 4 Sept. 1624.
[4] *Ibid.*, 'información de testigos', 9 Sept. 1622.   [5] *Geografía*, I, p. x.

study of Pedralba, meanwhile, suggests how narrow the margin of survival was, even in a resettlement, which was protected against distraint and which enjoyed a relative abundance of land. The low fertility of the womenfolk, the fact that they were widowed at an average age of 40, and the disappearance of two out of every five of their children before adulthood, paint a rather sombre picture of the 'new' Valencia which was born after 1609. This society, where so many girls married in their teens, continued to bear the marks of poverty and under-development more typical of African Societies. In this sense the fewness of its people was surely both cause and consequence of a more general social and economic backwardness.

2

Rich and poor

It has become fashionable in recent years to link depopulation in traditional societies with a narrowing of the gap between rich and poor. Le Roy Ladurie has made us familiar with the growth of a comfortable middling peasantry in the depopulated Languedoc of the fifteenth century; and Vilar has hinted at a somewhat similar picture for rural Catalonia in the wake of the Black Death, with the survivors of the epidemic tending to regroup and concentrate their holdings.[1] But it would be difficult to paint the age of the later Habsburgs in the same golden hues. Caxa de Leruela, writing in 1632, noted how the depopulation of Castile went hand in hand with the squeezing out of the middling, active peasantry, to the benefit of the very rich.[2] Indeed, even in France the demographic stagnation of the seventeenth century brought more, not less inequality in landholding.[3]

The problem in analysing Spanish developments, of course, is the extreme paucity of quantitative studies. The materials are fragmentary, often repellent because of the long drudgery of calculations, and always dangerous given the sheer inadequacy of much of the information. The sources for a study of property in Habsburg Valencia can be grouped under four headings. The most useful is undoubtedly the *peyta*, a tax levied on all forms of visible property, principally land but also houses, mills, herds and the like. The valuations used were (like those

[1] E. Le Roy Ladurie, *Paysans de Languedoc*, abridged edn (Paris 1969), 23–34; Pierre Vilar, *Catalunya dins l'Espanya moderna* (4 vols., Barcelona 1964–8), II, 47.
[2] Miguel Caxa de Leruela, *Restauración de la antigua abundancia de España* (Madrid 1632), 72, 109, 139 and 258.
[3] This is the solidly documented thesis of Jean Jacquart, *La crise rurale en Ile-de-France 1550–1670* (Paris 1974).

of the *taille réelle*) stereotyped, making it impossible to follow fluctuations over time. Nevertheless these records provide a unique insight into the distribution of property at any given period.[1] Less satisfactory are the terriers or *capbreus* drawn up every so often by the senyors to validate their claims to rent. Frequently the lord making the survey was not lord of all the land in the village; frequently his own peasants held part of their property in the jurisdictional limits of another village.[2] But the greatest drawback was probably that the lands were only measured by superficial area, and rarely valued. In some cases, indeed, only the intensively irrigated huertas were measured, and the arid secano was ignored altogether. This was the case, for example, in Valldigna. In general, with seigneurial *cadastres* one is reduced to surveying merely the huerta, because bringing in the much larger unirrigated tracts simply distorts the whole system of measurement. In a few cases, such as Segorbe and Cocentaina, rentals in the seventeenth century were directly related to the value of the individual property, whereas over most of the kingdom (and particularly in the resettlements) a blanket share-cropping arrangement applied. Thus, for example, any holding on the Gandía estates will simply be listed as so many *fanegadas* of huerta, at 4 *sous* per *fanegada* and one-eighth of the grain harvested. But on the Segorbe and Cocentaina domains, the *sous* and the fixed measure of grain required from each field fluctuate according to the quality of the soil or type of crop, and provide a rough index of values.

The third category of land survey to be found in Habsburg Valencia was made in connection with the taxes which had to be levied from time to time in the irrigation zones for the upkeep of the canals. These taxes relate exclusively to the huerta, cover both seigneurial and royal jurisdictions (unlike the *peyta*, for example, which was confined to the big towns of the royal demesne), but unfortunately also concern themselves only with

[1] An excellent introduction is provided by José Sánchez Adell, 'Estructura agraria de Castellón de la Plana en 1398', *Saitabi*, XXIII (1973), 147–75.

[2] For the widespread nature of this cross-border landownership at the present day cf. E. E. Malefakis, *Agrarian Reform and Peasant Revolution in Spain* (Yale University Press 1970), 25–6. This otherwise fine introduction to Spanish landholding tends to be somewhat misleading on Valencia, where the 10 hectare limit for a minifundia is simply inapplicable owing to the intensive nature of the agriculture of the irrigated zone.

superficial area since the taxes were raised – somewhat iniqui-
tously, given that not all irrigated fields were alike – at a flat
rate per *fanegada*. And finally, there are the valuations of
Morisco property made by the Crown after the expulsion in
1609. But these only relate to the royal demesne, where the
Moriscos were few in number. In fact there are really only two
communities of any size here – Játiva and Corbera.

Drawing on all these sources, I have attempted to construct
a table of property-holding in Habsburg Valencia. Ideally I
would have liked to include only those documents which give
values as well as area. In the end, the desire to have as wide
a sample as possible led me to include four communities where
there are no valuations and no rent-substitutes – Alberique,
Simat de Valldigna, Oliva and Guadasuar. In the case of the
last three the deformation is almost certainly minor, since we
are able to single out the huerta, a relatively homogeneous area
where values did not fluctuate too widely. As Cavanilles noted,
towards the end of the eighteenth century, the secano of Oliva
'is in great part of no use...The gem of the territory is the
huerta.'[1] Unfortunately in Alberique it is not always possible
to distinguish the irrigated land from the rest, and here – the
most dubious, therefore, of our examples – we are forced back
on the totality of the land area.

As it stands, table 5 groups disparate sources, but it may help
to give some idea of the distribution of property in seventeenth-
century Valencia. The population is grouped into deciles in each
case – that is, the proportion of the total assets in the cadastral
survey belonging to each ten per cent of the inhabitants,
starting with the worst-off (the 1st decile) and moving up to
the wealthiest (the 10th decile).

This table, with its picture of glaring inequality, may come
as something of a surprise. Valencia, after all, has been thought
of as the classic home of the contented medium peasantry.
However, as Eugenio Burriel, the best authority on Valencian
property structures, has argued, 'This huerta is generally
portrayed as the traditional home of the small proprietor...
Nothing could be further from the historical truth...The
greater part of the land [sc. round the city of Valencia] has

[1] Cavanilles, *Geografía*, II, 147.

Table 5. *Prope*

						Deciles				
		1	2	3	4	5	6	7	8	9

Proportions of surface area (s), land values (v) or rental value (r) pertain
of households listed in cadastral surveys (figures rounded up to n

Morisco communities

Játiva	1609 (v)	0	0	0	0	0	78	925	1,805	3,81
Corbera	1609 (v)	6	66	150	251	410	539	669	818	1,19

Resettlements

Muro	1611 (r)	198	338	395	437	483	548	553	601	65
	1759 (r)	11	34	70	123	180	217	284	364	51
Oliva	1614 (s)	108	140	163	190	212	238	250	264	27
	1664 (s)	62	90	116	155	178	218	257	323	4
Alberique	1667 (s)	101	271	421	545	681	839	1,022	1,307	1,82
Segorbe	1661 (r)	9	27	59	97	137	181	221	274	39
Simat	1677 (s)	9	36	52	72	85	98	98	110	14

Old-established Old Christian towns

Castellón	1608 (v)	1,965	2,580	2,580	2,946	4,801	7,654	12,150	15,029	26,78
	1702 (v)	3,483	3,660	3,660	3,680	5,018	7,641	11,568	17,416	27,87
Guadasuar	1609 (s)	53	128	194	289	391	516	728	1,022	1,44
	1762 (s)	131	222	308	400	495	653	820	1,085	1,62
Gandía	1724 (r)	0	72	327	584	962	1,353	2,052	2,574	4,33

* In 1611 rents in Muro were fixed at so many *barchillas* of wheat per *fanegada*, except
for tree-crops which were subjected to a share-cropping arrangement; by 1759 the
share-cropping had been commuted to a fixed sum in cash. Hence for 1759 I have
reduced the wheat dues to a cash equivalent and reckoned them in with the yield
from vines, etc. This explains the different values used in the table at the two dates,
the figures for 1611 covering essentially only the yield from grain-fields.

† The figure for Oliva in 1614 excludes inhabitants of the town with land in the
Moorish ghetto.

‡ Another 8,126 *fanegadas* in Alberique belonged to peasants from neighbouring
villages and have not been reckoned in here.

SOURCES: Játiva: ARV MR 10608 (fuller than the revised inventory in 10053);
Corbera: ARV MR 10034; Alberique: AHN Osuna leg. 1938; Simat: ARV Clero 3158

ructures in Valencia

10	Total	Number of households		1	2	3	4	5	6	7	8	9	10
xed percentages ole unit)			Percentage of total property belonging to each decile, to the nearest whole unit										
9,187	15,812 *lliures*	163	1609	0	0	0	0	0	1	6	11	24	58
2,479	6,525 *lliures*	59	1609	0	1	2	4	6	8	10	13	18	38
842	5,046 *barchillas**	148	1611	4	7	8	8	9	11	11	12	13	17
1,474	3,269 *lliures**	382	1759	0	1	2	4	5	7	9	11	16	45
364	2,200 *fanegadas*†	172	1614	5	6	7	9	10	11	11	12	12	17
734	2,552 *fanegadas*	363	1759	0	1	2	4	5	7	9	11	16	45
3,352	10,359 *fanegadas*‡	192	1667	1	3	4	5	7	8	10	13	17	32
659	2,062 *lliures*	407	1661	0	1	3	5	7	9	11	13	19	32
262	962 *fanegadas*	86	1677	1	4	5	8	9	10	10	11	15	27
59,309	135,795 *lliures*	1,276	1608	1	2	2	2	4	6	9	11	20	43
75,752	159,756 *lliures*	1,827	1702	2	2	2	2	3	5	7	11	18	48
1,894	6,658 *fanegadas*	228	1609	1	2	3	4	6	8	11	15	22	28
2,243	7,979 *fanegadas*	352	1762	2	3	4	5	6	8	10	14	20	28
1,210	23,471 *lliures*	390	1724	0	0	1	3	4	6	9	11	18	48

(huerta only); Muro 1611: ADM Cocentaina leg. 33 (grain-lands only); Muro 1759: ADM Cocentaina leg. 25; Oliva 1614: AHN Osuna leg. 602 n. 14 (huerta only; *terratenientes* missing); Oliva 1664: AHN Osuna leg. 1068 n. 2 (huerta only); Segorbe 1661/2: ADM Segorbe leg. 51 n. 1; Castellón 1608: AMC Llibre de Vàlues 1608 (first nine entries missing); Castellón 1702: AMC Llibre de Vàlues 1702; Guadasuar 1609: AMA 061/4; Guadasuar 1762: AMA 061/9 (wrongly catalogued as 1672); Gandía 1724: AHN Osuna leg. 811 n. 8, survey of incomes. All these calculations are based on property within a particular jurisdictional area held by the resident inhabitants thereof, except that in the ghettos of Oliva and Segorbe the proprietors from the old town are included since the resettlement communities there had ceased to exist as valid units by the 1660s. The Gandía figures include income from land worked on lease.

lain in the hands of big rentiers who lived in town and had little to do with the daily routine of farming.'[1] Játiva, Gandía and Castellón emerge from the table with the worst record of social and economic inequality. All three, of course, were big towns where the gulf between rich and poor was inevitably larger than in the countryside. The greater imbalance apparent in Játiva, though, is perhaps something of an illusion due to the imperfection of our sources. In the case of this community, it is possible to value land, but not possible to separate out the agricultural population from the rest. We know that some 3 per cent of the Morisco landless had workshops, and probably a large number had other, non-agricultural forms of activity. In Castellón the figures are less open to question because they reflect total property – houses, mills and shops as well as land. In Gandía, though the percentages refer only to income from land (including land worked on lease), we are able to separate out, more or less accurately, the agricultural population from the rest: 390 of the 610 households in the town either owned or leased a bit of land or were landless peasants and day-labourers. These modifications – imperfect though they are – probably give a more accurate reflection of social structure than the raw data from Játiva. Even so, one is still impressed with the great concentration of property in few hands in both Castellón and Gandía. The situation does not seem to change much after the expulsion of the Moriscos – rather the upper and lower deciles in Castellón (the very rich and the very poor) marginally increase in strength between 1608 and 1702 at the expense of the middling sectors.

The resettlements are in a class of their own. Here an attempt was made after 1609 to deal out the Morisco properties on a roughly equal basis – not entirely equal, though, because seigneurial favouritism and discrimination against artisans led to a certain deformity in these communities at their birth. Nevertheless, the figures for Oliva in 1614 and Muro in 1611 testify to the relative egalitarianism of the resettlement pro-

[1] Eugenio L. Burriel de Orueta, *La Huerta de Valencia, zona sur: estudio de geografía agraria* (Valencia 1971), 261–323. For the similar situation in the Júcar Valley, R. Courtot, 'Irrigation et propriété citadine dans l'Acequia Real del Júcar au milieu du XIXe siècle', *Etudes Rurales*, 45 (1972), 29–47.

gramme. What a contrast with Oliva in 1664 or Muro in 1759! The medium settler evidently failed to hold his own in Habsburg Valencia: this new world quickly became an old world of rich and poor. In Segorbe and Oliva, Morisco ghettos attached to big Old Christian towns, the resettlements simply disintegrated, with the properties falling partly into the hands of people from across the wall in the old part of the town. Admittedly by the 1660s the process of takeover and concentration had not yet gone all that far, and the upper decile controlled only between a quarter and a third of the ex-Morisco lands. Indeed this seems to be the general picture throughout the resettlements in the 1660s and 1670s: 10 per cent of the families managed to get hold of about 30 per cent of the property in the areas. To set this state of affairs in context, of course, one has to look at the situation before and afterwards – at Muro in 1759, at Morisco Corbera in 1609. In Muro the upper decile held 45 per cent of the lands. This, however, reflects not only the changing economic and demographic climate of Bourbon times, but also certain facts of geography. Muro was predominantly secano, and like other arid zones of the Spanish Mediterranean, was a hostile environment for the small, independent farmer, who could be ruined by a year of drought. This tended to encourage the formation of larger properties which were alone capable of withstanding adversity. By contrast, down on the irrigated plain of Guadasuar the less wealthy proved capable of holding their own a little better as late as 1762. At the other end of the chronological spectrum, the Morisco village of Corbera presented a somewhat more extreme picture of inequality than anything to be found in the resettlements at least before Bourbon times. But the difference is perhaps not all that marked, and anyway may have more to do with geographical than demographic factors – the village was situated in marshy terrain towards the mouth of the Júcar, where exposure to floods and the risk of harvest failure must have put a premium on large holdings from an early date.

Of course, the degree of concentration of property tells us nothing directly about the conditions of the majority of peasants. Were they more or less self-sufficient in terms of landholding during the age of depopulation? According to the *arbitrista* Jerónimo Ibáñez de Salt, writing in the 1630s, a family of three (father, mother and one child) would consume 36 *barchillas*, or 6 hectolitres, of wheat a year.[1] Had they been trying to cultivate this grain for themselves, they would have had to allow for a deduction of about one-tenth of the harvest to the church, and perhaps one-fifth (taking a frequent case) to the senyor. In other words, in order to keep their own table supplied they would have needed to harvest 51.4 *barchillas* at least. But to get this amount of grain they would have had to set aside about an eighth of the total for next year's seed – average seed yields in the fertile lands of Gandía working out at 8:1, according to documents of 1609 and 1724.[2] Thus, such a family would ideally need to harvest 62.6 *barchillas* of wheat in order to be able to eat 36 in a given year. From the document of 1609, we know that the huerta of Gandía could yield approximately 8 *barchillas* per *fanegada* (that is, just over 16 hectolitres per hectare). Thus in the most fertile part of Valencia, with very high yields for the epoch, a small peasant family might have required about 8 *fanegadas* (say two-thirds of an hectare) of huerta just to be self-sufficient in bread; and it must be remembered that even these high yields were diminished by inefficient, broadcast sowing which was more costly on seed than present day methods. Reassuringly enough, 9 *fanegadas* of huerta were promised to each settler in Valldigna after 1609; and in Gandía itself an ordinary settler's portion was fixed at 15 *fanegadas*. The seigneurial agent warned his master in the latter case: 'each peasant must be given at least half this amount...just to support his family'.[3]

The 8-*fanegada* limit only applies to the fertile huertas of Gandía, Valldigna, Játiva and Valencia itself. In other parts of

---

[1] 'El memorial del arbitrista Jerónimo Ibáñez de Salt', *Estudios de Historia Moderna*, IV (1954), ed. E. Asensio.

[2] AHN Osuna leg. 1033 nos. 87–9 (1724) – giving the amount of seed used in the whole of Gandía in an average year; leg. 1029 n. 3 (1609?) – an estimate of the average yield of grain from the huerta. My figure of 8:1 is a minimum, since we do not know the yield from the secano (though it can hardly have been very much since the document specifically refuses to put a figure on it, given the unreliability of this arid soil). The ratio will appear high for the Europe of the day; cf. B. H. Slicher van Bath, 'The Yields of Different Crops (mainly cereals) in relation to the seed, ca. 810–1820', *Acta Historiae Neerlandica*, III (1967), 35. But Vilar finds yields of 9 or 10:1 in the huertas round Barcelona in the late eighteenth century, *Catalunya dins l'Espanya moderna*, III, 643.   [3] AHN Osuna leg. 602 n. 14.

the kingdom the whole scale would have to be worked out anew to take account of different geographical conditions. Nevertheless, within its limited scope, we find, for example, that 136 of the 163 Morisco families inventoried in Játiva in 1609 had less than the 8-*fanegada* limit and that, when the place was resettled in 1623, only 8 of the 52 households were given less than this amount, and they were probably artisan families. Everywhere the higher demands of the Old Christian settlers in terms of land placed severe restrictions on the numbers which could be accommodated in the former Morisco communities. As another agent of the Duke of Gandía put it: 'the Morisco was happy with 2 *fanegadas* of land, and felt himself to be a rich man with so much...Now we give the new settlers 15 *fanegadas* of huerta...and still they are not satisfied, and find it impossible to live without some additional expedient.'[1]

In fact, the first generation of settlers was the last which enjoyed such favourable circumstances. By 1664 in Oliva some 312 of the 363 proprietors with holdings in the resettlement had less than the prescribed 15 *fanegadas* of huerta, while 230 of these had less even than 8 *fanegadas*. The figures here, though, are not really relevant, since the resettlement had ceased to exist as a separate unit by that date. But in Simat de Valldigna in 1677, 31 out of the 86 households had less than 8 *fanegadas* of huerta – less, therefore, than the minimum holding consistent with self sufficiency. For Gandía in 1724 we do not have any figures on the distribution of superficial area. But if we return to Ibáñez de Salt's estimate of the consumption needs of a small family (36 *barchillas* of wheat a year) and compare it with the prevailing price of wheat in Gandía in 1724 (9 *sous* 2 *diners* per *barchilla*), we can reckon that a man would have needed an income of around 330 *sous* in order to buy bread. In fact, 160 of the 390 people holding land or working in agriculture had a return of under 400 *sous* a year from the agricultural sector (though wage labour and artisan occupations boosted their income by an unknown amount).

In other words (allowing for the approximate nature of our calculations) it is likely that, even in this depopulated age, a third or more of the peasantry would have had a hard struggle

[1] AHN Osuna leg. 1027 n. 21.

to make ends meet. One begins to understand a little better, perhaps, the reasons for the low fertility and premature ageing of the population, discussed in the previous chapter. The problem in the first instance seems to have been that there was just not a great abundance of land to found a new, stable peasant prosperity. The Moriscos, inured to a wretched existence, had occupied the worst hill country where earlier generations of conquering Christians had not bothered to set foot. One is liable to be impressed by the fact that the seventeenth-century population – only two-thirds of the size of the old – was pretty fully stretched across the available surface area. Of 20,604 *fanegadas* of arable in Alberique, some 18,484½ were occupied in 1667; of 8,073 *fanegadas* belonging to Moriscos in Oliva, 6,917 were accounted for in 1664 (the difference is due to ricefields and hillside which were allowed to revert to marsh and scrub).[1] There was not a great deal of slack waiting to be taken up. The other factor influencing the property structure was the conditions in which the resettlements were made. The new communities started life with a clean bill of health in one respect: the debts of the Morisco population were offloaded onto the senyors, either directly in the case of community obligations, or indirectly in the case of a field or house which secured rent rebates on sums owing to old creditors; nevertheless the harshness of the new seigneurial rent terms created much poverty.[2] When combined with the general lack of resources of the settlers themselves, these heavier payments may have driven the smaller men quickly out of business. As the Council of Aragon's Resettlement Junta once remarked: 'most of the settlers are poor men, and those who have money will buy up their holdings'.[3] This seems to have been broadly what happened – though seigneurial rents in the resettlements acted as a discouragement to big investors and slowed up the process.

Who were these wealthy men? In the first or second genera-

[1] For Alberique AHN Osuna leg. 1938 (figures for the present day kindly communicated by the town council of Alberique); for Oliva leg. 1068 n. 2 and 562 n. 37.

[2] For the settlement of the Morisco debts, cf. the terms of the *asiento general* of 1614 in Pascual Boronat, *Los moriscos españoles y su expulsión* (2 vols., Valencia 1901), II, 611–34. For the subsequent interpretation of this decree, AMV Churat 1635, rescript of Philip III, 21 Dec. 1615, and ACA CA leg. 871, petition of the Duchess of Pastrana and others, 21 Jan. 1616.

[3] Quoted in Torres Morera, *Repoblación*, 19.

tion, they were often enough people who described themselves simply as *llauradors* (peasants). Only two or three of the wealthiest proprietors in Alberique in 1667 were in a higher social category – Jaime Andrés and Pere Gisbert, *ciutadans* ('citizens living off rents'), and perhaps their ward Llorens Abadia. In Muro by 1759 there was a greater sprinkling of titles. The giant holdings were in the hands of the Alonso and Abad families, whose various members could boast the noble prefix '*don*' or the clerical '*mossèn*'. The old community of equal peasants set up in 1611 had grown long in the tooth.

The rise of the Alonsos and Abads from (one presumes) the ranks of the peasantry reflects a more general social movement which was under way in later Habsburg Valencia. The 1630s witnessed the birth of a new expedient designed to raise money for a bankrupt royal treasury – the sale of noble status. There was no fixed tariff. The price varied inversely with the quality of the claimant (a tavern keeper had to pay more than a *ciutadà*), and with the level of demand (a peak in the 1640s, then a fall around mid-century, then a renewed rise in the last two decades of the century). But in general one could buy the status of a petty noble or *cavaller* for not less than 250 and not more than 700 *lliures;* the title of *don* for 300 *lliures* if one were already a petty noble, 1,300 if one were a commoner.[1] Turning to Gandía, where the document of 1724 lists income from land, one notes that 21 of the 390 people associated with agriculture had revenues of 250 *lliures* a year or more from this one source, and would thus have entered the ranks of those who could contemplate buying petty nobility. The document warns us, though, against overestimating fortunes based on land alone – at least in a seigneurial town, where much of the profit of exploitation had to go in feudal rent. No one in Gandía in 1724 got more than 650 *lliures* a year out of his farming or leases – which amounted to little when a lawyer could earn 1,000 *lliures* in Philip IV's reign and perhaps more in Philip V's time, and when the Duke of Gandía himself had an income of around 40,000 a year.[2] No wonder that as late as 1724, even after the

[1] ACA CA legs. 655–8, 'expedientes que se han beneficiado por la secretaría de Valencia'.
[2] ACA CA leg. 883, petition of Miguel Jerónimo Sanz, 9 Nov. 1641.

inflation of honours, some of the biggest landholders in the area were still plain *llauradors*. The shadow of the feudal senyors still loomed large.

Undoubtedly, though, the weight of the non-active, rentier sector had grown in the seventeenth century. In Castellón in 1608 the clergy, nobles and *ciutadans*, 29 of them, had controlled 133,175 of the total assessment of 2,715,893 *sous*; by 1702 they were 68 strong, and held 559,030 of the assessment of 3,195,080. Their share of the total had thus risen from 4.90 to 17.50 per cent. The expansion, it may be noted, was almost wholly in the ranks and fortunes of the nobles and *ciutadans*, not of the clergy. Of the 45 wealthiest proprietors in 1702, those with an assessment of over 10,000 *sous*, 20 had a similar family name to their predecessors in the upper tax bracket of 1608. But the unadorned Felius, Eguals and Sisternes of Philip III's reign had become *dons* by the age of the first Bourbon. One senses a considerable stability in the ranks of the elite over the seventeenth century – an absence of new fortunes, perhaps, but a consolidation of the old, now festooned with courtly honours.

Was Valencian agriculture becoming top-heavy? Not only the ranks of the nobility are involved here. Agriculture was the prime source of wealth in Castellón, yet one cannot help being impressed at how small the active peasant population was. Of the 1,276 household heads listed in 1608, only 779 were either peasants or agricultural labourers; 240 were what might be loosely classified as dependants (that is, widows and heirs), and the rest were nobles, rentiers, traders or artisans. The non-peasant sector, constituting 38.95 per cent of the population, controlled 35.69 per cent of the taxable wealth of the town. By 1702 the non-peasant sector had swelled to 42.56 per cent, but its control of the fortunes of the area had risen even further to 51.90 per cent. Almost all of the advance is accounted for by the rise of two groups: the nobility and distinguished citizens, and the lawyers and notaries. Castellón as the seat of a governor was an important centre for litigation, and it supported an ever-increasing number of lawyers – in 1608 34 lawyers held 145,225 *sous* worth of property, and in 1702 68 lawyers controlled 335,550 *sous* worth. Adding nobles, distinguished citizens, clergy and lawyers together, we find that their share of the whole was 28 per cent in 1702 as against 10.25 per cent in 1608. And the situation seems to have been much the same, interestingly enough, in Gandía in 1724, where the families of lawyers, nobles and *ciutadans* (but not clergy, missing from this survey) held 52,111½ of a total assessed income from land of 234,710 *reals*, a proportion of 22.20 per cent.

In other words, by the end of the Habsburg period between a quarter and a fifth of the property around some of the bigger towns was coming to be concentrated in the hands of an archetypal rentier class, a proportion which had doubled or tripled during the seventeenth century. If we include artisans and dependants in the reckoning, it may be that only about half the land was actually being worked by those who owned it. French historians have noted a parallel development in their own country during this period: the appropriation of between two-fifths and three-fifths of the land by the non-peasant (principally bourgeois and noble) sector.[1] No doubt when the information for big commercial towns like Alicante, Alcoy or Onteniente becomes available, we shall find that the mercantile group was also a big property-holder. But at the moment it would appear that the two wealthiest and most prestigious sections of the Valencian propertied class were the aristocracy and the lawyers. And, above all, these were local men, the sons of peasants who had made good. The wealthy outsider is a negligible factor in all the cadastral surveys which I have seen.[2] True, in Morisco Játiva or in the resettlement of Alberique, non-residents did indeed have as much as a half to two-thirds of the land. But they were peasants from neighbouring villages, who because of the hazards of the parish boundary found themselves closer to the fields in question than the people of the town to which the lands belonged. They merely confirm the general impression of an overwhelmingly localized pattern of landholding in Habsburg Valencia.

A similar conclusion emerges from a study of the sales which took place after 1609 of the former Morisco lands on royal

[1] Cf. H. Neveux, J. Jacquart and E. Le Roy Ladurie, *Histoire de la France Rurale* vol. 2, *L'Age Classique des Paysans 1340–1789* (Paris 1975), 266–7.
[2] This contrasts with the situation in the late nineteenth century when the bourgeoisie of the city of Valencia had acquired a third and more of the land in the Júcar Valley, Courtot, 'Irrigation et propriété citadine', 44.

demesne. The vast majority of Moriscos had lived on seigneurial estates, and here the Crown had formally prohibited sale, ordering the distribution of the property among a new population of peasant cultivators, with the avowed aim of restoring manpower ('so desirable for the sake of God and His Majesty').[1] But in the case of the scattered lands which lay within the boundaries of royal towns, the Crown felt free to dispose of its windfall for cash or favour – with the two notable exceptions of Játiva and Corbera, where an attempt was made to set up a new community of peasants holding land on feudal tenures. Approximately one-third of these Morisco spoils – 85,799 out of 262,265 lliures capital value – was granted as compensation to 42 senyors for their losses in the expulsion.[2] The rump of the property was then revalued upwards to 236,379 lliures, and most of this (excepting Játiva and Corbera) was sold off in a series of auctions by two special commissioners, Adrián Bayarte and Miguel Jerónimo Valero, between 1614 and 1618. It may be noted in passing that the Crown actually realized only about 100,000 lliures on the transaction (there were mortgages of 121,014 lliures to be paid off, and a proportion of the lands could not be sold at all but had to be established at quit-rents), and most of this was given away in cash grants to senyors who had lost in the expulsion.[3]

In general the volume of land changing hands in these deals was too small to make much difference to the pattern of property-holding in Valencia, except perhaps in two cases. Two towns accounted in fact for the bulk of the sales – Sagunto (mid-way between Valencia and Castellón) with 46,387 lliures, and Penáguila (in the hinterland of Alicante) with 31,310. In both cases, as in the rest of the auctions, local interests predominated, and a handful of wealthy families walked off with the lion's share (see table 6).

[1] Clause 4 of *asiento general* of 1614. For a case instance of royal intervention on seigneurial estates to overturn sales and establish a peasant commonwealth, AHN Osuna leg. 846 n. 2, decree of Salvador Fontanet for Gandía, 1 Oct. 1612.
[2] The most complete list of grants is in ARV MR 10113. For the valuations of Morisco property, ACA CA leg. 607 n. 28/2 and leg. 640 n. 4/35, and cf. Torres Morera, *Repoblación*, 145–6.
[3] For the cash grants, ACA CA leg. 593, memorandum (1620?); for the mortgages, leg. 654, consulta, 30 April 1617. The activities of the Bayarte commission are mostly contained in legs. 704 and 705, *passim*.

Table 6. *The sale of Morisco land in Sagunto in 1615*

Category of purchase (in lliures)	Number of purchasers	Total value of purchases (in lliures)
Under 500	342	28,378
Under 1,000	5	3,508
Over 1,000	7	14,551
Total	354	46,387

SOURCE: ARV MR 10081. I have included establishments on quit-rents in the figures for sales, as elsewhere in these calculations.

Thus 7 people acquired nearly a third of the land. They were the senyors of Castelnou, Rafelbuñol, Cuart, Gilet and Faura (all of whom had the bulk of their estates in the neighbourhood), the deputy finance officer of the kingdom, and a judge of the supreme court of the Audiencia. One notes again the predominance of the aristocracy and the legal profession as landowners. In Penáguila some 17,517 *lliures* worth of Morisco land (over half the total) was acquired by ten big interests, which included the local senyors of Benasau and Alcoleja, the *ciutadà* families of the Porta, Fenollar and Aracil, a priest, two *llauradors*, and (a unique instance of mercantile involvement) a trading company of nearby Alcoy. The rest of the property went to 55 people, mostly peasants from Penáguila itself or the neighbouring villages of Benifallim, Benilloba and Gorga.[1] In Liria, 7,086 *lliures* worth of Morisco land had already been given away to the neighbouring senyor of Benisanó. Of the 3,955 *lliures* which remained, two-fifths went to the local royal bailiff, a notary, a convent and a shoemaker. The balance was split into tiny fractions among 42 peasants from Liria and the neighbourhood.[2] In Guadasuar further south, just over half the lands went to 7 substantial interests (including again the royal bailiff), while the remainder was split into smaller plots among 15 others.[3] And so the story continued from one end of the kingdom to the other.

Developments in the seventeenth century, then, consolidated the position of a successful elite of landgrabbers. But Valencia

[1] ARV MR 10114.   [2] ARV MR 10098.   [3] ARV MR 10041.

was not yet a capitalist society. Over three-quarters of the land lay the shadow of the feudal senyors, propertyless themselves but with claims to perhaps a fifth of the agrarian product. One of the most delicate adjustments which had to be made – and one which explains much of the political as well as the economic evolution of the region – was the harmonization of interests between powerful landowners and their lordly masters. Plain Baltasar Oriola held 42 *fanegadas* of huerta along the banks of the River Alcoy in 1598. After the expulsion of the Moriscos he was given no less than 137 *fanegadas* of Morisco land rent free by the Duke of Gandía in return for loans and services rendered. By 1648 he held at least 220 *fanegadas* of huerta in Gandía, Benipeixcar and Alquería del Azoch. In 1645 he had purchased a patent of nobility from the needy Philip IV, and shortly afterwards became steward of the Borja estates, a position from which he could mastermind further land acquisitions round Gandía.[1] Another of the big property-owners in Gandía was don Francisco Escrivá, who was tied to the Borjas by the loans of money which he made to them and for which he was repaid with an illegally large holding of 64 *fanegadas* in the resettlement of Almoines. He held a further 29 *fanegadas* of huerta in Rafelcofer in the name of one of his servants (so as to comply with a royal edict against big holdings in the Gandian resettlements).[2] The territory of Oliva, also under the lordship of the Borjas, was dominated by the Císcar family, who, like Oriola and Escrivá, were closely involved in the financial affairs of the Duke of Gandía and very active in land purchase. Though relations were mostly harmonious, don Pedro Císcar had a great dispute with his master in 1658 over a rebate which he claimed for losses in farming the Duke's revenues.[3]

The social structure of post-expulsion Valencia, therefore, was a complex one. Feudal and traditional it certainly remained to a large extent. But the growth of a sturdy landowning elite under the shadow of the senyors – men who as lawyers or

[1] AMG Aguas de Alcoy III F 5/6; AHN Osuna leg. 1071 n. 1, *capbreu* of Gandía 1648–51; leg. 602 n. 40, Gandía v. Císcar, 1658; ACA CA leg. 658, *expediente*, 1645.
[2] AHN Osuna leg. 942 n. 54, accounts, 1665; leg. 1071 n. 2, *capbreu* of Almoines, 1668; leg. 1068, *capbreu* of Rafelcofer, 1638; leg. 4083, accounts, 1671–80.
[3] AHN Osuna leg. 1068 n. 2, *capbreu* of Oliva, 1664; leg. 602 n. 40, Gandía v. Císcar, 1658.

aristocrats in their own right could no longer be so easily dominated as the Morisco peasantry of old had been – was slowly beginning to crack open the existing framework. On the other hand, nothing is perhaps more significant in the whole story of seventeenth-century Valencia than the failure to grasp fully the opportunities for modernization. The Oriolas, Císcars and Escrivás became rural potentates who were just as obnoxious as the old Dukes of Gandía; they were mafia bosses (as we shall see), responsible for most of the violence and gang warfare which plagued the region, passive rentiers or tax-farmers (rather like the *gabelloti* who were behind much of the lawlessness in nineteenth-century Sicily), and not active cultivators. With their rise Valencia came to a crossroads and took a false turning.

3

The decline of agriculture

To outsiders the kingdom of Valencia appeared to be a green and prosperous land, perhaps – together with the valley of the Guadalquivir – one of the most flourishing agricultural areas in the peninsula. 'One of nature's orchards', Méndez Silva described it in 1645, 'blessed with a soft climate and the fairest and gentlest landscape in all Spain, and covered with gardens, plantations, shady arbours and villas, which echo to the babble of canals, fountains and streams.'[1] But the Valencians themselves were not so sure. Most of the territory, they had to remind Olivares once, was 'rough mountain and waste'.[2] The land of Valencia, in fact, offers great contrasts, above all between the irrigated huertas, where much of the intensive agriculture is and was carried on, and the dry secano. In a region where the annual rainfall is 17 inches and the summers are cloudless, access to water has meant the difference between life and death. 'Everybody who sowed this year in the waste lands of Segorbe has given his oath that no wheat or other grain could be harvested': thus the report of the authorities on the drought of 1613.[3] 'In the secano this year', declared the bailiff of Caudete in 1638, 'not a single crop could be saved.'[4] The fierce sun and the lack of rain could shrivel the grain which the peasants needed in order to survive. The weather was not the only factor; soil erosion in a hilly and poorly forested terrain was another problem typical of the Mediterranean area. Hence the importance of the alluvial clays which built up along the course of the rivers, and which, ribbed by a network of

[1] Rodrigo Méndez Silva, *Población general de España* (Madrid 1645), 201–2.
[2] ACA CA leg. 715, memorial of ambassador Verdalet, 1637.
[3] ARV MR 10117, *cuentas de bienes moriscos*, 1613.
[4] ARV MR 5650, *tercio diezmo*, 1638.

irrigation channels, constituted those islands of wealth, the huertas. Islands they always were, however: the biggest and most famous huerta of all, the delta of the river Turia half surrounding the city of Valencia, had a radius of only 10 to 15 kilometres, with its boundaries in Puzol, Catarroja and Manises (see map).

In Spain at the present day about a tenth of the arable is under irrigation, but this tenth accounts for nearly half the total value of the agricultural output.[1] In earlier ages the hold of the huerta was even more crucial. In the first place much of this irrigated land was used for basic subsistence agriculture and not, as today, for exportable luxuries. As the citizens of Alicante once put it, emphasizing their self-sufficiency in food, 'rain or no rain, there will be wheat in the huerta of Orihuela'.[2] And it was of breadstuffs that the chronicler Escolano was mainly thinking when he praised the huertas of Valencia, Játiva and Gandía with their 'two, three, and even four rotations of wheat, hemp, rice, barley or millet'.[3] Nor was the situation very different in the early nineteenth century when the French traveller Jaubert de Passa described the cycle of wheat (October to June), maize (June to October), hemp (March to July) and broad-beans (July to October) which in his day characterized the huerta of Valencia.[4]

The huerta, like the secano, was geared to the production of grain for a subsistence peasantry. One can verify the literary evidence by looking at the records of the tithe, perhaps the most precious surviving testimonial to life in rural Valencia under the old regime. We shall be concerned here with the *tercio diezmo*, the king's 'third of the tithe' (actually nearer a quarter) which was collected as follows. Out of what the cultivator handed over, the rector of the parish took the first cut, the *primicias*, equivalent to two-ninths of the full tithe; then the king took his third of what was left, and the balance went to the bishop and chapter of the diocese. For various reasons the tithe can never be a perfect guide to agricultural production. In the first place Philip II secured permission from the Pope to collect the

[1] OECD, *Agricultural Development in Southern Europe*, n.d., 269.
[2] BL Add. Mss. 28,380 fol. 393, petition of Alicante, n.d.
[3] Escolano, *Décadas*, I, 368.
[4] Jaubert de Passa, *Voyage en Espagne* (Paris 1823), 241–2.

Table 7. *Cultivations in the kingdom of Valencia 1600–50*

Category of crop	Value in lliures	Percentage of total
Wheat	14,402	59.40
Barley	1,417	5.84
Mixed wheat and barley	188	0.78
Millet and maize	639	2.64
Rye	110	0.45
Oats	361	1.49
Rice	892	3.68
Total grains	18,009	74.28
Wine	2,240	9.24
Olive oil	820	3.38
Silk	527	2.17
Almonds	244	1.01
Flax and hemp	460	1.90
Other fruits and vegetables	785	3.24
Total fruits	5,076	20.94
Cattle	1,161	4.78
General total	24,246	100.00

SOURCE: ARV MR 5413–5964, *tercio diezmo* of Alcira, Alcoy, Alfafara, Algemesí, Alpuente, Bañeres, Beniganim, Biar, Bocairente, Burriana, Carcagente, Castellón, Caudete, Corbera, Guadasuar, Ibi, Játiva and area, Jérica and area, Jijona, Liria, Morella and area, Molvedre (Sagunto), Onteniente, Penáguila, Ollería, Villajoyosa, Villanueva, Villareal and La Yesa, 1600–50.

tithe of the richest farm in the parish, and also tithes from newly irrigated fields, entirely for the Crown.[1] These, the *excusado* and the *novales*, came to be separately accounted for, and may thus slightly distort the picture of agricultural production derived from the main tithes. Less serious is the variation in the incidence of the impost from area to area – the proverbial tenth in Villarreal, but as much as an eighth in Villanueva de Castellón. A far bigger problem is that grain was everywhere the most efficiently taxed of products: wine or mulberry or olive, for example, were often commuted for a cash sum, and some crops, like mulberry and carob, were traditionally exempt or deliberately undertaxed in certain areas.[2] In short, there is a real danger that grain will be overweighted in any table of agricultural production based on the tithe. With this reservation, we may look at the analysis of crop distribution given in table

[1] RAH 9.4.4.1.43, fol. 268, Dr Luis Pastor to don Pedro Antonio de Aragón, 20 Oct. 1682; cf. ACA CA leg. 879, petition of chapter of Orihuela, 1638.
[2] ARV R 519, *acte de cort eclesiàstic* 2 and 3 of 1626.

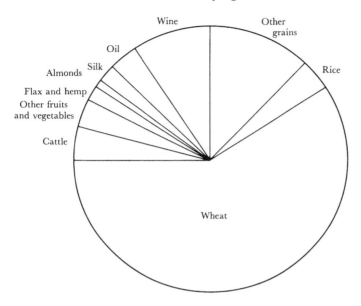

7; it is based on a systematic exploitation of all the *tercio diezmo* records for the period 1600–50. Each category is expressed in terms of average annual value, that is, volume multiplied by market price.

Thus approximately three-quarters of Valencian agricultural output, as measured by the *tercio diezmo*, was grain – a percentage which (reassuringly enough) is almost exactly the same as that for New Castile, according to the great survey of 1575.[1] One senses the self-sufficiency of rural Spain. As might be expected, the more arid inland areas of Valencia had the biggest weighting for grain – 90 per cent of the harvests in Morella, 77 per cent in the hilly secano to the west and south, but only 70 per cent in the lowlands of the Júcar Valley or Játiva, and only 60 per cent in the coastal plains of Castellón, Villarreal, Burriana and Sagunto. It is unfortunate that no records are available for the huerta of Valencia: there in the shadow of the great metropolis (which bought much of its bread in Sicily), luxury crops may possibly have outweighed grain. Within the overall figures, wheat has a striking preponderance. Of course,

[1] J. G. da Silva, *En Espagne: développement économique, subsistance, déclin* (Paris/The Hague 1965), 27.

as the most highly priced breadstuff, it tends to have an inflated importance in any table based on value. Very roughly it cost three times as much, volume for volume, as its nearest rival, barley. So if we divide its value total in the table by three, we have a more accurate measure of its ratio by harvest volume to the other grains – leaving it still three times as plentiful as barley, and just about equal to all other breadstuffs put together. In actual terms, barley was hardly grown at all round Morella, came to between a quarter and a fifth of the wheat harvest in the cold foothills of the *meseta*, and rose to between a third and a half in the milder climate of the Valencian south, where the soil was very poor and wheat grew less well on the stony hillsides. In the Júcar Valley barley gave way to rice and maize, and the paddy fields of Játiva and Corbera actually yielded as much unhusked rice as the grainfields yielded wheat – though the edible, shelled rice was considerably less plentiful. For one contemporary, writing in 1646, rice was 'of all foods in this kingdom, the most useful, profitable and necessary, and the one most ready to hand, being the main standby of the poor'.[1] This was considerably to overrate its importance. In fact it was not until the eighteenth century that the rice harvest in the Júcar Valley came to rival or surpass that of wheat. It remained in Habsburg times a rather despised and relegated crop, not so much for its taste as for the unhealthy conditions in which it was grown, and for its association with the Moors. Watching the Moriscos of Valldigna in 1603–4, the French traveller Barthélemy Joly sighed: 'it would move you to pity if they were Christians to see them bent over the rice, a foot deep in water'.[2]

Of other grains there is not much evidence in the *tercio diezmo* records. Oats were given to the hens in Bocairente; the little rye produced in Alpuente was reserved for the lambs in the spring; even the ubiquitous broad-beans, a major part of the crop rotation in the huertas, were used in Burriana 'for fattening up the pigs'.[3] It is clear that the daily bread of the Valencians in the early seventeenth century must have been

[1] 'El arbitrista Jerónimo Ibáñez de Salt', 262.
[2] 'Voyage en Espagne 1603–4', *Revue Hispanique*, xx (1909), 524.
[3] ARV MR 5594, 5475 and 5621.

largely good wheat, with some admixture of barley and rice.[1]
There are, however, a couple of reservations to be made.
Firstly, the *tercio diezmo* figures which we have come from royal
towns, where the diet and the economy were probably more
developed than in many a backward seigneurial village. Secondly, from the evidence of seigneurial rent-rolls, we can affirm
quite categorically that the Moriscos had a much worse diet than
the Old Christians. In five separate estates of the Duke of Gandía
before the expulsion – Jaraco, Castellón de Rugat, Lombay,
Chella and Turís, which were mostly populated by Moriscos
– wheat only averaged about a third by volume of the grains
paid over by the peasantry. The most important single harvest
there was some form of sorghum, millet or maize.[2] For once
Aznar Cardona was right: the Moriscos 'used to eat vile
things...such as pastes made out of lentils, maize, beans, millet,
and bread of the same sort'.[3] This situation changed after the
expulsion, with the Old Christian settlers moving over massively
to wheat and letting the inferior grains shrink in yield (see
appendix 2). It appears, therefore, that the *tercio diezmo* records
of the period 1600–50 catch the Valencian population at a
particularly favourable moment, when it had more land to
devote to a difficult and low-yield cultivation like wheat than
ever before or since. In this sense, the circumstances of the
peasantry may have been a little easier after 1609 than before.

But this was still essentially a subsistence economy. Grain
travelled only with difficulty out of or into the local neighbourhood. The administrators of the *tercio diezmo* of Alcoy, 108
kilometres to the south of the city of Valencia, had to decide
in 1625 whether to let the king's wheat sell locally at 6 *lliures*
and 6 *sous* per *cahiz*, or transport it by mule train to the capital
where it would fetch 8 *lliures* and 6 *sous* – 'but the cost of
carrying it will be more than the difference in price'.[4] The mule
trains from La Yesa towards the Aragonese frontier charged
a couple of *sous* per league on each *cahiz* – so that with wheat
selling in La Yesa in 1611 at 110 *sous*, it rose in price by just

[1] This seems to have been true of Castile also, cf. A. Domínguez Ortiz, *Alteraciones Andaluzas* (Madrid 1973), 29.
[2] AHN Osuna leg. 1027 n. 21, rents of the Duke of Gandía, 1609.
[3] *Expulsión justificada*, fol. 33.
[4] ARV MR 5443, Juan Gil Polo to bailiff of Alcoy, 27 May 1625.

under 2 per cent every 6 kilometres.[1] Often indeed, given the
poor state of communications, there was no mule train available
anyway; this was the case in Alcoy in 1625. In the circumstances
it is hardly surprising that the only large scale trade in grain
was to be found around Morella, where it linked up with a major
wheat exporting route from Aragon to the Mediterranean coast.
At the seaport of Vinaroz, the bread of Morella and Zaragoza
was embarked for Valencia, the biggest city in eastern Spain.
Elsewhere in the kingdom the overwhelming preponderance
of grain in the agriculture of the day is testimony to only one
thing: the subsistence nature of the rural economy. Nothing
changed here with the expulsion of the Moriscos (except for
the switch from maize to wheat). In particular the more equal
distribution of property in the resettlements may have reinforced self-sufficiency for a time. But even the bigger holdings
of aristocrats and lawyers round the Old Christian towns were
incapable of breaking the pattern of rural self-sufficiency –
hardly surprisingly, since many of them seem simply to have
been leased out to the poorer peasantry.

Of course one should not ignore the tender beginnings of
commercialization such as they appear in our table. Of the
considerable variety of commercial crops grown in the kingdom,
wine stands out as a market leader. Along the hills of western
Valencia where most of the best vineyards are now located, it
accounted for 14 per cent of the value of the harvests in the
early seventeenth century. Round Sagunto – thanks to access
to the sea and to cheap transport – it reached its maximum of
almost 50 per cent.

According to a government report of 1626 the kingdom of
Valencia produced between 80,000 and 150,000 *botas* (roughly
500,000 to 1,000,000 hectolitres) of wine every year. But much
of this considerable production – the government reckoned as
much as a quarter – was of very poor quality and liable to turn
into vinegar unless drunk within a few months of the vintage.[2]
Part of the problem was the sheer lack of markets, for wine
did not travel easily, being very bulky, and costly to transport

[1] ARV MR 5960, accounts of the bailiff of La Yesa, 1611. For costs in Andalusia, cf.
Domínguez Ortiz, *Alteraciones Andaluzas,* 32.
[2] ACA CA leg. 1352, 'advertimientos' (1627?).

overland.[1] Inevitably the really big commerce here was located near the coast, especially around Sagunto and Alicante. The wine produced elsewhere often lay untapped in its casks until it turned sour and had to be thrown away ('no use at all, not even for vinegar', as one disconsolate bailiff reported in 1645).[2] At best the vintage of the interior could be disposed of on a piecemeal basis; the peasants of Liria, for example, found a ready market among the thirsty charcoal-burners of nearby Benaguacil, and those of the north-west sold the occasional jar to the Aragonese herdsmen who came to winter their flocks in the Valencian lowlands.[3] Wine was important, in some places very important; but it failed to alter radically the traditional self-sufficiency of the local neighbourhood.

But of course Habsburg Valencia was noted not so much for its wine as for its silk – 'the chief product of the realm', as the Valencians grandiloquently described it about 1621, echoing almost word for word what their great grandfathers had claimed at the Cortes of 1547.[4] An estimate of 1580 suggested that Valencia produced 400,000 pounds of raw silk a year, worth, at an average price of 590.5 *diners* per pound between 1576 and 1587, 984,167 *lliures*.[5] With wine in the same period at 31.85 *diners* per jar, a maximum production of 150,000 *botas* would have been worth 1,194,375 *lliures*, and a minimum of 80,000 worth 637,000 *lliures*. A safe average would probably put the value of the Valencian vintage in Habsburg times at around 900,000 *lliures*, or just under the yield of the silk harvest. This may seem surprising, given that in the *tercio diezmo* silk ranks third behind wine and olive oil. But this reflects the limitation of the tithe as a source for the study of agricultural history, for when the tithing laws were promulgated in the thirteenth century there were so few mulberry trees in existence that the authorities did not think it worth while to lay down any 'definite rule' about them, which meant that the silk harvest was disgracefully

[1] ACA'CA leg. 707, petition of *jurats*, 21 Feb. 1622.
[2] ARV MR 5955, *tercio diezmo* of Villarreal, 1645.
[3] ARV MR 5764, *tercio diezmo* of Liria, 1620.
[4] ACA CA leg. 726, petition of *jurats* of Valencia (1621?); cf. cap.12 of the Cortes of 1547.
[5] Tulio Halperin Donghi, 'Un conflicto nacional en el siglo de oro: moriscos y cristianos viejos en Valencia', *Cuadernos de Historia de España*, XXIII-XXIV (1955), 31.

undertaxed.[1] Mulberry trees, like vineyards, tended to creep in on a small scale almost everywhere. Even in Játiva, which was an important silk centre, the cultivation of the mulberry was often haphazard and incidental. A good three-quarters of the Morisco lands in the huerta of Játiva had this type of tree lining the edges of the fields, but only 9 per cent were actually under plantation.[2] However, in the Júcar Valley mulberry had come close to transforming the face of the countryside. This was not so much the case in the old established capital of Alcira, but in places like Algemesí, Guadasuar, Carcagente and Alberique the silk harvest had come to assume a crucial importance. In Alberique in 1667, 22 per cent of the land was wholly planted with mulberry and another 11 per cent was partly so.[3] In Simat de Valldigna, on the fringes of the zone, between a fifth and a quarter of the huerta was wholly planted with mulberry, and another third was partly so.[4] 'Without question this area is a veritable Indies', wrote Escolano in 1610, 'what with its silk, rice, secondary grains, maize, wine and raisins. The silk trade is so important that populous towns have sprung out of tiny villages, such vast riches are there to be found'.[5] If the silk harvest was indeed Valencia's principal one, as the Cortes believed, then much of the profit was concentrated in the Júcar Valley.

The reason for this was partly the ease of access to the Castilian market from Alcira via Játiva and the Almansa Pass. For almost all of the production of the Júcar Valley was destined for Castile – indeed, for just one town in Castile: the great silk-weaving centre of Toledo. It was the economic dynamism of Castile, not of Valencia, which called the mulberry groves of the Ribera into existence. Part of the explanation is no doubt the inability of Murcia and Granada to keep pace with demand – in 1551 the Cortes of Castile were complaining about

[1] ARV R 519 cap. 3 of the Braç Eclesiàstic, 1626.
[2] ARV MR 10053, inventory of Morisco lands, 26 Dec. 1615. Of 1,187 *fanegadas* of huerta, 109 were wholly and 735 partly planted with mulberry trees.
[3] AHN Osuna leg. 1938, *capbreu* of Alberique. Of 18,484½ *fanegadas*, 4,208 were wholly, and 2,091 partly planted with mulberry trees.
[4] ARV Clero 3158, *capbreu* of Simat 1677. Of 931¼ *fanegadas* of huerta, 201 were wholly and 325¾ partly planted with mulberry trees.
[5] *Décadas*, I, 367.

the soaring prices for silk.[1] The situation must have deteriorated even further, to Valencia's advantage, after the rebellion of the Granadan Moriscos in 1568. The route from Alcira and Játiva to Toledo came to be one of the most frequented in that part of Spain, with its convoys of carts stuffed with silk thread, or the trains of mules with pack saddles strapped across their back (for silk was light to carry and precious in relation to its bulk).[2] For the Valencians, Toledo became their rendezvous in Castile; in 1656 that disorderly character the fifth Marquis of Guadalest, who had been exiled from Valencia, asked to be allowed to live in Toledo, 'where there are Valencian merchants whom he knows and who will succour him'.[3]

The magnificence of the Júcar Valley may make us forget that only there, and in the huertas of Valencia and Orihuela, did mulberry cultivation play a really large part in the agricultural scene – and even there it accounted at most for a fifth of the harvests as a whole. Ultimately one returns to the original picture: it was a basically subsistence economy, largely dependent on the bread it could grow for itself. It might be better to say unhealthily dependent, for the low rating of cattle in the *tercio diezmo* records – at most 10 per cent of the total round Morella, 5 per cent in other parts of the secano, and even less in the huertas of Játiva, the Júcar Valley or Sagunto – undermined the whole potential of arable cultivation. The huerta particularly required abundant supplies of manure to maintain its system of continuous rotation, and one finds contracts between peasants and saddlers or shepherds to secure this precious nutrient of the soil.[4] But the huerta would not tolerate a big animal population of its own, precisely because the soil never rested. In Valldigna there were repeated decrees in the seventeenth century against allowing cattle into the

[1] K. Garrad, 'The Causes of the Second Rebellion of the Alpujarras' (Cambridge University Ph.D. thesis 1955), 171.
[2] Both carts and pack-mules were used from Játiva; the silk is described in the customs records as being *en fardos de carro*, or *a coll de bestiar*. On occasion there is mention of a routing via Valencia and Requena, but the more common route must have been across the Almansa Pass to Albacete.
[3] ACA CA leg. 582 n. 25/18, petition, 8 Jan. 1656.
[4] APV Cosme Estanaga, inventory of Luis Pallardo, 2 Nov. 1636; ARV Clero leg. 770, Gomis v. Vell, 28 March 1631.

irrigated zone, 'where they wander off and browse in the grain fields'.[1] There was an additional problem: sheep and goats, even just passing through, 'clamber onto the banks [of the irrigation canals] and spill earth into them'.[2] One after another the huerta communities were forced to take action to protect the interests of the arable farmer – in Valencia as early as the fourteenth century, in Alcira in 1601, in Orihuela in 1625.[3]

The lack of a proper balance between arable and pasture was a serious drawback for Valencian agriculture, even into the age of depopulation after 1609. The problem, as we noted in the previous chapter, was that there was very little land going begging in seventeenth century Valencia. After that it was a question of resources. Since the aristocrats and lawyers who held the land did not farm it themselves, they seem to have shied away from the capital investment which herding demanded. In any case, the little kingdom had a tradition of depending on outsiders – the Aragonese and Castilian transhumants, who came looking for winter pasture in the Valencian lowlands every year, and who were accommodated in parts of the secano by proprietors in need of manure.[4] Unfortunately for the Valencians, their numbers had gone into sharp decline during the sixteenth century and were running under Philip IV at only about two-thirds of their old maximum under Charles V.[5] This stroke of misfortune – which had nothing to do with Valencian conditions – made the problem of manure more acute than ever.

One final point which should be noted in connection with the low level of the animal population is the sheer inadequacy of many of the ploughing techniques. Woefully short of cattle, many Valencian peasants found themselves thrown back on hoe

---

[1] ARV Clero leg. 739, *crida*, 5 Feb. 1645.

[2] ARV Clero leg. 770, Ferrandis v. Alfonso, 4 Feb. 1630. These are the records of the *justicia* of Valldigna. They provide a fascinating insight into agricultural practices in seventeenth-century Valencia.

[3] Thomas F. Glick, *Irrigation and Society in Medieval Valencia* (Cambridge, Mass., 1970), 23; AMA 03/131, 9 Sept. and 4 Nov. 1607; ACA CA leg.615 n.4/6, 'ordenanzas para el govierno de Orihuela', chapter 24.

[4] Vicente Fontavella González, *La Huerta de Gandía* (Zaragoza 1952), 112–13.

[5] J. P. Le Flem, 'Las cuentas de la Mesta 1510–1709', *Moneda y Crédito*, 121 (1972), 28. The numbers actually using Valencia are recorded for a few years in the seventeenth century, in ARV MR 10293–10297. I reckon they fell from a maximum of 268,460 head in 1620/21 to a low of 148,667 in 1662.

or spade cultivation. Bleda noted that the Moriscos 'concerned themselves only with their huertas and irrigated gardens, split into a myriad small holdings, for it would have broken their heart to work in a big, wide field'.[1] Broken their hearts – or their backs. The problem of getting to grips with the soil with no other tool than a hoe was a major handicap to the agriculture of the day. Our fullest information comes from the large and prosperous huerta community of Gandía in 1724, where the survey of that year listed 377 plough animals – 224 horses, 31 mules, 6 oxen, 6 cows, and 110 asses.[2] This may seem a good ratio for the 339 households which either owned or farmed any land in the town – but 119 of these families had no plough animal at all. Another 146 had just one meagre horse or ass – probably often (given the value of a few *lliures* or so) on its last legs. Only 74 families were in the fortunate position of having more than one animal, though some of these (lawyers and others) clearly used them for drawing a carriage rather than a plough. The situation appears to have been considerably worse in the more backward villages of the interior, especially in Morisco times. In Villamarchante on the morrow of the expulsion they found only 20 nags or mules and a few ploughs, for a population which had numbered 126 households; in the Sierra de Eslida there were no more than 24 draught-animals for 250 families.[3]

On the whole, if our analysis is correct, Valencian agriculture in the seventeenth century was overwhelmingly geared to providing bread for those who occupied or tilled the soil – and providing it badly. There is a rough method of demonstrating this by relating aggregate production to population level. The *tercio diezmo* fetched 24,246 *lliures* a year on average, making the full tithe equivalent to 93,520 ($x = 27y \div 7$), and total agricultural production (taking a simple multiplier of 10) equal to 935,200 *lliures*. The *tercio diezmo* areas in our table had around 19,045 households, a weighting of just over a fifth in a total population of 96,731 (the figures refer to 1609). Hence the total value of the agricultural product of the kingdom as a whole

[1] Bleda, *Crónica*, 1030.   [2] AHN Osuna leg. 811 n. 8, fiscal enquiry of 1724.
[3] ARV MR 10131 (Villamarchante); ADM Segorbe leg. 61 n. 9 (Sierra de Eslida). These figures may be too low, because the Moriscos had already sold off some of their stock before the inventory was taken.

may have been in the region of 4,676,000 *lliures*. This works out at around 11.13 per cent of the agrarian product of Castile, which da Silva has estimated at 15,000 million *maravedís* (or 42 million *lliures*).[1] Intriguingly, the population of Valencia, at 96,731 households, was about 8 per cent of that of Castile, which numbered 1,200,000 households in 1591. The agreement is close enough, and prompts us to reaffirm that agriculture in the peninsula in Habsburg times was closely tied to the number of mouths to be fed – or the number of hands at the plough. Therefore we must expect the fortunes of the rural economy to fluctuate, to a very large extent, according to the level of manpower.

Unfortunately, the *tercio diezmo* is not much use for charting these fluctuations, as it is largely confined by the hazards of the surviving documentation to the period 1600–50, and covers anyway only the major royal towns. For information about the rural economy the indispensable resort is to the tithe itself. In the cathedral archive of Valencia lie the records of 92 tithing areas into which the diocese was divided in the sixteenth-century (the number rose subsequently with the subdivision of some of the units), covering among them most of the modern province of Valencia and the northern half of that of Alicante. There is one great obstacle to using this documentation. Unlike the *tercio diezmo*, the main tithes were never directly adminis-tered but always farmed out to entrepreneurs. Hence we have no record of the state of the harvests, merely of the price which the tithe farmer was prepared to offer for them, once every four years in advance. The records of these tithe-farms are useless for any detailed work. They reflect at a distance the size of the expected harvest, the price which it would fetch on the market, and the margin of profit which the tithe-farmer intended to reserve for himself. We can never know what the first category amounted to in any one quadrennium; but we can at least get close to its fluctuation over a period of time by cancelling the element of price inflation.[2] There are three

[1] Da Silva, *En Espagne*, 91.
[2] For a discussion of the theoretical base underlying the use of tithe-farms, see Le Roy Ladurie, *Paysans de Languedoc*, 85–91. On the general question of Spanish tithes, see the contributions of Antonio Eiras Roel, Angel García Sanz, and others, in *Actas de las I Jornadas de Metodología Aplicada de las Ciencias Históricas*, 51–90 and 143–51.

groups of tithe-farms to be considered: the main ones ('of bread and wine', as they were called, out of sacramental as well as agricultural inspiration), the ancillary ones of cattle, separately accounted for in 11 areas where sheep were reared, and those of fruit and vegetables, important enough in the Middle Ages to have been also separately auctioned in three zones, Valencia, Sagunto and Játiva. I have deflated the main tithe-farms by a 7-year moving average of wheat prices (including the 4 years of the farm together with the preceding 3), those of fruits by a similar index of raw silk, and those of cattle by one of mutton prices (except after 1650 when an absence of mutton quotations forces us to use a general index of commodity prices).[1] A check on the deflated 'bread and wine' tithes is provided by the *tercio diezmo* of wheat, which is available for one part of Valencia – Morella, the 'granary of the kingdom' – between 1600 and 1700 in a long series which is continuous enough to be worth using. Here we are dealing with actual cuts taken of the harvest itself, which require no sleight of hand to make them speak (see figure 5).

As regards the main harvests the general pattern is clear enough: expansion up to the quadrennium 1573–6, an overall stagnation thereafter until the year of the expulsion of the Moriscos, then a fall, which was prolonged into the reign of Philip IV when the index reached a low point in the quadrennium 1645–8, and finally a gradual recovery in the reign of the last Habsburg, who seems to have presided over something of a minor golden age, in Valencia as in Catalonia.[2] The story is familiar enough from our survey of population trends. An agriculture which was 75 per cent grain based – grain which served mostly to feed the people who grew it – inevitably rose and fell more or less in accordance with the number of workers and the number of mouths they had to feed. However, the correlation is not perfect. Higher consumption by the Old Christians, man for man, than by the Moriscos made the

---

[1] All prices are based on Hamilton, *American Treasure*. Quotations for wheat and silk after 1650 come from the author's own manuscripts. I would like to thank Professor Hamilton most warmly for permission to use his figures, and also Richard Ling who communicated them to me in the first place. The tithe-farms themselves come from ACV *Libros de arriendos de diezmos*, 4388–97. Cf. appendix 1.

[2] Cf. Vilar, *Catalunya dins l'Espanya moderna*, II, 384 and III, 432.

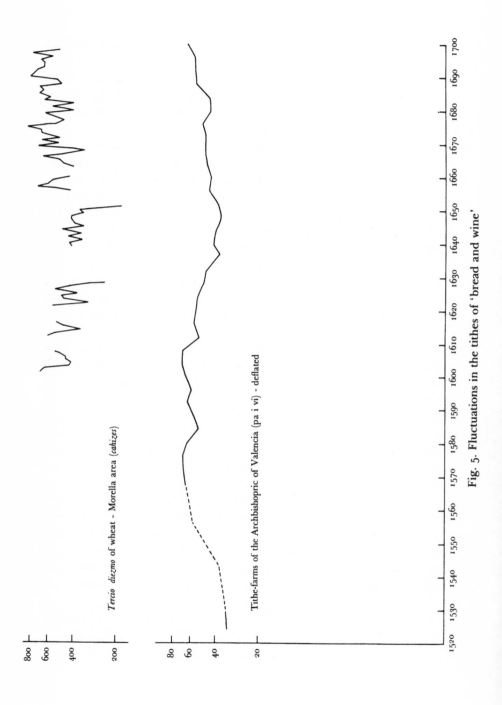

Tercio diezmo of wheat - Morella area (cahizes)

Tithe-farms of the Archbishopric of Valencia (pa i vi) - deflated

Fig. 5. Fluctuations in the tithes of 'bread and wine'

decline in agriculture around 1609 less pronounced than it would otherwise have been. The graph tends to bear out Jaime Bleda, who wrote in 1618: 'we hardly notice the absence of the Moriscos, for anyone can see that the tithes...are not yielding a great deal less (and soon will be yielding a great deal more) than before the expulsion'.[1] It was only after he wrote this that things began to go seriously wrong. There was even a certain optimism in some quarters that the Old Christians would farm land more efficiently than the Moriscos, who (grumbled Aznar Cardona) 'had many fine properties but never grew anything worthwhile on them'.[2] In Alberique it was hoped that land which had been neglected and left arid by an impoverished and backward Morisco peasantry would now be brought under irrigation, 'for this is feasible in many parts given the industry and application of the new settlers'.[3]

There were in fact many interlocking factors in the crisis which only became fully apparent around 1620. One might perhaps blame at the outset the policy of the Crown in distributing the Morisco lands to a mass of smallholders, overriding the opinion of some senyors that these small proprietors would lack the resources to tackle adequately the work of reclamation. As the agent of the Duke of Mandas noted in Picasent: 'we can see by experience that the ordinary settler has not the capital to clear 50 to 100 *cahizadas* [25 to 50 hectares] of scrub, whereas a big proprietor would spend money... tearing up the rosemary and dwarf palm...and anyway the new settlers would die of hunger were it not for the work which the big men provide in sowing, threshing, pruning and wine harvesting'. On this reckoning, the recovery of the tithes in the later seventeenth century was made possible by the re-alignment of property in the resettlements, by which the big interests among the second generation of settlers grabbed 30 or 40 per cent of the land for themselves.

Yet it may be doubted whether these larger proprietors had either the money or the interest to transform their new holdings, given that their one ambition was to become noble

[1] *Crónica*, 1030.   [2] *Expulsión justificada*, fol. 64v.
[3] AHN Osuna leg. 1926 n. 2, *carta puebla* of Alberique, 14 March 1612, cap. 12.
[4] AHN Osuna leg. 2980 n. 1, memorandum, 1 April 1619.

Table 8. *Income from land-owning in Gandía 1724 (in lliures)*

Direct exploitation	12,686
Leasing	2,876
Share-cropping	2,601

These totals refer only to income from land owned, another 5,308 *lliures* representing the actual benefits of the leaseholders and sharecroppers themselves (cf. table 5, p. 38).

rentiers, and given too that the bankruptcy of the former Morisco lords after 1609 destroyed a mass of bourgeois capital loaned to them. We can rarely tell, unfortunately, from the cadastral surveys what nobles, lawyers or artisans actually did with the land they held, except in one case. In Gandía the document of 1724 provides a somewhat haphazard breakdown of where agricultural income came from – whether from direct exploitation, leasing or share-cropping. The extent of the latter, being an ad hoc yearly arrangement, was almost certainly underestimated, so the figures have to be handled with extreme caution (see table 8). At the very least (and remember that the properties of the clergy, the archetypal rentiers, are not included in this survey) a quarter of the agricultural income of property-owners in Gandía came from rents – a proportion which corresponds very roughly to the weighting of lawyers, nobles and distinguished citizens in the landowning class. This Valencian bourgeoisie was not noted for its investing or productive zeal. As a group it was not all that wealthy. Recall the figure given in chapter 2, above: no one in Gandía got more than 650 *lliures* a year from land. Tithes, feudal rents, and (in 1724) the depressed state of the market severely restricted the resources of the big property-owners.

This poverty was very likely responsible for the failure to make better use of the land by irrigation. The seventeenth century is littered with projects for dams and irrigation channels, few of which were successful. The great dam of Tibi, which was completed in 1594 on such a magnificent scale 'that you might have thought it had been built by the Romans' (as the chronicler Escolano proudly informs us), broke open in 1601. Though repaired at enormous cost by 1604, it proved difficult to clean and maintain. The water came slowly, and many of the arid lands round Alicante which had been expected to benefit stayed dry.[1] A similar fate overtook the dam at Onteniente, built in 1686. It had been plagued from the outset by the opposition of powerful figures within the town 'who hold properties in the old irrigation zone and, as always happens, are eager to stop anyone else getting access to water'.[2] Owing to faulty engineering (the man in charge apparently 'couldn't handle a compass'), the great wall cracked open only a few years after completion and was never properly repaired. Technological inadequacy seems to have reinforced economic conservatism throughout Valencian agriculture.

The clearest proof of this is no doubt the disappointing performance of the tithes on commercial crops – the *paners* of Valencia, Játiva and Sagunto (see figure 6). The index of real value fell sharply here from its maximum in the quadrennium 1589–92, plumbing the depths in 1597–1600 and again in 1621–4 (when it coincided with a fierce crisis in the silk industry, which was plagued by a shortage of the raw material).[3] There was a revival in the 1630s, but the index stayed obstinately well below its old late-sixteenth-century level until the 1680s. Explaining the collapse of mulberry production in Algemesí, the authorities invoked 'the high cost of paying ploughboys or getting the special branches for the grubs to climb on, since these used to be brought to us by the Moriscos...Now everything is twice as dear'.[4] Hamilton, it is true, failed to find much evidence of pressure on wage labour in Valencia after the expulsion of the Moriscos, but his figures relate only to the capital city, where there was no immediate problem of depopulation. Around the old Morisco areas things appear to have been very different. It cost the abbey of Valldigna 60 *lliures* to have the grain reaped on its home farm of Benivaire in 1580 and over 156 in 1630; it cost some 500 *reals* to have the mulberry trees pruned there in an average year around 1600, and 750 around 1640 – all this over a period in which the estate itself was shrinking in size.[5] In 1585 the Duke of Gandía could get his vineyards dug for

[1] A. López Gómez, 'Riegos y cultivos en la huerta de Alicante', *Estudios Geográficos*, XII (1951), 713; Escolano, *Décadas*, II, 35; RAH 9.4.4.1.43, fol. 347.
[2] RAH 9.4.4.1.43, fol. 80, 'relación del desastrado fin de la fábrica del estanque eo pantano de Onteniente'. [3] Cf. below, chapter 4.
[4] ARV Comunes 1060, viceregal mandate, 21 Oct. 1639.
[5] ARV Clero legs. 795 and 730, *comptes*. Cf. Hamilton, *American Treasure*, 306.

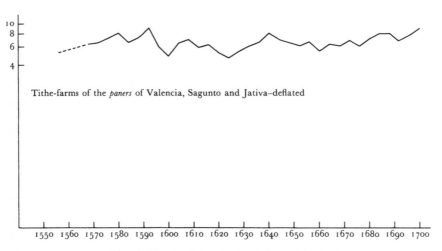

Fig. 6. Fluctuations in the tithes of fruits

just under 4 *sous* per man per day, and his wheat reaped for
5 (all this with free wage-labour; serfs cost him less), but in 1610
no man would touch a spade for under 8.[1] Round Orihuela
in 1640 they were moaning that 'the harvests of grain and
mulberry are being lost, for no man can be found at any price
to do the job'.[2] And finally even round Valencia city itself, with
the further depopulation of Philip IV's reign, agricultural wages
rose so steeply 'that even in the best years the most diligent
cultivator cannot get back from his grain what it cost him to
produce it'.[3] In the circumstances the trend towards rentier
status on the part of the big landowner of seventeenth-century
Valencia is readily comprehensible.

Of course the decline of manpower should have opened
opportunities for ranching. One of the most perplexing features
of the whole story is the catastrophically bad performance of
the cattle tithes (see figure 7). Even in terms of nominal value
they stayed obstinately depressed throughout the Habsburg
period (see appendix 1 B). It comes as little surprise, certainly,
to find the pastoralist losing ground in the later sixteenth
century as population expanded and took grazing land for

[1] AHN Osuna legs. 805 n. 1 and 1027 n. 21, accounts and memorial.
[2] ACA CA leg. 718, petition of Orihuela, 12 May 1640.
[3] ACA CA leg. 1355, petition of Valencia, 26 Nov. 1645.

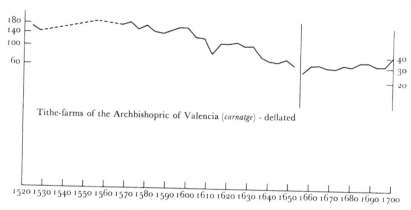

Fig. 7. Fluctuations in the tithes of cattle

arable. The cattle tithes reached their maximum in terms of real value as early as the quadrennium 1553–6 and then began to decline. But it is at first sight rather strange that the cattle-men failed to seize the opportunity of acquiring abandoned land in the wake of the expulsion of the Moriscos. Of course herding had never been, and was never to be, at the centre of this essentially arable economy: cattle were a continual menace to huerta crops. Another part of the problem seems to be that many of the pastoral tithing areas – Alcoy, Cocentaina, Calpe, Játiva, Penáguila, Perpunchent, Quesa and Bicorp – were situated in, or on the fringes of, the sierras of the south and west, where the Morisco population had been principally concentrated. To the already classic figure of the Morisco as muleteer it appears that we must add that of the Morisco shepherd and wool-shearer – embodied for example, in the famous Jerónimo Millini, 'king' of the rebels of the Vall de Laguar in 1609, whose domain was situated precisely in the sheep zone.[1] Certainly Cocentaina was complaining around 1620 that the wool trade of this whole area had been wrecked by the expulsion.[2] (See figure 8.) The especially grave economic disorganization of Valencia's chief pastoral zone appears to have destroyed the capital necessary to restock the herds.

The weather may also have been a complicating factor. Given

[1] Escolano, *Décadas*, II, 808.
[2] ACA CA leg. 869, petitions of Cocentaina, 1622–4.

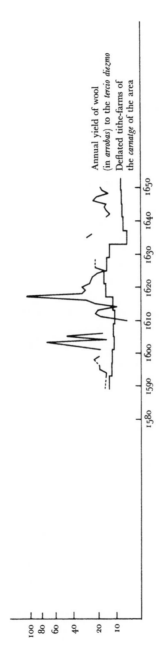

Fig. 8. Bocairente and Bañeres: decline of the herds

Annual yield of wool
(in *arrobas*) to the *tercio diezmo*
Deflated tithe-farms of
the *carnatge* of the area

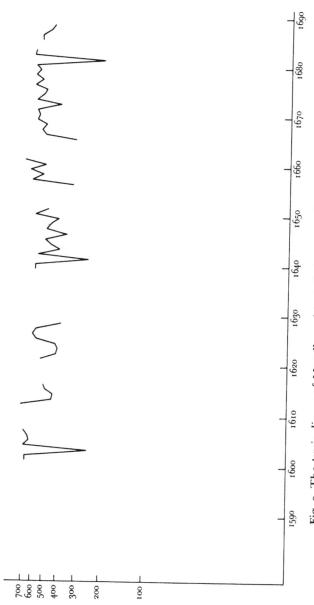

Fig. 9. The *tercio diezmo* of Morella and jurisdiction: annual total of new-born lambs

the poorly developed state of Valencian agriculture, a bad year – too dry or too wet – could wreak havoc. Its effects were more lasting than is the case nowadays, because cultivators had fewer reserves to fall back on. The crisis of the 1590s in the fruit tithes, for example, seems to have been precipitated by a spell of heavy, unseasonable rains, which caused the River Júcar to burst its banks several years in succession, laying waste some of the best mulberry in the kingdom.[1] The trouble with mulberry in Carcagente half a century later was 'the tragic way in which the leaf has shrivelled up', thanks to a run of dry years.[2] And it was the drought of the 1640s which prevented the cattle-men taking advantage of all the empty space in Valencia. 'With the lack of water and the great aridity this year', noted the Valencian magistrates in 1645, 'the sheep are under weight'.[3] The new-born lambs, declared the bailiff of Morella in 1651, 'will profit little because of the great drought, and will be hard to sell with the shortage of grass'.[4] (See figure 9.) Are these hard-luck stories credible or are they simply the eternal complaints of a peasantry for whom times were always bad?

A rough sort of record of bad weather can be assembled from a few miscellaneous sources for Valencia – in particular the comments of the bailiffs who administered the *tercio diezmo* (although these tend to come mostly after 1600 and before 1650), and the remarkable diary of a Valencian priest, running from 1589 to 1629.[5] The limitations of this testimony are only too obvious, especially the scarcity of data (except for Morella) after 1650. Nevertheless, if we take it at face value, we note a preoccupation with drought in very many years of the early seventeenth century – a preoccupation perhaps best summed up in the priest's comment on the rainfall of 11 August 1628: 'Thanks be to God, for we were sorely tried with the lack of rain and the lack of bread'.[6] Agriculture, then, was directly affected by exceptional aridity, in all or part of Valencia, in the following years: 1614, 1616, 1619, 1622, 1625, 1626, 1627, 1628,

[1] ARV Clero leg. 404, petition of the convent of La Murta, 21 April 1594.
[2] ARV MR 5632, bailiff of Carcagente to don Basilio Polo, 21 April 1646.
[3] AMV MC 174, deliberation of 3 Sept. 1645.
[4] ARV MR 5800, to Junta Patrimonial, 11 Oct. 1651.
[5] Porcar, *Coses evengudes, passim.*   [6] Ibid., II, cap. 3315.

1631, 1635, 1637, 1645, 1650 and 1683. And the inevitable counterpart of this dryness was a savage, intermittent rainfall, which caused flooding. The bad years for agriculture here, to judge from our sources, were 1589–90, 1605, 1612, 1617, 1624, 1627 (in spring, after a winter drought), 1631 (in June, after a spring drought) 1635 (in autumn after a summer drought), and 1651.

What information can we derive from these dates? It seems undeniable that the Valencians were critically concerned with the inroads which bad weather – a combination of drought and flooding – was making into their agriculture in the 1610s, 1620s, and 1630s, and also perhaps in the 1590s and the early 1600s. Bennassar, on the basis of a much more systematic study of dates of wine harvests, has hinted at a spell of dry weather in late-sixteenth and early-seventeenth-century Valladolid – a dryness punctuated by flooding.[1] This would seem to suggest that one of the troubles afflicting the rural Spain of Philip III and Philip IV was indeed an aggravation of that old problem of the Iberian farmer, drought. For example, in 1616 Bayarte was writing to the Crown of the problems facing the resettlements due to the lack of rain for several years past.[2]

In any case, as Bennassar suggests, there was no long-term worsening of the climate.[3] After 1650 colder years came to the vineyards of Valladolid; and after 1650 the mention of droughts in Valencia becomes less frequent. This may be just the defect of our sources, but I think not. The grain harvests of Morella – for which we have the longest continuous series – were really extremely good in most years of Charles II's reign. The period 1660–80 is probably the turning point – 'the fat corn years', as one authority has suggested calling it, because of the plethora of good harvests in the south of France.[4] It seems that another

[1] *Valladolid*, 39–51. On the other hand, the author himself prefers an explanation of the precocious vintages based on conscious marketing decisions.
[2] ACA CA leg. 704, Bayarte to king, 10 Aug. 1616.
[3] Any attempt to link Spain's troubles to that wider phenomenon, the 'Little Ice Age' of the seventeenth century, seems both unnecessary and impossible. I tend to agree with E. Le Roy Ladurie's playing-down of the impact of long-term climatic change on agriculture, in *Histoire du climat depuis l'an mil* (Paris 1967).
[4] Joseph Goy and Emmanuel Le Roy Ladurie, *Les fluctuations du produit de la dîme* (Paris/The Hague 1972), 362–4.

cycle of weather made its effects felt, not just in Valencia, but over the western Mediterranean seaboard. But this brought its own problems, for these excellent harvests were simply too big to be easily absorbed by the low level of population in Valencia. The scissors movement caused by rising output and falling market prices can be seen quite well in the case of Morella, where a good series for both exists. With more grain being harvested than ever before in Charles II's reign, and with only 1,591 households in the local *tercio diezmo* area in 1692 (as against 2,135 in 1609), the curve of prices for grain sank inexorably. 'One did not need to be a prophet or the son of a prophet', lamented the bailiff in 1663, to see that all this good weather would 'infallibly wreck the chances of selling this wheat'.[1] (See figure 10.)

Cheaper bread was perhaps a factor in the recovery of the Valencian population in Good King Charles' Golden Days, but the dismal result of this development was to burden the commercial farmers even more heavily. The French historians have noted how, around 1680, these wealthy men failed, victims of much the same circumstances as their contemporaries south of the Pyrenees – low prices for their goods and excessive overheads (in particular, high seigneurial rents).[2] The Oriolas, Císcars, Escrivás and their like, who had been busy accumulating property since the expulsion of the Moriscos, found themselves caught out. Their dissatisfaction was probably a key factor in the great peasant upheaval of 1693, the so-called Second Germania, which attempted to get seigneurial rents lowered during this troubled period. Do not put your money in agriculture, the Queen Regent had advised them in 1669 as she launched a grand project for a trading company, 'for farming is nothing but slavery, or a sure way of going mad'.[3] The wealthy men in Valencia seem to have taken her advice. Little money, in the end, was forthcoming for the sort of commercial agriculture – mulberry or cattle – which might have transformed Habsburg Valencia. Nothing is more striking in the whole

[1] ARV MR 5806, to the Junta Patrimonial, 10 Jan. 1663.
[2] Le Roy Ladurie, *Paysans de Languedoc*, 304–8; Jacquart, *Crise rurale*, 707–15.
[3] AMV Churat 1634 vol. III n. 121, 15 Jan. 1669.

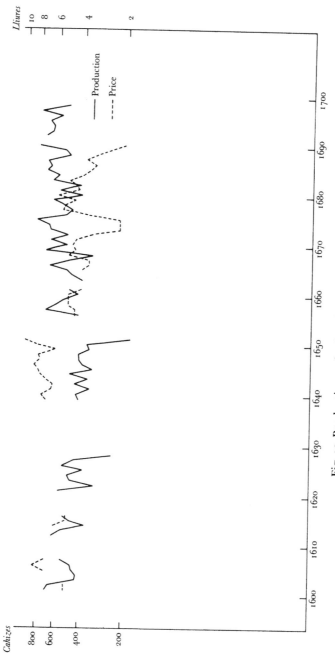

Fig. 10. Production and price of wheat: Morella and district

story, in fact, than the permanence of a traditional agrarian structure, even while factors such as wind, rain and manpower alternately increased and diminished the size of the end product.[1]

[1] A general pattern of stagnation appears to have characterized Castilian agriculture in this century also. On the other hand Castile has a different, more violent price history, and a different, less violent population history, so the tithe curves seem to sink less in the early seventeenth century, and behave less buoyantly under Charles II. Cf. Pierre Ponsot, 'En Andalousie occidentale: les fluctuations de la production du blé sous l'ancien régime', in Goy and Le Roy Ladurie, *Fluctuations de la dîme*, 304–19; and Gonzalo Anes and Jean-Paul Le Flem, 'La crisis del siglo XVII: producción agrícola, precios e ingresos en tierras de Segovia', *Moneda y Crédito*, 92–5 (1965), 6–23.

4

Paying their way in the world

'We in this city and kingdom of Valencia', the committee of the Estates reminded Philip IV, 'live for the most part by trade, and on the victuals and merchandise brought from other realms.'[1] This brave declaration, contradicting any facile assumption that the Valencians lived wholly within a subsistence economy, was founded on the notorious fact that the kingdom could not feed itself. 'Our wheat harvest is so small', wrote one viceroy in 1609, 'that it does not last half the year.'[2] Two centuries later the geographer Cavanilles was to arrive at a remarkably similar assessment: 'the kingdom hardly grows enough wheat to feed its big population for six months of the year'.[3] Though the expulsion of the Moriscos might seem to have eased the pressure for a while, the deficit in fact remained a major feature of the seventeenth-century economy. For the prime culprit was the great city of Valencia, which was still consuming – even when its population had fallen to around 10,000 households – some 36,500 *cahizes* (say 73,000 hectolitres) of wheat a year, most of which had to be imported from overseas.[4]

But it was not simply a question of the bread supply; the dependence of the Valencians on outside supplies of essential food and materials was fatal. 'For the provisioning of this city with meat', declared the magistrates in 1629, 'more than 80,000 head of sheep are needed every year', almost all of which, given the underdevelopment of Valencia's pastoral economy, had to come from the *meseta*.[5] True, mutton did not figure largely in

[1] ARV G 1957 fol. 77, Diputats to king, 23 April 1624.
[2] ACA CA leg. 607 n. 13/2, viceroy to king, 7 Nov. 1609.
[3] Cavanilles, *Geografía*, I, 203. [4] ACA CA leg. 710, viceroy to king, 14 Aug. 1635.
[5] AMV CM 59 jurats to king, 27 March 1629.

79

the diet of the poor, who turned instead to fish ('even on days which are not of fast and abstinence'). But this 'most essential food' had to be brought in from the Atlantic, mainly in the form of stockfish, by English or Breton skippers.[1] In 1627 the government looked at the whole range of Valencia's foreign imports, preparatory to imposing a new duty on the trade. It found the most important imports to be wheat, meat, olive oil and fish, with linen and spices making up most of the balance.[2]

Linen is a generic term covering the coarse canvas ware which was a basic article of dress over much of Valencia. Towards the end of the eighteenth century Cavanilles was to remark that the peasants of the huerta wore hardly anything else; and in the *tercio diezmo* records, flax and hemp account for nearly 10 per cent of the value of the harvests in the coastal plain between Castellón and Sagunto.[3] Away from the coast the importance of flax diminished. Up in the sierras clothes were mostly woven out of the local wool, because the weavers of Alcoy and Onda were able to turn out enough 'mountain cloth' to satisfy 'a large part of the common people of our kingdom as well as of Murcia and La Mancha'.[4] Thus there are two Valencias to be considered with respect to textiles – the hill country which was largely self-sufficient, and the plain which depended heavily on imports. Most of the cheaper linen came from France, handled by the merchants and shippers of Arles and St Malo.

With spices we enter the realm of commodities which Valencia did not merely consume herself, but passed on as intermediary to other parts of the peninsula. Most of the 'pepper, cloves and drugs' landed in the kingdom came, in fact, through one port, Alicante, and were destined for distribution throughout the Crown of Aragon. The Portuguese, of course, were supposed to have a monopoly of spice imports into the Spanish Monarchy, at least after the union of the two crowns in 1580. Olivares, the powerful favourite of Philip IV, learned to his horror in 1622 that it was English interlopers who were providing Alicante and Mediterranean Spain generally with these precious commodities. As part of his general programme of reform, he insisted

---

[1] ACA CA leg. 724, petition of *jurats* (1645?).
[2] ACA CA leg. 1352, don Francisco de Castelví to don Nicolás Mensa, 9 Feb. 1627.
[3] *Geografía*, I, 141.   [4] Escolano, *Décadas*, I, 366.

that the men of Alicante should deal directly with Lisbon. But
he found that he had brought a hornets' nest about his ears,
for the merchants of Alicante let him know in no uncertain
terms that they had no intention of sailing out into the broad
Atlantic, because of 'the enormous peril to life and fortune from
storms at sea and from the many pirates who are on the prowl'.[1]

The story of Alicante and her spices illustrates the strengths
and weakness of the mercantile community in Habsburg Spain.
The town grew rapidly and by the 1620s its trade had acquired
such dimensions that 'it is more valuable than that coming
through the customs of Valencia city'.[2] Situated in poor, arid
country to the far south of the kingdom, it had few natural
resources apart from its wines and its soap (made out of olive
oil), and it retained into modern times something of the air
of a colonial factory, of the kind which might have been found
in the somnolent hinterlands of Asia or Africa. First, there was
its diminutive size – barely 1,500 families at the peak of its glory
in Habsburg times. Then too, there was its lopsided occupational
structure (lopsided at least for the seventeenth century). 'If you
take our trade away', her spokesman warned Olivares, with
some exaggeration but more than a grain of truth, 'the town,
or the greater part of it anyway, will empty overnight, for it
is our whole livelihood.'[3]

The rise of Alicante was above all a result of her geographical
situation as one of the best natural harbours along the Mediterranean coastline, linked by good roads (suitable for carts as
well as mules) to the heartland of Spain. Her triumph over her
potential rival Cartagena was sealed in 1550 by a treaty between
Valencia and Castile reducing duties by half on Castilian goods
in transit through the port.[4] As the agreement made clear,
Castile was primarily interested in Alicante as a port of embarkation for raw wool from the Meseta en route for the
weaving centres of North Italy. In the reign of Philip II it became
a regular port of call for Atlantic shipping bound for Leghorn,
and sometimes served as a staging post for Indies goods carried

[1] ACA CA leg. 603, petitions of Gerónimo Claros, Lorenzo Ivorra and others (1624),
and cf. leg. 592, consulta, 19 Jan. 1634.
[2] ACA CA leg. 1352, petition of the Diputats, 1627.
[3] ACA CA leg. 603, petition of Lorenzo Ivorra, 1624.
[4] ACA CA leg. 1352, copy of *concordia* of 1550.

on mule-back from Seville, before they were loaded in Mediterranean waters for Italy.[1]

Apart from Alicante, though – whose history really belongs to all Spain – the ports of the Valencian littoral were mostly cramped and backward places. Of course the city of Valencia depended on overseas trade for its very existence, but this was essentially as a consumer – and not a very active consumer at that. 'Almost all the profit on the sale of linen', noted the Cortes of 1645 sourly, 'goes to the French and not to us.'[2] For not only did most of the stuff come from France in the first place, but even its sale over the counter within the city walls was virtually monopolized by Gallic residents. Somewhat earlier the Council of Aragon had bewailed the fact that the Valencians were not men of enterprise, either in trade or in agriculture. In words which prefigure with some accuracy those of the Alicante spice-dealers, it noted that same numbing fear of 'fog, hailstorms, drought, tempests at sea, corsairs, bankruptcies and suchlike perils'.[3] The Valencians preferred to sit at home while the French or the English took the risks and pocketed the profits.

'The greater part of the merchants and businessmen of this kingdom', noted the assembly of the nobility in 1609, 'are active in revenue farms, handling seigneurial rents, tithes and first fruits.'[4] The statement was perhaps something of an exaggeration. In fact a majority of the tithe-farmers were often nobles, and – increasingly in the seventeenth century – just plain peasants, as the merchants retreated from an ever more unprofitable agricultural market (see table 9). On the other hand some big mercantile fortunes were made in or pledged to the tithes. One can think of a few such cases. The partnership of Miguel Vaquero and Juan Bautista Bandrés – which virtually dominated Valencian finance in the 1620s until they went bankrupt in 1626 – emerged in a modest way by farming the rents of the Duke of Segorbe in the 1590s and spread into farms of 29 different tithing areas (over a quarter of the total) in the

[1] F. Braudel and R. Romano, *Navires et marchandises à Livourne 1547–1611* (Paris 1951), 36; Valentín Vázquez de Prada, 'Actividad económica del Levante español en el siglo XVI', VI° *Congreso de Historia de la Corona de Aragón* (1957), 902–3.
[2] ARV R 521, cap. 207 of Braç Real, 1645.
[3] ACA CA leg. 607 n. 16, consulta, 30 Nov. 1613.
[4] ARV R 527 fol. 403, 18 Sept. 1609.

Table 9. *Tithe-farmers by status group*

	1521/24		1620/23		1697/1700	
	Number	Percentage	Number	Percentage	Number	Percentage
Nobles	41	14	85	29	14	4
Ciutadans (bourgeois rentiers)	15	5	13	5	44	11
Professions	32	11	13	5	12	3
Clergy	9	3	Nil		3	1
Merchants	84	29	87	30	25	6
Artisans	64	22	53	18	66	17
Peasants	16	5	37	13	220	56
Women	31	11	1		9	2
Total	292	100	289	100	393	100
No indication	35		106		35	
Total	327		395		428	

quadrennium 1620–3; a farm of the excise of the city of Valencia in 1624; and – the biggest prize of all – a farm of the royal customs dues between 1621 and 1626.[1] At a more modest level were the Sanz family, Baltasar and Gabriel, father and son, who dominated the life of the seaport of Peñíscola under Philip III and Philip IV. As well as dabbling in the trade of Peñíscola, they farmed out the *tercio diezmo* of the rural hinterland in 1624; contracted to victual the king's troops awaiting embarkation at Vinaroz in 1633, and to supply meat at a guaranteed price to the city of Valencia in the same year; and then made the leap into the big time (also in 1633) with an offer to farm out the royal salt monopoly in the kingdom.[2]

In rural Valencia, time and money were differently spent. It is difficult to recapture the tranquil pace of life in this other Valencia, which by its sheer bulk also counted in the glittering world of the trader. The merchant Francisco Baso of Játiva had 2 hectares of mulberry and grain, as well as his two spinning wheels, 60 *lliures* in cash, and the 'chestnut coloured nag' on which (one presumes) he made the rounds of the little villages

[1] Their career can be pieced together from ADM Segorbe leg. 61 n. 9; ACA CA leg. 709, petition, 7 Feb. 1631; leg. 1372 fols. 109–117, memorandum of don Francisco de Castelví (1627?).

[2] The details are scattered through AMV MC 160, 6 April 1634, and 162, 14 Aug. 1635; ACA CA legs. 712, *pagos*, 1631–5, and 716, viceroy to king, 24 Sept. 1637; ARV B 131, 18 July 1639; and, finally, BL Add. MSS. 28,373 fol. 141, petition, 19 Dec. 1604.

of the neighbourhood, buying and selling the silk and linen for which the huerta of Játiva was noted.[1] Again, landed property figures large in the holdings of the Baya Mallux brothers, Vicente and Juan, who decided in 1571 to form a company 'after the mercantile fashion' (keeping the accounts, incidentally, in Arabic). The Baya Mallux were the third biggest landowners in the upper valley of Valldigna, according to my reading of the cadastral survey of 1548, and they were the biggest herd-owners after their master, the abbot of Valldigna, in the early 1600s, with around an eighth of the total flocks of sheep and goats.[2] Between 1571 and 1577 the mercantile company of Vicente and Juan made a profit of 2,479 *lliures* on the sale of silk and wool, 1,166 on sugar (cultivated on a large scale in Valldigna at the time), 915 on cattle, and 420 from farming the rents of the abbot.[3] But this activity was hardly significant in the context of the rural economy. In all, these prosperous Morisco peasants-turned-traders had earned in eight years only a third of the 15,000 *lliures* which their master, the abbot, drew in seigneurial rents in one year alone.

Valencia was a naturally rich agricultural land, but its commercial potential was only feebly developed. Foreign merchants came from time to time to scour the hinterland in the harvest months – men like Isaac Ponset, consul of the French nation, who rode round Játiva in 1619 buying up olive oil for France.[4] But it would hardly have paid him to make the same trip every year, for the badly tended olive trees often gave no fruit at all.[5] This was still pioneering country over much of its length and breadth, where travellers ventured cautiously, if at all. Ponset's companion in 1619, Jaime Tricaut, turns up again in 1631, this time combing the sierras for wool; but he took good care to arm himself against the 'hordes of robbers' who had tried several times to relieve him of his strongbox.[6] Such men, at not

[1] ARV Clero leg. 735, inventory, 6 May 1596.
[2] ARV Clero 1423, *capbreu* of Simat de Valldigna, 1548; leg. 732, 'manifest dels cabrits', 1603–4.
[3] ARV Clero leg. 752, 'procés de compte y rahó de la compañia mercantinalment [*sic*] entre'l quondam Vicent Baya Mallux de una y Joan Mallux jermà de aquell de part altre', 21 Oct. 1578.
[4] ARV MR 10610, *Peatge* of Játiva, 1619.
[5] ARV R 530 fols. 39v–40v, declaration of the Estament Militar, 8 Feb. 1620.
[6] ACA CA leg. 875, petition of Jaime Tricaut, 26 May 1631.

Table 10. *Raw and spun silk exported from Alcira and Játiva (average yearly totals in pounds weight)*

	Alcira				Játiva			
	Fina	Adúcar	Esqueixada	Total	Fina	Adúcar	Esqueixada	Total
1553–8	10,539	1,415	Nil	11,954				
1592–5					14,319	16	592	14,927
1596–7	9,260	1,162	15,218	25,640				
1606–8	4,302	455	45,282	50,039	7,915	333	Nil	8,248
1619–25					13,099	3,697	4,594	21,390
1626–33	773	2,418	14,543	17,734	7,684	4,366	3,602	15,652
1691–9	12,577	3,686	Nil	16,263	9,645	2,084	100	11,829

A blank in the table indicates that no information is available.
SOURCES: ARV MR 10447–10458 (Alcira), and 10603–10629 (Játiva).

much more than a day's ride out of the city of Valencia, were in a real enough sense merchant venturers.

If, as the committee of the Estates grandiloquently proclaimed, Valencia could only procure her daily bread by trade, what had she got to give in return? Her trump card was the range of tempting delicacies for which the Levante was famed throughout the peninsula – rice, raisins, figs, aniseed, wine, esparto, even flax, but above all silk, according to one list of 1622.[1] Without doubt it was silk, 'the chief fruit of the realm', which served as Valencia's lifeline with the outside world. Silk for bread: put crudely, that was the strategy of Valencian trade in Habsburg times. Here the Valencian story appears to overlap with that of the peninsula as a whole. One of the major symptoms of the decline of Spain – as it appeared to contemporaries no less than to later historians – was a fatal inability to balance its books in the world of international trade. The treasure of the Americas drained away through a thousand channels on reaching Seville and went to pay for the goods which the *arbitristas* kept urging the Spaniards to provide for themselves.[2] The problem of the empire was reflected in microcosm in the Valencian experience after 1609 – a decline

[1] ACA CA leg. 707, *jurats* of Valencia to king, 21 Feb. 1622.
[2] Sancho de Moncada, *Restauración política de España* (Madrid 1619) fols. 5–6v; Pedro Fernández Navarrete, *Conservación de Monarquías* (Madrid 1626), 93–5.

of local industry, a fall in exports and an inability finally to maintain an accustomed style of life.

Table 10 lists the quantities of silk in transit through the customs of Alcira and Játiva, two of the prime centres of mulberry cultivation, in the seventeenth century. It is based on the *Peatge* and *Quema* records and perhaps tends to over-emphasize exports to Castile (the most thoroughly and efficiently taxed of all the trades) at the expense of intra-Valencian transit, or sales to the French and the Italians. Native Valencians were in theory exempt from duty, except on exports to Castile, and Frenchmen or Italians sometimes paid their silk bills in the seaports of Denia or Cullera rather than in Alcira or Játiva – though in these cases they were supposed to get a certificate recording the exemption or the payment of the duty elsewhere, and these certificates were duly entered, in most cases at least, in the customs register. There are three qualities of silk to be distinguished: the *fina* or fine silk thread which comes from the inner cocoon spun by the silkworm, costing between 50 and 80 *sous* per pound weight; the *adúcar* or rough outer shell of the cocoon, worth 15 to 20 *sous;* and finally the broken thread which could be got from smashed or perforated cocoons, the *seda esqueixada* or *capell foradat* of our records, which fetched 5 to 7 *sous.*

Two great floods punctuate the sad story of falling silk exports – those of 1589 and 1627, when the Júcar burst its banks, ruining mulberry production for years to come. The decline is particularly visible in the case of best quality silk, though the use of *adúcar* and *esqueixada* on an increasingly massive scale during the early seventeenth century helped to conceal the magnitude of the collapse for a while. In 1647 and again in 1657 we find the abbot of Valldigna fulminating against the growing abuse of adulterating the fine thread with a mixture of *adúcar*.[1] By the 1690s, paralleling the revival of population and production in the countryside generally, silk exports had begun to revive. *Esqueixada* fell away to almost nothing, *adúcar* maintained the important position it had built up in the early part of the century, but the true measure of the recovery is the more buoyant performance of the fine silk thread from

[1] ARV Clero legs. 727 and 751, *cridas* of 1647 and 1657.

inside the cocoon. In terms of value and quality of output, the silkgrowers of the Júcar Valley were well on the way to reestablishing their old splendour by the end of the Habsburg period, preparing for the full flowering of the industry in the Levante under the Bourbons.

Surprisingly enough for a region so rich in raw silk, only a fraction of this material was actually woven into cloth in Valencia itself – 40,000 to 60,000 of the 400,000 pounds of thread teased from the cocoons, at a time when output was at its peak around 1580.[1] The Valencians were conscious enough themselves of their inferiority in this respect – 'for it is highly desirable that the silk we grow should be worked up before it is sent outside the kingdom, thereby creating more jobs... and swelling the incomes of our people, as well as benefiting Your Majesty's treasury'.[2] Though there was a lot of spinning done in the Júcar Valley, virtually all the cloth manufacture as such was concentrated within the walls of the capital, which had a long and glorious tradition as one of the homes of European velvet.

Though the fortunes of manufactured silk are perhaps less easy to chart than those of raw silk, something can be learned from looking at the customs records of the city of Valencia. In the Habsburg period, Castile was the best customer for Valencian silk cloth as it was for the unworked thread. Of some 96,620 ells of silk textiles manufactured in the city of Valencia in 1529, between 35,000 and 45,000 eventually found their way to Castile; of some 297,902 ells despatched in the same way in 1598, about 153,000 were destined ultimately for Castile.[3] In other words, Valencia's big neighbour regularly took a half of her silk manufactures. The history of this trade in silk cloth to Castile has recently been charted in an outstanding study by Richard Ling.[4] Ling finds that exports more than trebled in volume, from around 45,000 ells a year in the early 1520s to around 150,000 in the later 1570s. Then trouble occurred.

---

[1] Halperin Donghi, 'moriscos y cristianos viejos', xxiii-xxiv, 4.
[2] ACA CA leg. 726, petition of the *jurats* (1621?).
[3] ARV G 4807 & 4808, 'libres del despaig de les sedes teixides del General del Tall'. The *Tall* was a tax falling on the manufacture of cloth for sale.
[4] Richard Ling, 'Long Term Movements in the Trade of Valencia, Alicante and the Western Mediterranean 1450–1700' (University of California Ph.D. thesis 1974), 65–77.

After the peak year of 1579 a serious recession appears to have set in and, though there was a revival by the 1620s, the vivacity of the mid-sixteenth century was not recaptured.

The bare statistics do not fully convey the sense of tragedy which contemporaries felt at the difficulties of their main industry. In 1587 an official enquiry was mounted to find out what was wrong. By the 1620s the magistrates of the city were bewailing the slump in the number of weavers from 4,000 to barely 400.[1] And as the weavers disappeared, so did the ancillary trades, 'for the working and handling of silk sustained a whole host of people, including women of quality who did some spinning to bring in a little more house-keeping money and to give their children a good and honourable education'.[2] These were days, of course, in which the population of the city was falling (from 12,327 households in 1609 to 10,000 by 1646), and our sources blame the abandoning of 1,000 houses on the troubles of the silk industry.[3]

At first sight the figures for the export of silk cloth to Castile do not seem to support their case, for they were running only a little below the level of the mid-sixteenth century peak. But beyond the question of quantity is that of quality. In the early sixteenth century the bulk of the textiles manufactured in the city had been velvets – full, heavy silk cloths which were highly priced. By the later sixteenth century these had virtually disappeared, giving way to satins, which were less full and less highly priced. By the 1620s satins had given up half the market to a bastard silk tissue called taffeta, which went on to account for 80 per cent of exports to Castile by 1630–1.[4] Taffeta is a material which uses relatively little silk to the ell, and its rise probably largely reflects the decline in mulberry production within the kingdom. For the Valencians themselves the problem around 1620 was clear: too much silk was leaving the territory unworked.[5] By edicts of 1623 and 1638 the monarchy of Philip IV went some way towards meeting their complaints, by in effect forcing all raw silk grown in the jurisdictional area of the city

[1] ACA CA leg. 714, 'pragmática de la seda', 1623.
[2] Ibid.; cf. ARV R 593 fols. 198v–211, memorial of Gerónimo Guaras, 1688.
[3] AMV CM 59, jurats to king, 19 Oct. 1619.
[4] Ling, 'The Trade of Valencia', 65–73.
[5] ACA CA leg. 726, petition of jurats (1621?).

of Valencia to be at least spun into thread within the city walls.[1] To demands for a general export tariff, however, it turned a deaf ear – for that would have cut off the sources of supply of the imperial city of Toledo, mistress of the Júcar Valley.

While the difficulties of the rural economy and the fall in mulberry output must bear much of the blame for this situation, a lot of the trouble probably stemmed from the sheer uncompetitiveness of the city industry. Vilar has remarked of the complaints about the decline in the Barcelona woollen manufactures around 1620 that a shift was taking place from the high-cost guilds to a putting-out system among the peasantry.[2] Something similar can be detected in Valencia. The proud, rather somnolent spinners' guild of the city of Valencia spun silk according to a time-honoured, labour-intensive method known – appropriately enough – as 'the long method' (*a la larga*). It required the assistance of woman, who, 'not having beards, can knot the thread in their teeth without getting it tangled up'.[3] The peasants in the Júcar Valley had faster techniques – the *gorra y cubillo* or *cubillo y bandera pequeña*, terms whose exact significance is unfortunately unknown. Possibly these were variants on the machine 'with five spindles' which turns up in Játiva in 1601, and whose chief merit was 'to allow much more silk to be spun in an extraordinarily short space of time than ever could have been or was spun before'.[4] The exclusive guild of the city of Valencia would have nothing to do with these inventions, which were manned 'by peasants and other untrained hands who have never been taught to spin properly'.[5] It tried time after time to have them banned, without success. Eventually in 1640, bowing to the inevitable, it offered the king a handsome subsidy for permission to use the *gorra y cubillo* method itself.[6]

The gradual removal of spinning to the countryside need not have been a disaster had the Valencian weavers had the capital

[1] ACA CA leg. 714, 'pragmática de la seda', 1623; leg. 880, petition of the spinners, 17 Dec. 1638; RAH 9.4.4.1.45, fol. 288, *crida* of 1638.
[2] *Catalunya dins l'Espanya moderna*, II, 318–25.
[3] ACA CA leg. 726, petition of *jurats* (1621?).
[4] AMV Churat 1634 vol. I n. 35, *crida* of 1601.
[5] ACA CA leg. 726, petition of *jurats* (1621?).
[6] ACA CA leg. 657, memorandum, 29 Aug. 1640.

to buy back the thread. But the sheer poverty of the business sector after 1609 seems to have led to an increase in the export of this thread to Toledo – whose own weavers were not exactly a model of efficiency at the time, but who evidently had a slight edge in purchasing power on the Valencians.[1] The Valencia area was thus sinking by 1620 to the level of the Júcar Valley – a mere exporter of raw or half-worked silk. By 1650 a glorious medieval industry had been relegated to the status of a minor taffeta producer, 'supplying only the city itself and part of the kingdom...and exporting only the double taffetas which sold well at court'.[2] It was during this period that French silk cloth probably established its hegemony in Spain, destroying not only the more prosperous sectors of the Valencian manufacture, but also those of Toledo and Seville.[3] The irony is that these foreign textiles managed to infiltrate despite a protectionist law of 1623 specifically excluding them; because they were partly woven out of Spanish raw silk they were exempt from the prohibition.

But the Valencian industry had sunk further by the 1650s than the talents and tradition of her people warranted. Once the sharp financial crisis of Philip IV's reign was past, and as mulberry production began to revive, so the native silk manufactures began to expand again from about 1670. Above all there was an improvement in quality; satins re-emerged as market leaders, pushing taffeta down to 43 per cent of the exports to Castile by 1701. Unfortunately the recovery of Charles II's reign is hard to document. The figures for exports to Castile, our main source of information, only become available in 1699 after a long break since 1633. As they stand, they suggest little or no increase in quantity over the level of the 1620s, merely an improvement in quality.[4] But by all accounts the 1690s are the wrong time to look at the industry, which, contemporaries agreed, took a tremendous buffeting when the Castilian silver

---

[1] Toledo was complaining about the decline of its own industry around 1617; see A. Domínguez Ortiz, *La Sociedad española en el siglo XVII*, I (Madrid 1963), 138–9. Cf. Weisser, 'The Decline of Castile', 634–5.

[2] ACA CA leg. 602 n. 57/1, 'explicación del estado del trato de los texidos de seda' (1700?).

[3] AMS I vol. 25 n. 3, and III vol. 35 n. 49, complaints of 1620 and 1684 on the decline of the Seville manufacture.

[4] Ling, 'The Trade of Valencia', appendix.

currency was devalued by a quarter in 1686. Valencian merchants became less interested in working the exchanges and withdrew their capital from the weavers. All the familiar signs of crisis, visible around 1620, reappeared: an alleged fall in the number of weavers from 1,000 to 450, the folding up of a host of ancillary trades and the queues of silk-workers' wives outside the doors of the magistrates, begging for relief.[1] If we can believe one estimate that Valencia was exporting over 300,000 yards of silk cloth to Castile at the peak of the silk boom before 1686, this would represent a doubling of the previous high point of 1579. Since the highest recorded total in the customs for the late 1690s was 139,106½ ells in 1699, it may well be that the manufacture had been cut by half in a decade. On the other hand the crisis in the city was matched by a further extension of the putting-out industry in the hinterland, and this time weaving was involved as well as spinning. 'For a short while now', claimed the authorities in 1712, 'many weavers of satins, velvets, damasks and other silks have set up their looms in the cities, towns and villages of this kingdom.'[2] Enquiries were opened in the 1690s into why so little raw silk was now paying the customs for Castile. In Carcagente and Alcira only about half the production was found to be going any longer to the looms of Toledo, perhaps a quarter to the city of Valencia, and to France and Italy, while the remainder stayed behind to be woven into cloth by local weavers.[3]

Behind the ambiguity of some of the figures and behind the complaints of crisis, one senses the enduring stability of the Valencian silk industry. The Habsburg period was no doubt a low point in its fortunes – an interval between the glory of the fifteenth century and the renewed dynamism of the eighteenth century. It is intriguing to note, though, that an excellent recent study of the late-eighteenth-century manufacture finds that the giant still had feet of clay – clay which has the authentic character of the 1620s or the 1690s. The industry was under-capitalized, short on technological innovation, worried by its

[1] ACA CA leg. 602 n. 57/1, 14, 18 & 25; ARV R 593 fols. 198v–211.
[2] ARV G 4637, para. lix of *Tall*, 1712.
[3] ARV MR 10503 and 10459. I calculate that 25,588 of the 40,634 pounds of raw and spun silk changing hands in Carcagente in 1694–5 were destined for Castile, but only 3,112 of the 31,522 pounds changing hands in Alcira in 1699.

incapacity to hold on to the raw silk of its hinterland and uncompetitive in the face of French competition.[1] The diagnosis might have come straight from Habsburg times. Apart from the temporary crisis caused by a shortage of mulberry in the early seventeenth century, there is a fatal, recurring theme: the sheer lack of capital of the Valencian weavers. 'We go to Madrid to sell our cloth', they complained around 1700, 'but we cannot return home without the money to lay in new stock, and so we have to sell off our wares cheaply or on long credit terms.'[2] Another authority at the same period suggested that this was a short-term phenomenon. Previously the weavers had worked with material given to them by merchants, who then marketed the finished product. Dissatisfied with this arrangement, the weavers tried to set up in business for themselves, with disastrous results. They had to cheapen the quality of their product, lay off workers and use apprentices instead of journeymen, with the consequence that Valencian silk cloth 'came to be held in inferior esteem for texture and durability of any marketed in Madrid, Cadiz or other parts'.[3] One may question whether this 'withdrawal of mercantile capital' was motivated by a revolt of the weavers, or by the devaluation of the Castilian currency in 1686. In any case the crisis (if such it was) of the 1690s was merely an aggravation of a long-standing problem, which can be traced in the late eighteenth as well as the early seventeenth centuries: the Valencian silk industry was just very poor and backward.

The inadequacy of working capital seems to have been a general phenomenon throughout Valencian industry. Echoing the thoughts of some Castilian *arbitristas* on the parallel decline of manufactures in other parts of Spain, the president of the Audiencia denounced the tendency of businessmen to retire prematurely and sink their finances in *censals* – long-term loans to peasants, nobles and town councils, or anyone else who had real estate to mortgage as security. 'One of the reasons why this kingdom and its commerce are in such a ruinous state', he thundered, 'is that everybody wants to live off rents, so that the shoemaker, the tanner, and anybody else who has saved

[1] Vicente Martínez Santos, 'La sedería de Valencia 1750–1800', *Moneda y Crédito*, 134 (1975), 115–35.
[2] ACA CA leg. 602 n. 57/18.   [3] *Ibid.*, n. 57/1.

up 100 or 200 ducats puts them into a *censal*.'[1] The practice was not, of course, peculiar to the Habsburg period. Two centuries later Cavanilles was to castigate 'this vain ambition to quit the ranks of the artisan and swell those of the idle who live off rents'.[2] Nor was the creditor class necessarily precluded from investing in large-scale trade. A distinguished citizen of Carcagente, Antonio Juan Matoses, who died in 1609, left *censals* worth 7,218 *lliures* but also silk valued at 2,100 which he had despatched that year to the looms of Toledo.[3] If seventeenth-century industry was particularly undercapitalized, it is perhaps due less to the practice of living off rents than to the fact that those rents often proved unrecoverable after the expulsion of the Moriscos.

Any attempt to assess the losses of the *censalistas* after 1609 must be very tentative. We know that 121,014 *lliures* worth of mortgages were claimed against the remnant of royal demesne which had once belonged to Morisco peasants and which remained in the Crown's hands after alienations to the senyors had taken place. In general, these credits seem to have been paid, either by transference of the land to the creditor, or out of the proceeds of sale. Something may have been lost, especially since rigorous proofs were required of the existence of these mortgages, and some of the land anyway went out of cultivation. But one has the impression that this class of creditor came out of the expulsion relatively unscathed.[4] Those who had lent money to the far more sizeable Morisco population which lived on seigneurial estates, or to their masters, the feudal aristocracy, met a rather different fate. The debts owed by this sector totalled 4,000,000 ducats (4,200,000 *lliures*), according to the generally agreed estimate.[5] Although it was accepted that mortgages on individual Morisco lands could and should be paid off (as on the royal domain) by switching the rents due from the new settler to the creditor, or, if necessary, surrendering the land itself while reserving seigneurial rights over it, in

[1] ACA CA leg. 607 n. 48, memorandum (1610?).
[2] *Geografía*, I, 22; cf. II, 165.
[3] ARV Clero leg. 404, inventory, 20 March 1609.
[4] ACA CA legs. 704–5, correspondence and papers of Adrián Bayarte, 1614–16, *passim*.
[5] ARV R 698, memorial of mossèn Bartolomé Sebastián (1613?); AHN Osuna leg. 899 n. 1, petition of don Francisco Roca (1624?).

practice such individual debts were only a small proportion of the total. The overwhelming mass of the borrowing had been done by the senyors in the name of the Morisco communities, and neither the lords nor the communities had, after the expulsion, assets adequate to meet the obligations. By 1624 scarcely a sixtieth part of the debts in this sector were being paid, according to the embittered spokesman of the creditors.

But there was worse to come. Around 1620 the depopulation and economic decline of even the Old Christian towns was entering a critical phase. Here there were 12,000,000 ducats worth of *censals* at stake in loans to individuals and to municipal councils. The inability of the latter to pay their way was an outstanding feature of the later Habsburg period. It was hoped that the creditors of the city of Valencia would accept voluntary cuts in the capital owing to them as a way of getting at least something from the debacle, but such hopes were unfounded, and the metropolis fell thirteen years in arrears on interest payments during the reign of Charles II.[1]

It ought to be possible to gauge the importance of these investments to the Valencian economy. From the figures quoted above, it can be seen that there was a capital of just over 16,000,000 ducats sunk in *censals*, say about 16,921,014 *lliures*. Taking the most common rate of interest of 6⅔ per cent, this represents an income of 1,128,068 *lliures* a year – roughly equivalent to a quarter of the total annual output of the agrarian sector which we estimated earlier at 4,676,000 *lliures*. The great importance of the *censals* as a lifeline attaching the feeble urban economy to the matrix of wealth, the land, emerges clearly enough from these admittedly very crude calculations. When the agrarian sector lost its footing only slightly in 1609, an economic landslide was touched off throughout the kingdom: the *censals* became too heavy to pay, and with their non-payment the urban economy began to suffocate.

Two major consequences flowed from all this. In the first place, after the expulsion fresh credit became hard for anybody to find, whether idle noble or industrious artisan. The *censal* had normally been borrowed at 6⅔ per cent. Partly to discourage

---

[1] ARV R 541, king to viceroy, 22 Dec. 1660; 593, fol. 52, 'memorial de los acrehedores censalistas de la Ciudad y Deputación'; and cf. below, chapter 7.

investment in what it considered to be a sterile sector, partly to help a bankrupt nobility and partly to bring Valencia into line with Castile, the government fixed a maximum of 5 per cent for future borrowing from 1614.[1] The result was a fall in the popularity of this kind of loan, until in 1645, bowing to pressure from borrowers, the Crown began to ease the restrictions, and allowed the mortgage to find its own level. Interest rates duly drifted upwards again until it reached the old level of around 6⅔ per cent under Charles II.[2] With the temporary eclipse of the *censal* under Philip IV, the letter of exchange (*cambio*) – an unsecured, short-term loan from one trimestrial fair at Medina del Campo to the next – came into its own. The only trouble was that the *cambio* was prohibitively expensive, fetching up to 19 per cent interest a year, until the government intervened in 1619 to fix the rate at 10.[3] But it was only in the easier credit circumstances of the later seventeenth century that the rate did come down significantly in practice – to 12 or even 8 per cent, paralleling developments in the rest of Europe.[4] No story of the financial woe of early-seventeenth-century Valencia would be complete without reference to the successive bankruptcies of the *Taula*, the bank of the city of Valencia, which defaulted on payments three times in little more than the space of a generation: in 1614, 1634 and 1649.[5] Though not directly related to the expulsion of the Moriscos, these bankruptcies reflected the general tightening of credit and a drying up of confidence (in its widest sense), which were characteristic of the age.

The second major consequence of the collapse of the agrarian sector after 1609 was a reduction in the demand for manufactured goods. 'All those who live off rents', noted the city

[1] Boronat, *Moriscos*, II, 611–34.
[2] ARV R 521, chapter 203 of Braç Real, 1645, and 598, fols. 22–22v, king to viceroy, 30 Oct. 1652; AHN Osuna leg. 1030 n. 6/2, borrowings of the Duke of Gandía, 1695.
[3] AMV Churat 1635 n. 105, *pragmática* of 1619. Cf. ACA CA leg. 611 n. 4/1, consulta, 16 Feb. 1639.
[4] AHN Osuna leg. 1030 n. 7/1, steward to Duke of Gandía, 10 Jan. 1695. On the general fall in interest rates, see Geoffrey Parker, 'The Emergence of Modern Finance in Europe 1500–1730', in C. M. Cipolla, ed., *The Fontana Economic History of Europe* (1974), II, 539–40.
[5] ACA CA legs. 653, 678 and 679, documents related to the Taula. And see the very useful little study by S. Carreres i Zacarés, *La Taula de Cambis de Valencia 1408–1719* (Valencia 1957).

fathers in 1624, 'are trying to cut back as far as possible on food and clothing, often leaving the artisan...little option but to join the queues for bread outside the monasteries'.[1] What faced Valencia during the immediate post-expulsion era was a gradual, collective impoverishment as the decline of agriculture began to affect the urban economy.

The impoverishment of the business elite and industrial workers must bear a large share of the blame for the difficulties of the silk trade – and not only silk, for the woollen manufacture also appears to have fallen on hard times.[2] These reverses were serious for a kingdom which depended so much on outsiders for essential supplies of bread, meat and linen. One has the impression that the Valencian balance of trade worsened in the early seventeenth century. As Fray Gaspar Prieto, General of the Mercedarian Order and one of Olivares' trusted confidants, put it in 1626: 'more silver leaves this realm than comes into it, for we buy abroad more than we sell'.[3] The phenomenon evidently persisted into the easier circumstances of Charles II's reign. In 1693 the Audiencia sent to Madrid a major report on the drain of money from Valencia, which provides an interesting insight into where contemporaries thought the problem lay. The report blamed three main factors – the purchase of victuals abroad, the anomaly whereby an absentee bishop and chapter (Tortosa) drew tithes from nearly a third of the kingdom and the technical point that Valencian coins were understamped in relation to their true value.[4] Of course one may feel that the obsessive concern with bullion was somewhat misplaced. After all, in the case of spices Valencia got back some of the coin which she paid out to the English by marketing the product in other parts of Spain. This, however, was just the problem from the point of view of Madrid: Valencia's gain was Spain's loss.

Bullionism had always been an important part of state policy, and there were medieval prohibitions on the export of money from Valencia (except, after 1545, for the buying of wheat or meat). But it was more honoured in the breach than the observance. It was under Olivares that a last, determined effort

[1] AMV CM 59, *jurats* to king, 6 Feb. 1624.
[2] ACA CA leg. 1357, memorial of Gerónimo Ibáñez de Salt and J. B. Doñol, 1646.
[3] ACA CA leg. 1372, memorial, 1626.
[4] ARV R 594 fol. 137, 10 March 1693.

was made to make the policy work. Already in 1622 he had fallen foul of the merchants of Alicante by his attempt to break the English spice ring. In 1625 he set up the *almirantazgo* or admiralty court in Madrid, to supervise the closure of the ports of Castile to hostile nations and to prevent the export of bullion even to friends; and in 1628 the court's jurisdiction was extended – under protest – to the Crown of Aragon.[1] In future no merchant was to land goods on Spanish soil without entering into a bond that he would export native products of equivalent value within the year.

The vision of Olivares was not that of the Valencian mercantile community. 'In the whole world', protested the city fathers, 'men are allowed to trade freely from one town and one kingdom to another with no questions asked, and to receive payment in cash for what they sell, such being the law of nations.'[2] Ultimately all the plans hatched in Madrid foundered on this fundamental obstacle that without Valencian cooperation – above all, without the loyalty of a bureaucracy recruited exclusively from natives of the kingdom – no policy could actually be enforced in the eastern ports. One man did try. Judge Marcos Antonio Bisse, a harsh, lonely character, was seconded in 1640 from the king's fiscal office in Orihuela to the admiralty commission in Alicante, and ordered to crack down on the illegal trades. The Bisse commission was an unmitigated disaster. The unlucky man narrowly escaped assassination. But what finally destroyed him was partly the intrigue mounted through the Audiencia and the Council of Aragon by the Mingots, a family of Alicante potentates and royal ministers – and partly the fall in the customs of the great trading port as the English and Dutch boycotted the place. The slump in revenue was something the hard-pressed treasury of Philip IV could not allow, and at the beginning of 1642, on the recommendation of the viceroy, Bisse was relieved of his commission for interpreting the *almirantazgo* 'too rigorously'.[3]

The problems which dogged Bisse to the end were twofold.

[1] ARV R 698 fols. 343–346v, decree of 23 June 1628. On the general history of the *almirantazgo*, see A. Domínguez Ortiz, 'Guerra económica y comercio extranjero en el reinado de Felipe IV', *Hispania*, 23 (1963), 71–110.
[2] ACA CA leg. 707, petition of *jurats*, 21 Feb. 1622.
[3] ACA CA legs. 719–22, petitions and correspondence of Marcos Antonio Bisse with the king and the Protonotario, 1640–2; leg. 882, Bisse to king, 28 May 1641.

Firstly, Valencia could only continue importing if she exported treasure, and bullionist policy could only lead to an overall trade slump; secondly the attack on hostile shipping, particularly the French, cut communications with Valencia's best trading partners. Who would provide the fish to feed the king's own army in transit through Valencia if not the cod fishermen of St Malo?[1] And who would clothe the peasants of the huerta if not the merchants of Arles, whose linen grew coarser, more costly and harder to find with every year the *almirantazgo* lasted?[2] 'It is not just the trades with France that suffer', claimed the city fathers, 'for trade is one and indivisible, and the Italians, Flemish and English have been tending to pull out as well.'[3] The admiralty commission continued in theory to hang like a shadow over Valencian commerce for the rest of Philip IV's reign; but the failure of Bisse in Alicante meant that it could never be rigorously enforced. In particular the system was abandoned by which outward-bound ships were made to enter into a bond that they would sail only to friendly ports. But above all the whole policy was undermined by an expedient which began to be adopted as early as 1638, of issuing so-called 'contraband licences' to individuals to import so much Breton fish or Rhône linen.[4]

The failure of Olivares' mercantilist policy (such as it was) left the structural dependence of Valencia on the foreigner pretty much unaltered. The kingdom went on buying its daily bread overseas and settling the bill to a large extent with the bullion extracted from Castile in return for silkstuffs. It is inevitably somewhat difficult to pin down the precise damage which this state of affairs inflicted on the Valencian economy. What role did a balance of payments deficit play in the notorious phenomenon of the Decline of Spain? Probably it contributed to the fact (noted in an earlier chapter) that Valencian – and Spanish – bread prices were, and remained, the highest in Europe. Paying out so much for the means of

[1] ACA CA leg. 724, viceroy to king, 9 Sept. 1643.
[2] ARV R 521, chapter 1 of Braços Militar and Real, 1645.
[3] ACA CA leg. 715, Juan Bautista Polo to king, 28 Sept. 1637.
[4] ACA CA leg. 717, viceroy to king, 3 Jan. 1640, and leg. 724, viceroy to king, 28 April 1644. For a different assessment of the efficacy of the Spanish trade embargoes see J. L. Israel, 'A Conflict of Empires: Spain and the Netherlands 1618–48', *Past and Present*, 76 (Aug. 1977), 34–74.

Table 11. *Farms of the royal customs of Peatge and Quema: average yield per year (in lliures)*

1514–19	9,005	1621	20,700
1546–9	9,000	1634–8	15,200
1554	12,000	1643–9	16,575
1576–7	20,450	1654–8	16,655
1580–8	22,357	1664–9	17,244
1592–8	24,661	1674–9	21,632
1602	25,535	1684–9	21,408
1611–16	19,200		

SOURCE: ARV B *arrendamientos* 124–34. From 1592 the Crown had to begin giving bonuses (*exaus*) to tax-farmers, and I have deducted their import from the value of the farm. The re-incorporation of the seaport of Denia, whose customs were alienated to the Duke of Lerma in 1604, tends to boost the figures from 1674. My figures may be compared with those assembled by Alvaro Castillo, working with the actual port books of Valencia itself, 'Coyuntura de la economía valenciana', 21–34.

existence itself, the Spanish population must have had less of a surplus to devote to other goods, and this may explain (as the *jurats* of Valencia hinted in 1624) some of the troubles of manufacturing industry. Besides this, the sheer shortage of good coin (for there was plenty of bad 'black' or unstamped copper circulating) played its part in keeping interest rates high, and further depressing manufactures. But to paint the trading economy in uniformly dark colours would be misleading. After all, importers themselves seem to have been prospering. The merchants of Valencia and particularly of Alicante picked up important 'invisible earnings' as agents for French linen or English spices. Unfortunately, no good series for the Alicante customs has yet come to light. But if we look at the farms of the royal customs of the city of Valencia and her outports – which reflect both imports and (to a lesser extent, since native Valencians were exempt) exports – we can see that some people were prospering in this depressed age (see table 11).

The familiar ebb and flow of the Valencian economy is clearly visible in this table – the great age of expansion between 1550 and 1580; the stagnation which followed it; the decline after the expulsion of the Moriscos (not so grave as was the case with the rural tithes); the accentuation of this decline under Philip IV (more pronounced perhaps than in the case of agriculture, because of the *almirantazgo* of 1628); and finally the recuperation under Charles II (which is artificially inflated on our table, owing to the inclusion of the customs of Denia and Játiva after 1674). The figures, of course, lend themselves to several interpretations: the fall in the customs under Philip IV may have been because the Valencians were exporting less, or because they were too poor to go on importing at the old, high levels, or because the long wars with Flanders and France frightened off trade. Most probably the true explanation is a mixture of all three. The same will probably hold for the recovery under Charles II. Though this monarch also found himself embroiled in long and costly wars against Louis XIV, the demise of the *almirantazgo* was not apparently called in question. Only in 1692, following the destruction of Alicante by the French fleet, did the government of Madrid once more steel itself to interfere in the commercial affairs of the eastern provinces. Protesting against the new prohibitions on trade with the perfidious Gauls, the Valencians expostulated: 'we have never known anything like this for fifty years, not even for a hundred years, no indeed, say some (though they exaggerate), not for the last thousand years'.[1] Valencia was accustomed to taking its wars – like its responsibilities to the Monarchy – with more than a pinch of salt.

[1]   ACA CA leg. 670 n. 42/2, 'informe jurídico', 15 May 1692.

5

The seigneurial reaction

'Sire', the Valencian deputy Aparici told the Cortes of Cádiz in 1811, 'the peasants of Valencia who live on seigneurial estates cannot be called peasants at all, for they are in truth mere slaves.' Two hundred years after the event, Aparici had no hesitation in blaming the expulsion of the Moriscos for this state of affairs, 'for it was then that the ills which our people are still suffering took root'.[1] It is a commonplace of historical writing on the subject to castigate the resettlements after 1609 as unstable and unfair. In an age of economic decline the senyors reinforced their own position, turning Valencia into a hotbed of peasant unrest. Unable to pay the high rents introduced after the expulsion, the peasants took to the hills, providing recruits for the bandit gangs which were so active in the kingdom in the seventeenth century. Finally on 10 July 1693 the powder keg exploded, in what was probably the greatest *jacquerie* witnessed by Habsburg Spain, the so-called Second Germania. After years of litigation about rents, the peasants of the Duke of Gandía refused payment, their ringleaders were imprisoned, and a rustic army gathered to secure their release. By 13 July the royal governor of Játiva, at the head of the local militia, had succeeded in cornering the rebels in the mountains near Muro. Here on 15 July the popular forces, some 4,000 strong, recruited from among the vassals of the Duke of Gandía, the Count of Cocentaina and other lords of the area, were dispersed in a short, one-sided engagement. The peasants fled in disarray leaving ten or twenty of their number dead or dying on the battlefield.[2]

[1] Manuel Ardit, *Els Valencians de les Corts de Cadis* (Barcelona 1968), 37 and 41.
[2] ACA CA legs. 579–81, *passim.*; F. Momblanch, *La Segunda Germanía del Reino de Valencia* (Valencia 1957); S. García Martínez, *Valencia bajo Carlos II: bandolerismo, reivindicaciones agrarias y servicios a la monarquía*, II (Valencia 1974).

According to figures presented to the Cortes of Cádiz, Valencia was, with Cantabria, Galicia and Andalusia, one of the regions in the peninsula where the nobles were most powerful. About three-quarters of the surface area, at least, lay under seigneurial jurisdiction – more if we include ecclesiastical fiefs.[1] But the landed hierarchy was essentially a secular one in Valencia. Ecclesiastical lordships were relatively few, probably because by the time the kingdom was conquered in the mid-thirteenth century the great wave of donations to the church which had characterized early medieval Europe was drawing to a close, and governments were everywhere introducing strict new laws against mortmain. There were approximately 186 fief-holders in Valencia at the time of the expulsion of the Moriscos.[2] Nine of these were bishops or monasteries, whose manorial income (as distinct from their claim on tithes) must have been around 70,000 *lliures* a year in all.[3] Then there were 13 *encomiendas* of the Military Order of Montesa, 3 of Santiago, 2 of Calatrava, and 1 of St John. These life-tenured fiefs, distributed by the king to favoured servants, rented 26,565 *lliures* in all.[4] Finally, the city of Valencia held one lordship, while the 157 others were all lay nobles. At the top of the secular hierarchy came 8 magnates – the Dukes of Segorbe, Gandía, Maqueda, Infantado, Lerma and Mandas, the Marquis of Guadalest and the Count of Cocentaina – whose Valencian revenues collectively totalled some 289,000 *lliures*.[5] Below them was an intermediate grouping of 20 important, mostly native houses, holding rents amounting to 202,000 *lliures* or thereabouts. Finally at the base of the pyramid came 129 gentry families with lordship over one or two villages, and a total

[1] S. de Moxó, *La disolución del régimen señorial en España* (Madrid 1965), 9–10.
[2] See the list in Boronat, *Moriscos*, I, 428–42. Wrongly dated by Boronat, the list actually belongs to the year 1609.
[3] Escolano, *Décadas*, I, 101. The calculation is only approximate. If we include tithes, then the archbishopric of Valencia alone was worth 70,000 *lliures*; cf. ACA CA leg. 686, consulta, 4 Dec. 1616.
[4] BL Harl. MSS. 3569 fol. 107, list of *encomiendas* (1600?).
[5] Escolano, *Décadas*, I, 102. Again, as with the ecclesiastical revenues, Escolano's figures require some reworking; for example, the last Count of Oliva, separately listed here, had actually died insane in 1569 and his estates were, most of them, bundled in with the *mayorazgo* of Gandía by 1609; and the Segorbe rents are improbably high. But otherwise the figures are reasonably accurate, as I have been able to verify from the Gandía, Infantado, Cocentaina and other archives.

income in the region of 387,000 *lliures*. To see these figures in perspective, one should recall the figure advanced in an earlier chapter for the total agrarian product of the kingdom – 4,676,000 *lliures*. The fief-holders, with rents in excess of 974,565, would thus have pocketed about one-fifth of the output of the rural economy. Possibly this was one of the harshest rates of exploitation in the peninsula. We know, for example, that the titled nobility of Spain as a whole had an income of around 5,000,000 ducats, whereas their Valencian equivalents (counts, marquises, dukes) enjoyed 427,000 *lliures*, around 8 per cent of the total when the currencies have been converted.[1] But the Valencian population was only 5 per cent of that of Spain at its peak in 1609. Therefore 5 per cent of the people were paying 8 per cent of the tax bill for the idle nabobs of the Monarchy. The problem was worsened by the absenteeism of the greater part of the magnates, like Infantado, Lerma or Maqueda. 'The best part of the aristocracy', complained the Valencian magistrates in 1623, 'lives in other realms and spends there the rents it draws from us.'[2]

Widely diverse in fortune, this aristocracy was equally diverse in terms of origin. It included men of small substance whose social position had improved since the Middle Ages as well as wealthier families whose fortunes had declined. As the chronicler Viciana put it, 'there is no constancy in fortune: the wheel of fate is never still an instant, and we have seen many lineages prosper and rise swiftly to the top only to fall again even more suddenly and abruptly'.[3] Actually the great families of Habsburg Valencia were a relatively 'new' aristocracy – a mixture of apanaged princes like the Duke of Segorbe (created 1469) or the Duke of Villahermosa (1476); politicians who had intrigued to take advantage of the weakness of the fifteenth-century monarch, like the ancestor of the Duke of Lerma (created Marquis of Denia in 1431) or the Count of Cocentaina

[1] Domínguez Ortiz, *La sociedad española en el siglo XVII*, I, 220. As regards purely feudal dues, Valencia accounted for about half the Spanish total; cf. Pierre Vilar, in *L'abolition de la féodalité dans le monde occidental*, Colloques Internationaux du C.N.R.S., Toulouse, 12–16 Nov. 1968 (2 vols., Paris 1971), II, 746.
[2] AMV CM 59, *jurats* to king, 27 Feb. 1624.
[3] Martín de Viciana, *Crónica de la Inclita y Coronada Ciudad de Valencia* (4 vols., Valencia 1564–6), II, fol. 25v. There is a facsimile edition, prepared by Sebastián García Martínez (3 vols., Valencia 1972).

(1448); and wealthy speculators like Pope Alexander VI, who bought the sugar-rich Duchy of Gandía for his illegitimate son, Pedro Luis de Borja, in 1485, or his contemporary, Pedro González de Mendoza, the Great Cardinal and primate of Spain, who must have helped purchase Alberique (the nucleus of the later Valencian patrimony of the Dukes of Infantado) for his bastard, the Marquis of Cenete, in 1491. But by the time Viciana wrote in the 1560s, such easy acquisitions were a thing of the past. The new men of the fifteenth century climbed, and then kicked the ladder away from beneath them. The age of the Habsburgs proved to be one of stability and consolidation for the great families, as one by one they brought their estates under the cover of *mayorazgo*, the rigid, perpetual, well-nigh unbreakable entail of imperial Spain.

Grandiose and steadfast, the Borjas, Mendozas and others lorded it over an infidel population in a semi-colonial fashion. Some time after the expulsion the agent of the Duke of Gandía looked back on a golden age, as it seemed in retrospect, when the Moriscos had been there 'to plough the duke's fields and work on his castles, houses and other buildings, and come with their mules and pack animals when his baggage had to be carried from one place to another, even to points outside the kingdom, while their womenfolk would be busy spinning or weaving for the ducal household'.[1] Yet this world came suddenly and fairly painlessly to an end in 1609. To later historians, no less than to contemporaries, it has always seemed hard to explain how the senyors came to accept the expulsion of the Moriscos, 'for though it cost them...much ease and fortune, yet they showed themselves very obliging in word and deed'.[2] This raises the question of the whole structure of Valencian feudalism as it evolved over the Habsburg period.

The most important thing to remember about aristocratic revenues is that they came largely from traditional feudal dues. There is no parallel in the eastern provinces to the case of a Duke of Béjar in Castile, who drew over a third of his rents in the seventeenth century from property which he actually

[1] AHN Osuna leg. 846 n. 2, memorial of Cristóbal Monterde, 1613.
[2] Bleda, *Crónica* 992.

owned himself.[1] Out of rents of 1,796 *lliures* which he drew
before the expulsion from Luchent, Cuatretonda, Pinet and
Benicolet, the Duke of Mandas got only 2 *lliures* from fields
of his own![2] The Duke of Segorbe, who owned no property
in the Sierra de Espadán, had some houses and orchards of
his own in the big town of Segorbe itself, but they brought
him only 292 of the 3,400 *lliures* income he enjoyed from there.[3]
The Duke of Villahermosa, in addition to his widely extending
but unprofitable lordships in the barren north-west, could count
a pine grove, a garden and several fields of his own in the
village of Artana, but the yield was only sufficient to pay the
local bailiff for administering them.[4] The wealthier Duke of
Gandía was actually the biggest single landowner in his barony
of Jaraco and Jeresa in Morisco days – but Jaraco and Jeresa
were only one estate, accounting at the most for a twentieth
of the ducal income, and even there the demesne was not all
that large, since it produced only about 55 of the 1,380 *cahizes*
of wheat, rice and barley cultivated in the area.[5]

Even where sizeable demesnes did exist – and the abbey of
Valldigna, in good Cistercian tradition, was a classic example
of the kind – they tended to be run down over the Habsburg
period. The busy monks drew about a sixth of their income
(2,538 out of 15,323 *lliures* in the 1580s) from the grainfields,
vineyards and mulberry groves which they farmed for
themselves.[6] Unfortunately there are no figures for demesne
profits after that date, but we know that their biggest farm, the
grange of Benivaire, was gradually being wound up. In 1607
it could boast 15 mules, 9 ploughs, 8 yokes, 7 hoes and spades;
by 1665 only 4 ploughs, 4 mules, 1 horse and a hoe; and by
1708 the whole property had been given out to share-croppers.[7]

[1] C. J. Jago, 'Aristocracy, War and Finance in Castile 1621–65' (Cambridge University Ph.D. thesis 1969), 201. For the much smaller demesnes of Catalonia, see Vilar, *Catalunya dins l'Espanya moderna*, II, 65–6, and III, 551.
[2] AHN Osuna leg. 4100 n. 3, accounts of 1601.
[3] ARV MR 9723–9732, sequestration of Segorbe, 1576–84.
[4] ARV MR 9625–9632, sequestration of Villahermosa, 1553–98.
[5] AHN Osuna leg. 1021 n. 8, accounts of 1586.
[6] ARV Clero leg. 795, 'rentas del monasterio', 1582–91.
[7] ARV Clero legs. 732 and 778, inventories of 1607 and 1708; *libro* 3953, inventory of 1665.

It is no doubt tempting to blame some of this decline on the ending of serfdom after the expulsion of the Moriscos. In 1614 the Crown ordered that all labour services in resettlement areas should be commuted to a 'moderate' sum in cash, noting with some disgust (for such things were largely unknown in the more enlightened lands of Castile) that the Moors had been 'more like slaves than vassals'.[1] But one should not overstate the changes which came about in this sphere as a result of the expulsion. In the first place, the Moriscos were not the only ones who owed labour dues; the Old Christians of Alacuás, a progressive village in the shadow of the great city of Valencia, owed one or two days' ploughing a year on the lord's fields, an obligation which they kept into the 1620s and probably beyond.[2] Secondly, the Moriscos (like the Old Christians) had put up a stiff and successful fight to get these services reduced to a minimum – not a difficult exercise, perhaps, since seigneurial demesnes were so exiguous. The biggest landowner of them all, the abbey of Valldigna, had had to surrender most of its dues as long ago as 1557. In Benivaire the Moriscos were only to gather wood and in Lo Pator only to dig and weed twice in the year; in the grange of Barig alone did full, unlimited labour persist.[3] By the 1580s Benivaire was working quite profitably on wage-labour, with a gross turnover of 2,538 *lliures* and a salary bill of only 569. What destroyed this big farm, and so many others, during the seventeenth century was not the ending of serfdom after the expulsion, but the steep rise in agricultural wages which accompanied depopulation, and the drop in market prices for foodstuffs in the reign of Charles II.

This phenomenon is particularly evident in the one area where forced labour had had some importance in pre-expulsion Valencia, in connection with the refining of sugar. Sugar cane, which had been extensively planted in the fifteenth century, had retreated by Habsburg times, in the face of Portuguese competition, to the huertas of Valldigna, Gandía and Villalonga. It was not cultivated by the senyors themselves but by their peasantry, who were obliged (round Gandía) to plant a quarter

[1] ACA CA leg. 607 nos. 46/1, 49/1 and 49/16, consultas and correspondence on the resettlement, 1610–13.
[2] ARV Alacuás, *expediente* 54, *capbreu* of 1629.
[3] ARV Clero leg. 789, *concordia*, 14 May 1557.

of their own fields with cane and give one half of the harvest to their lord. It was the refining and marketing end of the business which directly interested the abbot of Valldigna, the Duke of Gandía, and don Pedro Franqueza, the notorious court favourite of Philip III's time, who was Count of Villalonga. Sugar provided the Borjas with 14,120 of the 65,000 *lliures* (or more) rents they drew from all sources before the expulsion; and it accounted for nearly a quarter of the Valldigna receipts, 3,749 *lliures* out of 15,323 – more even than the demesne.[1] The mills were kept turning by gangs of swarthy serfs, several hundred strong, who were whipped up from their villages before Christmas every year for two months' work at crushing, boiling and moulding.[2] But the industry was engaged in an unequal contest with history; increasingly large quantities of cheap sugar were arriving from the New World, where the crop could be grown in more favourable climatic conditions. For example, labour costs in Valencia, even with serfdom, seem to have been pretty high, eating up 5,190 *lliures* in Gandía (over a third of the turnover), and 2,159 in Valldigna (over half of a much smaller turnover).[3] Faced with the collapse of the mills after the expulsion, the Crown decided to modify its declared policy of abolishing serfdom, and not only allowed labour services to continue in Gandía but kept them going in Villalonga, which was resettled by a royal commissioner after it had been confiscated from the recently disgraced Franqueza.[4] But all these efforts came to nothing. Valencian sugar continued its ineluctable decline. By the late seventeenth century there was so little of it cultivated in Villalonga that labour services there had become a dead letter.[5]

If one concentrates, however, on the mills or the seigneurial demesne, the real significance of labour dues in the Valencian context will be missed. It was, noted the Council of Aragon, 'especially in the season when the lords retired to their estates', that the Morisco serfs proved their worth.[6] Don Agapito

[1] AHN Osuna leg. 805 n. 70, accounts, 1607–9; ARV Clero leg. 795, 'rentas del monasterio', 1582–91.
[2] See the description of the operation in Viciana, *Crónica*, II, fols. 13–13v.
[3] AHN Osuna leg. 805 n. 70, and ARV Clero leg. 795, 'rentas'.
[4] AHN Osuna leg. 562 n. 41, *carta puebla* of Villalonga, 1612.
[5] *Ibid.*, marginal notes on late seventeenth-century copy.
[6] ACA CA leg. 607 n. 49/16, consulta, 30 Nov. 1613.

Salvador bemoaned the loss of his infidel peasantry, not for their ploughing, but for the hens they gave him and for the linen woven by their women, when he arrived in his castle of Favareta for the summer.[1] Alvaro Vives, senyor of Pamies, reckoned that his official rents of 1,000 ducats were swelled by another 500 at least, 'thanks to the favours and odd jobs which his Moriscos did for him'.[2] But it has to be emphasized that this sort of service mostly benefited the smaller senyors. A great courtier like the Duke of Segorbe, for example, got nothing out of his Moriscos in the Vall de Uxó, 'because he never came up to the valley any more'.[3] At the most we may hazard a guess that for some lords their villages became colder places to live in after the expulsion. The old *casa del senyor* which still dominates the market square in many a Valencian town is predominantly a late medieval construction, with its massive grey stone walls and towers.[4] The seventeenth century saw few new buildings or improvements – with some notable exceptions, such as the handsome palace of the marquises in Albaida. Though changing life styles and the extinction of families also contributed to seigneurial absenteeism, perhaps the disappearance of Moriscos bearing gifts tended to hasten the process. 'If His Majesty could only see the state into which this castle has fallen since the Moriscos left', lamented the Marquis of Guadalest (who had been sentenced to house arrest), 'I am sure he would not have told me to live here.'[5]

Men like Guadalest or Segorbe were what was known as manorial lords (*senyors de llocs*). This was not necessarily the same thing as being lords of the land (*senyors directes*). Round Gandía, for example, many peasants held land, not of the Duke, but of the convent of La Merced; round Segorbe, not of the house of Aragon, but of the monastery of Vall de Cristo; in Muro, not of the Count of Concentaina but of the convent of La Concepción.[6] One of the features of the resettlement was that

1 ARV Clero leg. 770, testimony of doña Marcela Pujades, 17 May 1630.
2 ACA CA leg. 874, petition of Alvaro Vives (1620?).
3 ADM Segorbe leg. 61 n. 9, 'testimonis ex officio rebuts en la vila de Onda', 1612.
4 One of the best guides to surviving seigneurial dwellings in the Valencian countryside is Luis Guarner, *Valencia: Tierra y Alma de un País* (Madrid 1974).
5 ACA CA leg. 715, Guadalest to don Melchor Sisternes, 23 Feb. 1637.
6 AHN Osuna leg. 846 n. 2, memorial of Cristóbal Monterde, 1613; ADM Segorbe leg. 51 n. 1, *capbreu*, 1661–2; ARV MR 7935, *amortización*, 1617.

the manorial lords, with the permission of the Crown, established lordship over all the land in the area, leaving the old
senyors directes largely with their traditional and by now devalued
quit-rents. But before the expulsion, lordship was extraordinarily fragmented, and some senyors – like the Duke of Segorbe
– had to rely principally on their so-called *regalías*, which gave
them control of the local courts (although without jurisdiction
over rents or property in the case of those peasants who held
land of a different *senyor directe*), and a monopoly of ovens, mills
and shops in the area.

The expulsion and the resettlements gave some manorial
lords the chance to extend control here. In the deep south –
the territory overshadowed by the fiefs of the Duke of Maqueda
and the Count of Elda – they began taking over shops and ovens
which had formerly belonged to the Morisco communities
themselves.[1] In Valldigna the *regalías* rented 1,712 *lliures* in 1582
and half as much again, 2,481, in 1648, rising from a ninth of
the total income to a fifth – a remarkable achievement, since
the population of the area had dropped by half in the interval.[2]
Not only sharp practice by the monks was at stake here.
Everyone agreed that the Old Christians consumed more
anyway than the lean followers of Islam. The records of the
Valldigna butcher show that this worthy despatched on average
7.7 kilos of meat per household per year to his Old Christian
customers in 1603 and 1604, but only 4.33 to the Moriscos.[3] Again
in the Marquesate of Lombay, where no new charges were
introduced after 1609, the ovens, mills and shops rented 1,870
lliures on the eve of the expulsion and only 931 in 1641 (because
of the drop in population), but a good 2,655 in 1700, even though
the number of inhabitants – larger, of course, than in 1641 –
was still only two-thirds of its size in Morisco times.[4]

Many of these manorial lords of old Valencia, no doubt, would
have liked to think of themselves as princelings, especially those
who had erected a gallows at the entrance to their estates
(although the profits of criminal jurisdiction were everywhere

[1] ACA CA leg. 703, bishop of Orihuela to king, 19 March 1614.
[2] ARV Clero legs. 795 and 785, accounts of 1582 and 1648.
[3] ARV Clero leg. 732, accounts of Lorens Lido, 1603–5. The accounts do not
distinguish Old Christians and Moriscos as such, merely the Upper Valley and the
Lower Valley. [4] See appendix 2.

small and treated as pocket money for the senyor). But their grandiosely named 'regalian rights' hardly permitted them much economic power, for in general they were able only to nibble at the really valuable trades that were carried on in the kingdom. The Duke of Mandas had a ·'chain' across the Castilian frontier at the Mogente crossing, at which he charged a small toll, but the main customs dues in Mogente went to the king.[1] The Duke of Gandía had a 'boat' which ferried people across the mighty Júcar at Albalat, but Albalat was only a secondary crossing, and the boat was anyway confiscated by the Crown in about 1580.[2]

The rents paid by hereditary peasant small-holders constituted, in fact, the basis of the seigneurial system in Valencia after the expulsion, as before it. When the senyors were attacked, then and now, for harshness in the resettlements, it was because they increased these copyhold dues, and above all because they switched over from fixed payments in coin (the *censos*) to percentage cuts (*partició*) of the harvest. 'One cannot deny', wrote don Diego Clavero to the Duke of Lerma in 1610, 'that by the expulsion of the Moriscos many lords here have suffered. But it is clear too that some – not a few either – have done well for themselves, for anyone who was only getting quit-rents before is now twice or four times as rich.'[3] This, combined with the fact that all lands in a resettlement now owed rent to the manorial or jurisdictional lord, who became universal *senyor directe* (alongside and in addition to those already there), is where the main seigneurial reaction is generally held to lie.[4]

Under the inclusive heading of *censos*, contemporaries tended to group two different kinds of tax. One actually belonged to the senyor as jurisdictional lord and was really part of the regalian rights. It included various cash tributes – often for the

[1] AHN Osuna leg. 4100 n. 3, accounts of Mogente, 1600.
[2] AHN Osuna leg. 696 n. 22, 'evençut de la baronia de Corbera, Riola y Albalat', 1579–80.
[3] ACA CA leg. 607 n. 46/1, Clavero to Lerma, 9 Jan. 1610.
[4] The *senyors directes* as a separate entity tend to fade out of the picture after the Crown confirmed that new settlers in a village would have to pay four-fifths of all new land rents to the manorial lord, leaving any independent landlord with one-fifth plus what he was getting before the expulsion. Cf. chapter 13 of the *asiento general* of 1614, in Boronat, *Moriscos*, II, 620–2. In fact, what happened where there was a separate *senyor directe* was that the manorial lords reduced their own demands on the peasant by an amount proportionate to the sum the former was entitled to collect before the expulsion. See, for example, ADM Segorbe leg. 51 n. 1, *capbreu* of Segorbe, 1661–2.

upkeep of the local castle or mosque (the latter in Vall de Uxó even after the conversion to Christianity). In Villahermosa such tributes were still very valuable in the last decades of Morisco Valencia, and brought the Duke well over a third of his income, while in Vall de Uxó they accounted for about a quarter of the Duke of Segorbe's receipts.[1] But these two estates were located in some of the worst hill country in Valencia. Their masters were absentees, the Moriscos ruled their own lives, and very little had changed since the Middle Ages. In the more valuable lands of Valldigna, such poll taxes were of infinitesimal value before the expulsion – a bare 332 *lliures* out of rents of 15,323. In Lombay they accounted for 460 of the total revenues of 5,518 *lliures*. In accordance with the trend throughout the kingdom, many of these tributes in Lombay were given up after the expulsion, sank to 55 *lliures* all told in the 1640s, and disappeared completely by the time the Bourbons came to the throne.[2] An era was closing.

This left the true quit-rents, which were payable by the peasant to his *senyor directe* for the land he tilled. In many a medieval charter it appears that share-cropping had been the rule – in Vall de Uxó in 1260 and in Valldigna in 1366.[3] But in harmony with a general trend throughout Europe in the later Middle Ages these rents had often been commuted for fixed cash payments, enshrined in documents and charters which no subsequent senyor could set aside.[4] In Valldigna by the later sixteenth century the huerta was all parcelled out for about 1,000 *lliures* a year, and in Vall de Uxó both huerta and secano were given out for about 486.[5] On the other hand, *partició* of the harvests remained very common in the secano – in Lombay, Planes and Valldigna itself – where the yield was simply too uncertain from one year to the next to make fixed commutation a viable proposition. And one has to remember that most of

---

[1] 568 out of 1,362 *lliures* rental all told in Villahermosa, ARV MR 9625; 298 out of 1,172 *lliures* in Vall de Uxó, ADM Segorbe leg. 14 n. 10.
[2] See appendix 2.
[3] ARV Clero leg. 741, charter of 14 May 1366; for that of Vall de Uxó, Florencio Janer, *Condición social de los moriscos de España* (Madrid 1857), appendix XVII.
[4] Cf. G. Duby, *L'économie rurale et la vie des campagnes dans l'occident médiéval* (2 vols., Paris 1962), II, 479 and 599.
[5] ARV Clero leg. 789, charter of 14 May 1557 (referring to earlier custom); ADM Segorbe leg. 14 n. 10, accounts of Vall de Uxó, 1553.

the bigger manorial lords – all those with full criminal jurisdiction – were allowed to collect the king's share of the tithe,
the *tercio diezmo*, within their own villages. Occasionally (as in
Vall de Uxó), even this was commuted, but generally it was not,
and it provided a flexible source of income for many senyors.

At most, therefore, one can say that the resettlements saw
the generalization and consolidation of payments in kind. This
was perhaps not entirely a reaction on the part of the senyors
to the devaluation of their old quit-rents by the steep price
inflation of the sixteenth century. Share-cropping appeared to
make sense when there were poor peasants arriving in the
resettlements without resources. Advising the Duke of Segorbe
against charging simply new, higher quit-rents in Benaguacil,
one witness pointed out that 'these poverty-stricken fellows',
the new settlers, would simply not be able to pay them. The
best chance for the senyor was to grab what grain he could,
'there on the threshing floor'.[1] Interestingly enough, Jovellanos
defended share-cropping at a later date as the best arrangement
for a poor peasantry.[2] Everything depended, of course, on the
rate – and it was this factor which really stamped the Valencian
resettlements as unstable and unfair. Two centuries later, in
the course of his peregrinations around the kingdom, Cavanilles
came on the old Morisco village where the peasantry had to
part with as much as a quarter of their grain after tithe to the
senyor: 'that does seem too much', he noted.[3]

In trying to assess what really happened after 1609, one has
to remember the official criteria for 'fair rent' in Valencia at
the time. The judges of the supreme court deemed a third to
be the maximum which the senyor could demand; and the
Council of Aragon actually asked for a fifth of grain in the royal
resettlement in Játiva.[4] It would be wrong to imagine the
resettlements taking place in a sort of free-for-all, with each
wicked baron taking what he could get. Certainly the bigger
senyors seem to have conformed fairly closely with the common
practice of the court. In Alberique the Duke of Infantado asked

---

[1] ADM Segorbe leg. 61 n. 9, testimony of a notary, 30 March 1613.
[2] Gaspar Melchor de Jovellanos, 'Agricultura y propiedades de Asturias', *Obras Escogidas* (1956 ed.) III, 205.   [3] *Geografía*, II, 34.
[4] ACA CA leg. 607 n. 49/1, consulta of Audiencia, 1610; and leg. 708, *carta puebla* of Játiva, 1623.

for a fifth of grain; so did the Duke of Mandas in Picasent, and the Duke of Segorbe in Paterna.[1] Though the rates differed for tree fruits and for the secano, it was really the share-cropping of wheat grown on the irrigated lands of a village which set the tone for the whole charter of resettlement. And the smaller the estate, roughly speaking, the higher the rate here seems to have been – it stood at one-third in Negrals, Sagra and Senet, and at one-quarter in Cárcer, Valldigna and Genovés.[2] These lesser men could, of course, act more independently of the court. But geography played a part too. The Duke of Gandía was warned by his agents that no Old Christian would want to come in to the arid hill country behind Gandía and Oliva at the *partició* of one-third which had obtained before the expulsion, and he duly lowered the rate to one-sixth, or, as in the especially forbidding Vall de Laguar, one-seventh.[3] On the plain, his interest was in sugar, so that grain was allowed to escape with only a one-eighth cut.[4] On the estates of the Duke of Segorbe, similar pressures were at work. The Duke had to settle for a sixth of grain in Vall de Uxó because the huerta was poorer than in Paterna, where he had got a fifth. And in Benaguacil the original settlement was so badly mismanaged – the Duke's agent was allegedly 'frequenting women in the pay of the settlers, and taking gifts of money, jewels and the like' – that the peasants got away with paying only a seventh.[5] Conditions varied, therefore, according to the quality of the land, the efficiency of the senyor, and his ability to ignore the Council of Aragon and its concept of fair rents. A thorough recent study of the *cartas pueblas* finds that the most frequent request was for a sixth; thirds, fourths and fifths were also very

[1] AHN Osuna leg. 1926 n. 2 (Alberique); leg. 3146 n. 2 (Picasent); ADM Segorbe leg. 6 n. 6 (Paterna).
[2] *El Archivo*, IV, 38 (Negrals); ARV Clero leg. 801, Valldigna, 12 Dec. 1609; Halperin Donghi, 'moriscos y cristianos viejos', *Cuadernos de Historia de España*, XXV–XXVI (1957), 199–200 (Cárcer, Sagra and Senet); Rafael García, *Geografía e historia de Genovés*, colección 'Pueblos de España', n.d., 143.
[3] AHN Osuna leg. 562 n. 6, memorandum of Dr Avargues, 1729, and n. 44a and 44b, *cartas pueblas* of Lombay, Ebo and Gallinera, and Vall de Laguar. For Catadau, leg. 722 n. 6.
[4] This was nevertheless an improvement on the situation there in Morisco times, when there had been no *partició* of grain at all; AHN Osuna leg. 1029 n. 3, memorandum (1610?).
[5] ADM Segorbe leg. 61 n. 9, 'información de testigos', 27 Sept. 1615. For Vall de Uxó, leg. 6 n. 3.

common, but sevenths and eighths obtained in only 12 of the 61 charters covered.[1]

These rates, on top of tithe, small cash payments and seigneurial monopolies, were really pretty harsh. They should be compared with percentages of one-sixth to one-eighth of the harvest which appear to have been generally demanded of tenants in Old Castile and León.[2] Writing after two decades of peasant unrest, Melchor de Macanaz warned Philip V that social conditions in Valencia were very bad and a poor foundation for Bourbon rule. 'The senyors in this kingdom enjoy such exorbitant taxes and dues from many of their vassals that they turn them from free men into slaves, or else into desperadoes, who take to robbing on the highways and stirring up trouble rather than work in the fields.'[3] Nothing was done, however, by the Bourbons, and the peasants remained as one of the thorniest questions facing the liberal reformers of the nineteenth century. But is it accurate to date the trouble to the resettlements after 1609? After all, the words of Macanaz can be matched almost exactly by those of Bleda, who wrote of the excessive rents payable by the Moriscos, 'such that the wretches could no longer bear the burden, and were continually plotting rebellion to shake off the yoke'.[4] It is interesting to note that a cut of one-fifth of huerta crops for the senyor can be found in thirteenth-century Valencia under the Crusaders; it is probable that they were merely following earlier Moslem practice here.[5]

It is only by bearing in mind the long tradition of servitude in the Valencian countryside that we can understand perhaps why the Old Christians were prepared to accept harsh terms of resettlement in 1610 and later. The *cartas pueblas* were not simply dictated by the lord to the peasant; they were, at least in theory, negotiated contracts; this posed a serious problem for the liberal reformers of the nineteenth century when they came to undo them.[6] The charter of Cocentaina, for example,

---

[1] Eugenio Císcar, 'Tierra y señorío en una etapa crítica de la historia valenciana 1570–1620' (Tesis doctoral, Facultad de Filosofía y Letras, Valencia 1976), 447–8.
[2] Antonio Domínguez Ortiz, *La sociedad española en el siglo XVIII* (Madrid 1965), 288.
[3] BUV Ms. 24, 'Relación del antiguo gobierno de Aragón, Cataluña y Valencia' (1713), fol. 5.   [4] *Crónica*, 1031.
[5] Robert Burns, S. J., *Medieval Colonialism: Postcrusade Exploitation of Islamic Valencia* (Princeton 1975), 110–13.   [6] Moxó, *Disolución del régimen señorial*, 170.

had been hammered out by the Count's agent and the peasants in the church of the old Moorish ghetto; and the count wondered whether it might not be a good idea to state clearly all the dues for which the Moriscos were liable, 'so that people can see what a lot of tributes and labour services I am ready to give up'.[1] Curiously enough, two of the prime centres of the great peasant revolt of 1693, the villages of Petres and Villalonga, had not been settled by private senyors at all, but by Salvador Fontanet and the royal Junta Patrimonial respectively, acting in the name of the Crown.[2] It was only later that these two estates, by then under royal sequestration, were restored (with their charters intact) to seigneurial hands.

If the new feudal regime which emerged in seventeenth-century Valencia was harsh, yet it enjoyed the approval of the Crown (which intervened actively throughout the resettlements) and had the sanction of tradition. What did the peasants themselves feel about it? In the Vall de Uxó, the new settlers had rejected the first set of terms which the Duke of Segorbe submitted to them. Their most radical stand was perhaps on those clauses which they considered unusual rather than burdensome. They attacked a proposed tax on straw ('for who has ever heard of such a thing?'), they would not pay anything for their beehives ('for these have never paid anything in the valley, nor outside either'), and they demanded their own butcher's shop ('for that is the law of the land'). On the more fundamental question of land-rents they had to tread warily, impugning not the legal principle but the practical issues involved. The Duke asked for a quarter of huerta grains, the peasants countered with the offer of a twelfth ('given that the lands of the huerta are so poor and barren, and so short of water'), and the two sides eventually settled on a sixth.[3] The great protest of the peasants of Valldigna against the abbot in 1667 recalls very much the tone of the Vall de Uxó document. The peasants were aware of their legal rights – the fact that the abbey had made no provision for a municipal grazing area or *bovalar* was directly

[1] ADM Cocentaina leg. 2 n. 15, 'advertimientos para el señor don Francisco Corella tocantes a la nueva población' (1611?).
[2] ACA CA leg. 607 n. 17 (Petres); AHN Osuna leg. 562 n. 41 (Villalonga).
[3] ADM Segorbe leg. 62 n. 5, 'memorial de lo que dizen los pobladores de la Vall de Uxó'.

attacked as against the law, and the incidental activities of the abbot, such as measuring paths and canals and charging a rent for them, or getting the rice *partició* after rather than before the rice was dried, came under a confident, sustained assault as unfair and unjust. But on the main issue of *partició* itself, the peasants had to be cautious: one-quarter of huerta crops, one-seventh of secano and one-third of carob are challenged as being too high, for 'the harvests are so full of chaff'.[1] We find similar phrases in the petition submitted by the peasant deputies to the Crown in 1693 against the Valencian senyors: 'the harvests are so small that the poor have reached a point where they can no longer support such heavy obligations'.[2] True, the Second Germania had more radical overtones than the general run of rural protests. Basing themselves on royal edicts of 1268 to 1363 (carefully purloined from the viceroy's own archives), the leaders alleged that they were not only exempt from paying 'the exorbitant rents which are now current, but from any other whatsoever, for only Your Majesty had the power to impose them'.[3] But even here one notes the attention to legal argument. Without a document, there would have been no peasant revolt.

The point is simply that the peasant communities of Valencia were politically well organized, and had a long tradition, since at least the later Middle Ages, of using the royal courts to defend their interests. Asked to intervene on the side of the Moriscos against the senyors, the bishops of Valencia refused: 'The Moriscos were very well able to take their case before the king's judges when they had any grievances to complain of, and there they received a fair hearing.'[4] This was no idle claim. The account books of the community of Tabernes de Valldigna for 1607–8 record the expenditure of the community on trips to Valencia to consult with Dr Arinyo (later a judge of the Audiencia) on the terms of an agreement with the abbey limiting labour services in the sugar mill, and to find out from Dr Just whether they or the abbey were legally liable for the

[1] ARV Clero leg. 726, petition of Vicente Casaña, 15 July 1667.
[2] ACA CA leg. 579 n. 45/3, petition of Felix Rubio and others, 1693.
[3] ACA CA leg. 580 n. 5/37, consulta, 17 April 1693.
[4] Quoted in Boronat, *Moriscos*, II, 135.

excusado tithe payable to the king.[1] In 1583 and again in 1595 the abbey was blocked by royal intervention in its attempts to enforce a *partició* of mulberry and carob; the Moriscos took their stand on immemorial tradition, and the judges backed their refusal to pay. Angrily the abbot of the day began to insist on the strict letter of his own rights, 'since these vassals are so free, and there is so little point in being their lord'.[2] In 1589 the senyor of Gestalgar was thrown into prison for chopping down the peasants' peach trees, when they refused to give him a share of the fruit.[3] In Muro the Count of Cocentaina was at logger-heads with his Moriscos over rents in the years before the expulsion.[4] In Fansara, the Moriscos 'had a lawsuit with the duchess [of Segorbe], and defended themselves with the charters in their possession'.[5]

If documents rather than armed force ruled the relationship between lord and peasant in Valencia, this was perhaps to a large extent because the peasant communities had a legal existence of their own; this was not the situation in parts of western France, for example, where the parish priest seems to have been the only spokesman for the peasants to the outside world.[6] Day-to-day government in the Valencian villages was in the hands of officially appointed magistrates – the *justicia* and the *jurats*. True, these were mostly designated by the senyors, but in the majority of cases only from a list of three candidates for each office forwarded by the peasants themselves.[7] The list was usually drawn up by the outgoing magistrates, either on their own or in consultation with a restricted inner council (Consell Particular), which was itself appointed by the senyor, again usually from a list of names submitted by the community.[8]

[1] ARV Clero leg. 759, 'procés de comptes de la aljama de Taverna', 1607–8.
[2] ARV Clero leg. 781, 'memorial de los agravios', 1594; leg. 736, abbot v. peasants, 1583, and leg. 750, proceedings before the bishop of Utica, 20 Dec. 1593.
[3] ACA CA leg. 581 n. 55, consulta, 1 June 1589.
[4] Francisco Momblanch, *Historia de la villa de Muro* (Alicante 1959), 61–83.
[5] ADM Segorbe leg. 61 n. 9, testimony of Pere Farlet, 1612.
[6] Neveux *et al.*, *Histoire de la France rurale*, II, 284–8.
[7] Eugenio Císcar, 'Tierra y señorío', 339–42.
[8] In Valldigna the peasants as a whole were apparently allowed to choose any names they liked with the abbot picking one of two, ARV Clero leg. 741, *carta puebla* of 1609, c. 3. In Vall de Uxó the Duke of Segorbe arrogated to himself the right of nominating the Consell Particular directly, with this body then responsible for forwarding him three names for each office; ADM Segorbe leg. 6 n. 3, *carta puebla* of 1613, c. 46. It may be interesting to note that, in Cocentaina, elections after the

Government in the villages, therefore, was fairly oligarchic: it involved a delicate adjustment of interests between the feudal lord and the more important landowning families on whom he would depend to staff the Consell Particular and forward suitable candidates for public office. When the village elite deserted their master, they would appeal to the Consell General, the general assembly of all the local heads of households, which had to ratify the decision to appoint lawyers to take the senyors before the royal courts. There was a clause in most resettlement charters requiring the lord's authorization for such an open assembly to be held – even, in Cocentaina, prohibiting secret voting but requiring each peasant to run the gauntlet of seigneurial anger by stating his opinions openly.[1] In the circumstances it is perhaps surprising that the villagers were able to move against their master, yet move they did, and the whole of Valencian history is littered with their lawsuits. In the first instance the peasants would state their case formally before the Audiencia, alleging abuse by the senyor. The Audiencia might cautiously instruct the latter to appoint an arbiter acceptable to both sides (a way of avoiding a clash with the feudal lords, who were all entitled legally to full civil jurisdiction within their own demesnes). But if the arbiter failed to give satisfaction, the peasants could appeal again to the royal judges, and finally, if they were turned down again, they could appeal to another chamber within the Audiencia.[2] Suits could drag on inconclusively for years, until either the senyor or his vassals ran out of patience or money, and most of them seem to have ended in a compromise.

It was as one of a series of lawsuits against the senyors alleging injustice and abuse in the resettlements that the Second Germania began. Some of the early leaders were lawyers, like the notary Felix Vilanova and the advocate Dr Leonardo Pintor, or professional men, like the archivist of the viceregal palace who dug out copies of the *furs* of Jaime the Conqueror and his son King Pedro for the peasant leaders, and who was sacked

expulsion – by the Count from names proposed by his vassals – were specifically designed to follow existing practice in the old quarter, and to follow 'the laws and customs of the present kingdom'; ADM Cocentaina leg. 2 n. 15, *carta puebla* of 1611, c. 20.   [1] *Ibid.*, Cocentaina, c. 24.
[2] A good example of the procedure is ARV Clero leg. 751, Almusafes v. abbot of Valldigna 1584–92. Almusafes was not allowed a third appeal.

for his pains.[1] The wealthy peasants can be detected lurking in the background – Vicente Alonso of Muro, for example, whose family were *ciutadans*, tithe-farmers, and the biggest landholders in the village, and who intervened unsuccessfully with the governor of Játiva on the fatal morning of 15 July 1693 for an amnesty for the insurgents; or the bailiff of Castellón de Rugat, who had played a similar role as intermediary a day or so before, and who was to turn up again in 1695 leading a peaceful deputation of village *magnates* (as the Duke of Gandía somewhat contemptuously called them) to try and get the Borjas to commute rents for a fixed sum.[2] These men had special grievances at this period, of course, because prices for agricultural produce were wretchedly low. But the passage from litigation to armed force – the bypassing of the lawyers, and the military promenade with guns, banners of Saint Vincent Ferrer and Our Lady, and cries of 'long live the poor and down with bad government' – went beyond what they had bargained for. The men actually captured and tried by the courts were mostly without property, except for one of the ringleaders, the surgeon barber Josep Navarro of Muro.[3] As the authorities pointed out at the time, the revolt was mostly confined to 'the poorest and most backward villages' in the kingdom, the rough mountain territory of the Marina which runs inland from Gandía to Cocentaina and Alcoy. As they also noted, this was prime bandit country.[4] The real intellectual influence here was exerted not by lawyers but by priests – the rectors of Ráfol de Almunia, Almudaina, Almoines, Ebo, Villalonga, Ráfol de Salem, Catamarruc, Ondara, and Muro, who taught openly that the peasants paid too high rents and that 'they should have no scruple in stealing from the senyors'.[5] Just what relationship Vicente Alonso and the bailiff of Castellón de Rugat had to these

---

[1] ACA CA leg. 579 n. 53/2 (Vilanova), and 580 n. 5/13 (Pintor and the archivist).
[2] On the Alonsos, governor of Játiva to viceroy, see García Martínez, *Valencia bajo Carlos II*, II, 257–8, ACV *arriendos de diezmos* 4397, 1697–1700, and ADM Cocentaina leg. 25, *capbreu* of 1759; on the bailiff of Castellón, ACA CA leg. 581, n. 2/13, governor of Játiva to the viceroy, 13 July 1693, and AHN Osuna leg. 1030 n. 6/2, steward to Duke of Gandía, 28 Nov. 1695.
[3] Henry Kamen, 'Nueva luz sobre la segunda Germanía de Valencia en 1693', *Homenaje a Juan Reglá* (2 vols., Valencia 1975), I, 655.
[4] ACA CA leg. 581 n. 2/17, informe de la junta de ministros, 21 July 1693; leg. 579 n. 53/2, viceroy to king, 17 Feb. 1693.
[5] ACA CA leg. 581 n. 2/10, 'lista de los nombres de los curas que imbió el exmo. señor marqués de Castel Rodrigo al exmo. señor arçobispo'.

rustic holy men is unclear: some of the priests may have been outsiders, aggrieved at having to sink their talents and end their days in such god-forsaken places, but most were probably native sons, from the wealthy peasant families of the area.[1] In any case, it is clear enough that the rejection of the peasant arguments on the resettlement charters by the government-appointed panel of legal arbiters on 12 February 1693, and the refusal of the Council of Aragon on 20 April to get directly involved, probably finished the agitation in the more urbanized parts of Valencia, although they led to greater radicalism in the isolated mountains.[2] Rumours flew round, and of course could not be checked, that the senyors had stolen or hidden the papers recording all the concessions made by the good king; the tradition of violent independence and the vendetta led directly to the use of a rent-strike in the early summer, in defiance of the lawyers; and finally retaliation by the authorities in the form of troop billets and the arrest of strikers led to the inevitable confrontation between 10 and 15 July.

The Second Germania was an inglorious fiasco and not at all typical of the methods of ordered opposition to the senyors which characterize Valencia. But it casts an interesting light, nonetheless, on the structure of rural society. Above all, per-haps, it underlines the relative weakness of the feudal lords, who had, in the end, to be bailed out by the royal militia – a particular grievance here for the Crown was that the senyors would not or could not give any money to defray the cost of the military operation.[3] Though litigation through the courts could be slow and ultimately unsuccessful, the sullen hostility of the village (ruled by the local men of property rather than by the landless, absentee senyor) could force the lord to come to a compromise. In 1630 the Duke of Gandía had reduced the main *partició* in Catadau from one-eighth to one-eleventh.[4] In

---

[1] On the fringes of the troubled zone, the rector of Orcheta, for example, was the son of a wealthy peasant of the same village, farmer of the seigneurial rents in the area; APV 1376–II, 29 Jan. 1639. And see the matrimonial connections of the clergy in another part of the neighbourhood, in Joaquín Mestre, *Alcalalí* (Alicante 1970), 431–52.

[2] ACA CA leg. 580 n. 5/38, 'informe de los abogados', 12 Feb. 1693; leg. 579 n. 45/1, consulta, 20 April 1693.

[3] ACA CA leg. 580 n. 5/32, viceroy to secretary Haro, 14 April 1693.

[4] AHN Osuna leg. 722 n. 6/25.

1649 the Duke of Segorbe reduced that in Benaguacil from one-seventh to one-ninth; and in 1658 he brought that of Vall de Uxó down from one-sixth to one-eighth.[1] There were, it is true, some moves in the opposite direction – the abbey of Valldigna, for example, managed gradually to twist the arms of old-established families between 1631 and 1675, and got them to agree to the new, higher rents laid down in the resettlement charter of 1609.[2] But even Valldigna had to make some concessions – reducing the *partició* on wine in 1622, amalgamating the fifths and eighths characteristic of share-cropping in the secano into a uniform seventh in 1645 and finally in 1700 giving way on some of the incidental grievances listed above in the protest of 1667.[3]

It is against this background of unrest that the actual evolution of seigneurial fortunes has to be seen – for the amount of rent coming in is the ultimate test of 'seigneurial reaction'. There was something like a doubling of feudal incomes in the half-century before the expulsion of the Moriscos – the 13 *encomiendas* of Montesa moved up in value from 7,400 *lliures* a year in 1564 to 15,100 round 1600, the Duchy of Villahermosa from an average of 1,414 *lliures* in the period 1553–7 to an average of 2,663 in 1593–1600.[4] These probably resembled most estates in being a mixture of feudal dues, regalian rights and some share-cropping, even if only the *tercio diezmo*. But in Vall de Uxó and Sierra de Eslida, where there were no rents in kind at all, the revenues of the Duke of Segorbe edged up from 2,619 to 3,363 *lliures* between 1553 and 1609, a barely perceptible change over an interval in which prices doubled.[5]

Even where share-cropping was the rule, the stagnation of population and production after about 1580 badly affected seigneurial receipts (see table 12). Everywhere a highwater mark seems to have been reached in the 1580s. Seigneurial coffers (at least in the better-run estates) can never have been so full. And then came the time of disillusionment, when even the healthiest rents appear to have been blocked – a particularly

[1] ADM Segorbe leg. 6 n. 7.   [2] ARV Clero leg. 740, acts of renunciation, 1631–75.
[3] ARV Clero leg. 781 and 784, *concordias* 7 May 1645 and 18 March 1700.
[4] For the *encomiendas* of Montesa, Viciana, *Crónica*, vol. III, and BL Harl. 3569 fol. 107; for Villahermosa, ARV MR 9625–9632.
[5] ADM Segorbe legs. 62 n. 1 (1553) and 61 n. 9 (1609).

Table 12. *Revenues of selected share-cropping estates: average yearly receipts (in lliures)*

	Turís	Lombay	Planes
1559–63	1,108	3,913	—
1565–8	—	—	2,506
1575–80	2,176	—	3,175
1582–6	2,369	—	4,000
1587–90	2,281	5,242	3,830
1591–4	—	5,905	3,819
1600–9	2,405	5,517	—

A blank in the table indicates that no information is available.
SOURCES: AHN Osuna legs. 1027 nos. 18 and 21, and 1036 n. 1 (Lombay and Turís); ARV MR 10168–10180, and ACA CA leg. 646 n. 2/2 (Planes – farms only).

unfortunate occurrence at a moment when prices were rising faster than ever. Not surprisingly these decades saw a sharp increase in seigneurial borrowing. They also witnessed an intensification of the age-old conflict between lord and peasant, for almost all the disputes listed above between the Moriscos and their senyors come from the period after 1580 – surely no coincidence. Nor perhaps is it wholly a coincidence that the first proposals for getting rid of the Moriscos began to be mooted around 1580 in government circles, and gathered strength with every year, as the weakness of the Moriscos' erstwhile protectors, the senyors, became apparent. When the blow fell at last in 1609, the nobles, after some early opposition to the expulsion – 'declaiming loudly against the king and his ministers' – quickly tried to turn the situation to their advantage, writing little letters of loyalty and claiming compensation of the Crown, and turning themselves into the most efficient agents of royal policy by rounding up the Moriscos on their own estates.[1] A delighted Duke of Lerma praised their docility, noting 'how convinced they are that we had no choice but to take the decision we have – a point which they will appreciate all the more clearly when they see how sizeable the Morisco spoils are, and the profit to be got from their estates'.[2]

Certainly rents after the expulsion proved resilient in some

[1] Fonseca, *Justa expulsión*, 53–4.
[2] To the archbishop of Valencia, in Boronat, *Moriscos*, II, 208 n. 30.

places. The Vall de Uxó and Sierra de Eslida rented 5,034 *lliures* in 1640 as against 3,363 on the eve of the expulsion.[1] Here the switch from fixed tributes to share-cropping paid dividends. In Valldigna the abbey could count on about 12,000 *lliures* rent in the 1640s as against 15,000 in its sixteenth-century heyday – not a bad performance, all things considered, for it was taking approximately three-quarters of its old revenues from a population no more than half the size of the old.[2] This was in theory – in practice only 7,000 or 8,000 of this sum could actually be collected in any one year. The poverty of the peasantry and their sullen resistance to high rents served to draw the teeth of the seigneurial reaction.

In fact, if we leave aside exceptional cases like Vall de Uxó where any change could only have been for the better (given the blockage of seigneurial dues before the expulsion), rents fell after 1609 – and stayed low into the reign of Philip IV. 'You must not look at what the settlers are obliged to pay on paper', alleged the Duke of Segorbe on one occasion, 'but at what they can and do pay. For example, the wheat they hand over is the worst they can get away with...and they do not pay anything for the secano since it is never ploughed.'[3] The receipts of the Count of Castellar dropped from 13,650 *lliures* a year to 1,050, those of the Count of Buñol from 14,000 to 3,000, of the Count of Real from 'more than 10,000' to 2,700, of the Marquis of Navarrés from 4,000 to 755, and of the Marquis of Guadalest from 20,000 to 8,325.[4] These were probably the worst affected estates, located in the predominantly Morisco crescent of hills which swept round the plain of Valencia. Their lands were poor and attracted few settlers, and the switch from quit-rents to share-cropping made little difference. Less serious were the losses of the Duke of Infantado, master of the most valuable community in the kingdom, Alberique: his receipts fell from 20,000 to 10,830 a year.[5] Similarly, the Count of Elda managed

---

[1] ADM Segorbe leg. 14 n. 12 (1640) and leg. 61 n. 9 (1609).
[2] ARV Clero leg. 785, 'carta cuenta del llibre de la col. lecta major', 1648–90.
[3] ADM Segorbe leg. 42 n. 2, Duke v. chapter of Segorbe, 1621.
[4] ACA CA leg. 875, Castellar, 15 Nov. 1631; leg. 654, Buñol, 28 March 1621; ARV Diversorum 385 fols. 92v–112v, Real, 1615; ARV Clero leg. 735, Navarrés, 1631; leg. 404, Guadalest, 1619.
[5] AHN Osuna leg. 3146 n. 2, accounts of 1619.

to salvage 7,500 a year from his old rentroll of 12,000.[1] The Count of Cocentaina, who was pointed out by the Council of Aragon as one of those who had done best out of the expulsion and the resettlements, was getting 16,117 *lliures* in 1615 as against some 21,000 when he still had Moriscos. But he had achieved this tour de force by overburdening his new settlers, and eventually the edifice cracked under the strain, the peasants left, and the rents fell to as little as 9,450 by 1623.[2] This was the dilemma at the heart of the seigneurial reaction. Advising the Crown to charge low rentals for the Morisco lands of Játiva, the Deputy Maestre Racional wrote: 'where the resettlements are onerous people will just not stay, except for those wretches who have neither the tools nor the wherewithal to live, and these places get one batch of settlers after the next, each lot worse than the one before'.[3]

Higher dues after 1609 contributed to the disorder in the countryside, but the malady itself had deeper roots. Once population, trade and agriculture began to revive under Charles II so too did seigneurial rents. The longest series we have is for the revenues of the Dukes of Gandía.[4] Their permanent Valencian patrimony – if we ignore new acquisitions and alienations over the seventeenth century – fetched around 45,114 *lliures* a year on the eve of the expulsion, only 20,943 in 1634, but then 27,465½ by 1705. The pre-expulsion figure is actually inflated artificially compared with the others. It should be reduced by 5,190 *lliures* to allow for labour costs in the sugar mills, which were directly administered by the dukes before 1609. Indeed, much of the drop in the Borja revenues depends on the disastrous performance of this one crop – sugar. If we leave aside the old Duchy of Gandía, where this cultivation had been all important to the Borjas, we find that Oliva and the resettlements, renting 23,365 *lliures* before the expulsion, were cut back to 14,943 by 1634, but then recovered strongly to 19,035½ by 1705. In other words, the non-sugar revenues were healthy enough in the late seventeenth century. The detailed

[1] ARV Clerol leg. 764, Elda, 1612.
[2] ACA CA leg. 657, report of don Baltasar Sanz (1630?).
[3] ACA CA leg. 640 n. 4/71, to king, 29 Jan. 1619.
[4] Calculations based on AHN Osuna legs. 602 n. 28, 806, 1021 n. 16, 1027 n. 21, 1028 n. 98 and 1033 n. 38. Cf. appendix 3.

breakdown of the Borja rents in the Marquesate of Lombay give some insight into the mechanism of growth.[1] Even though the population of Lombay in 1700 was still only about two-thirds of its level in Morisco days, and even though the rate of share-cropping here on the main crops had actually been reduced from one-third to one-sixth after the expulsion, more money was coming into the seigneurial coffers than ever before. The explanation for this was partly (unfortunately for the historian), a fluke harvest of olives in 1700 which artificially increased the oil revenue, and partly the fact that the senyor was now taking his share of the mulberry leaf harvest in kind, whereas it had been largely commuted before the expulsion. But also the Old Christians were spending more, man for man, in the village shops than the Moriscos had done, and were cultivating the more valuable wheat rather than that standby of the poor, millet. These two factors seem to have played a key role in boosting seigneurial revenues.

On the other hand, if the Lombay rents were actually worth 5,989 *lliures* in 1700, they could only be farmed out to contractors for 3,705 in the 1690s, rising to 4,810 by 1705.[3] Similarly, the barony of Cofrentes was worth 5,309 *lliures* a year around 1660, yet it could only be farmed out for 3,700 in 1634, and 3,290 in 1674.[3] This gap was serious, because almost all Valencian senyors negotiated their rents away to contractors in return for a lump sum. The situation is an almost exact parallel with that in France at the time, where seigneurial rents began to fall because the big commercial farmers who administered them under contract were going out of business, victims of the price collapse of late seventeenth-century Europe.[4] It is during this period that we find the wealthy propertied men of Gandía and Oliva, like don Pedro Císcar, complaining that they were losing money on the rent farms of the Borjas.[5] Good harvests had to be offset against a bad market, and both tax-contractors and senyors suffered.

In general, then, the seigneurial reaction of seventeenth-

[1] See appendix 2.
[2] AHN Osuna legs. 1033 n. 48, 1021 n. 16 and 1028 n. 98, farms, c. 1690–1705.
[3] AHN Osuna leg. 806, rents of Cofrentes, 1659–62.
[4] Le Roy Ladurie, *Paysans de Languedoc*, 304–11.
[5] AHN Osuna leg. 602 n. 40, Gandía v. Císcar, 1658.

century Valencia was far from justifying its promise. The higher dues introduced after 1609 – in particular a switch from quit-rents to share-cropping – never did succeed in bringing the receipts of the senyors back to their old sixteenth-century peaks. 'From our investigations and enquiries', noted the Resettlement Junta in 1613, 'it would appear beyond doubt that extremely few of the lords in this kingdom have not suffered serious financial loss as a result of the expulsion, though some more than others, and some temporarily and others for good.'[5] In the end, all the ambitions of the resettlements tended to founder on the depressed state of the seventeenth-century economy.

[5] ACA CA leg. 607 n. 16, 1st consulta of Junta de Población, 1613.

6

The bankruptcy of the senyors

The concept of 'the aristocracy in crisis' is an old one for the early modern period. Already in 1912 Lucien Febvre had painted the dire plight of the nobility of the Franche-Comté, whose old feudal rents failed to meet the needs of the new age and who were forced increasingly to sell out to bourgeois creditors.[1] More recent studies have cast a lurid light on the financial predicament of the great families of France, Spain and England.[2] The exact implications of the phenomenon, however, are not all that clear. Perhaps only in England was there a massive transfer of estates out of the hands of the old nobility, a development which would help explain the uniquely radical nature of the challenge to the social and political hierarchy which is associated with the Civil War. In France as in Spain the great families still seem to have been as firmly in the saddle in 1640 as in 1540. Jago has noticed in the case of Castile how the Crown intervened time after time to save the big houses by staggering, postponing or reducing their debt payments, and Tricoli has observed much the same phenomenon (though royal intervention was more informal) in the case of Sicily.[3] The Castilian and Sicilian nobles kept their estates, but at the cost of subservience to their protector, the king.

In Valencia by the beginning of the seventeenth century the all-too-familiar outlines of the debt problem were clearly visible.

[1] Lucien Febvre, *Philippe II et la Franche-Comté*, 1912, 2nd edn (Paris 1970), 130–6 and 183–9.
[2] L. Stone, *The Crisis of the Aristocracy* (Oxford 1965); C. Jago, 'The Influence of Debt on the Relations between Crown and Aristocracy in 17th century Castile', *Economic History Review*, XXVI (1973), 218–36; Goubert, *Cent Mille Provinciaux*, 240–2; J.-P. Labatut, *Les Ducs et Pairs de France au XVIIᵉ siècle* (Paris 1972), 260, 269 and 277.
[3] G. Tricoli, *La Deputazione degli Stati e la Crisi del Baronaggio Siciliano del XVI al XIX secolo* (Palermo 1966), 141–6, 161, and *passim*.

Unfortunately the only inclusive figures for the nobility come from after the expulsion of the Moriscos, when the senyors were saddled with the debts of the old communities, thus aggravating their burden. But the generally agreed total owed at that time by the 130 or so lords who had once had any Moriscos on their estates was a staggering 4,000,000 ducats.[1] Assuming standard interest at 15 *mil el millar* or 6⅔ per cent (the rate that generally obtained in Valencia before the expulsion), the annual charges on these debts must have amounted to around 280,000 *lliures*. As noted earlier, the total landed revenue of the 186 lay and ecclesiastical fief-holders in the kingdom was in the region of 974,565 *lliures*. Given that the majority of the Morisco debts represented the borrowing of the feudal nobility, the Valencian senyors may have been paying over to their creditors between a quarter and a third of their revenues every year before the expulsion. This may be compared with the situation in England, where Stone calculates that by 1641 one-sixth of the gross rentals of the peerage was pledged in interest payments, 'which is approaching the limit which an estate could comfortably support'.[2] By this reckoning the Valencian situation was very bad indeed.

Overall estimates are inevitably somewhat misleading. It is a fair guess that most of the 157 lay and almost all the ecclesiastical fief-holders were in fact living more or less within their means. The lords of the Vall de Alcalá, with rents of 2,604 *lliures*, were well able to meet interest payments of 292 – at least until the expulsion of the Moriscos cut the rentals of this barbarous mountain domain to only 299.[3] The senyor of Alboy was comfortably enough off with rents of 1,300 and debts of only 246 *lliures* a year – again, until the expulsion cut his revenues to a mere 450.[4] How typical these cases were we do not know, though it may be significant that the lord of Alboy was one of only a handful of senyors actually to attend the meeting of the assembly of the nobility which protested against the expulsion on 16 September 1609. The higher up the social

---

[1] AHN Osuna leg. 899 n. 1, petition of don Francisco Roca (1624); ARV R 698, memorial of mossèn Bartolomé Sebastián (1613?).
[2] *Crisis of the Aristocracy*, 246. All references are to the abridged 1967 edn.
[3] ACA CA leg. 612, consulta, 16 Jan. 1618.
[4] ACA CA leg. 627, consulta, 16 Jan. 1618.

ladder we go, in fact, the darker the financial prospect. The senyor (soon to be created Count) of Faura was already, before the expulsion, paying out a quarter of his 4,000 *lliures* a year income in interest charges on his debts.[1] So too the Count of Carlet must have been handing over 2,000 *lliures* a year to his creditors from revenues of 6,000.[2] Such men may not have seen the point of fighting to the death to hold on to their Moriscos.

It was the magnates, however, who seem to have been in the worst plight. Out of projected receipts of 68,848 *lliures* around 1605, the Duke of Gandía reckoned to set aside 35,546 simply to service his funded debts (see appendix 3). There are no overall figures for the premier nobleman of Valencia, the Duke of Segorbe. But his estates of Benaguacil, Pobla and Paterna rented 6,350 *lliures* just before the expulsion, and of this sum no less than 6,265 went to satisfy interest on mortgages lying against this particular patrimony; in his other baronies of Vall de Uxó and Sierra de Eslida the interest was greater than the rents – 3,693 as against 3,363 *lliures*, with the peasants making up the difference out of their own pockets.[3] The Duke of Mandas, with revenues of 13,600 *lliures* (aside from his estates of Mogente and Sardinia for which no statement of liabilities is available), had to meet interest payments of 8,470.[4] The Count of Cocentaina owed his creditors about 12,056 *lliures* a year out of rents of 21,000.[5] The Marquis of Guadalest, Philip III's ambassador to Flanders after 1604, had long-term mortgages of 350,000 ducats lying against his patrimony, plus 50,000 ducats of short-term debts. Assuming that these were charged at the standard rate of 6⅔ per cent, interest on them must have been in the region of 28,000 *lliures*. But the Guadalest estates were only worth 20,000 to 25,000 *lliures* a year.[6] As don Diego Clavero reported grimly to the Duke of Lerma on the morrow of the expulsion, some Valencian nobles had 'as much in the way of

[1] ACA CA leg. 868, petition, 16 May 1618.
[2] ARV Procesos de Madrid, P 751, 1623.
[3] ADM Segorbe leg. 61 n. 9, memorandum of 1609.
[4] AHN Osuna legs. 2980 n. 1, 764 n. 28, and 3146 n. 2; ACA CA leg. 654, petition of Duke of Infantado, 11 March 1622.
[5] ACA CA leg. 657, report of don Baltasar Sanz (1630?); leg. 869, petition of Countess of Cocentaina, 6 Sept. 1622.
[6] ACA CA leg. 654, petition of Guadalest, 28 March 1622; ARV Clero leg. 404, *concordia* with creditors, 13 Sept. 1617.

debts as of rents, and others probably more, like the Marquises of Guadalest, Aytona and Navarrés, or the Counts of Buñol, Elda and Real'.[1]

The figures which I have quoted are all for long-term debts, *censals*, which were secured against mortgage of property. The process by which the Valencian aristocracy found it necessary during the later sixteenth century to convert short-term obligations into non-redeemable, interest-bearing bonds like the *censals*, parallels to some extent the similar conversions which the Spanish Monarchy was forced to operate over the same period. The rise of the *censal* parallels, in effect, the rise of the *juro*. In neither case can one take these bonds as evidence of total borrowing. What tended to happen was that a large number of short-term debts piled up and became unrepayable. Thus, when Carlos, seventh Duke of Gandía, saddled his estate with 75,000 ducats worth of bonds after his succession to the title in 1595, he was merely funding earlier, loose obligations of his father, Francisco.[2] Unfortunately, for a view of what the nobility was borrowing, we are mainly reduced to the *censals* alone, because the short-term letter of exchange (*cambio*), drawn usually on one of the Castilian fairs, tended to escape the attention of seigneurial accountants – or rather it would come under the jurisdiction of the men charged with irregular household expenditure – the private, 'cameral' treasurer of the fifth Duke of Segorbe, for example, in the 1560s.[3] At the most, we can say that the rise of the *censal* reflects the breakdown of a more traditional, haphazard system of borrowing. If we look at the bonded obligations of the Borjas, we can see that by the 1590s the family simply had no longer the money to pay back capital on short-term commitments, but had increasingly to go in for funding its debts (see table 13). In the case of the Dukes of Segorbe a roughly similar pattern is noticeable. Against their so-called 'old patrimony' of Benaguacil, Pobla and Paterna lay many bonds dating back to the fifteenth century; the earliest was apparently contracted in 1357. But in the Vall de Uxó and Sierra de Eslida almost all of the *censals* belong

---

[1] ACA CA leg. 607 n. 46/1, 9 Jan. 1610.
[2] AHN Osuna leg. 1035 n. 20; and cf. leg. 896 n. 5.
[3] ARV MR 10187, Francisco Hierónimo Metaller, 1566–8.

Table 13. *Censals of the Dukes of Gandía (to the nearest lliura)*

Before about 1570	213,920
Carlos, fifth Duke *c.* 1571–92	90,809
Francisco, sixth Duke 1592–5	125,169
Carlos, seventh Duke, borrowings between 1595 and 1604	111,595
Total obligations of the family by 1604	541,493

SOURCE: AHN Osuna leg. 1033 n. 75, and leg. 805 n. 2. There is an alternative, less satisfactory breakdown in leg. 899 n. 1, which I used in my article, 'La situación económica de la nobleza valenciana en vísperas de la expulsión de los moriscos', *Homenaje a Juan Reglá* (2 vols., Valencia 1975) I, 522. It is misleading on the whole chronology of Borja borrowing, since it is a document drawn up around 1622 and very imprecise about the dates of older debts.

to the period 1586–1607.[1] It would appear, therefore, that the last couple of decades of Morisco Valencia – a time of stagnation in seigneurial revenues – witnessed, not so much an increase in aristocratic borrowing, as an inability to pay off loans and a growing need to fund debts.

The problem, of course, with this operation was finding the security. There was a lot of bluff but some truth in the seventh Duke of Gandía's remark to his creditors that when he died they would find themselves 'on the street' ('*en la calle*'), for in theory no individual nobleman had the right to burden entailed estates with mortgages.[2] In Castile the obstacle was circumvented increasingly with royal dispensations.[3] In Valencia a more traditional system persisted (abolished in Castile in 1594) by which the peasant communities contracted the loan against the security of the property of the inhabitants, with the senyor slipping his vassals a 'letter of safeguard' acknowledging that the money had really been for his use and promising to pay the interest. But it availed the peasants of Gandía not at all to wave their letters of safeguard after 1604 when their ducal master went bankrupt and stopped payments to his creditors. 'We have not done business or negotiated with this duke', came the latter's reply, as they sued out writs of distraint, 'but with your communities.'[4] What happened, however, when matters

[1] ADM Segorbe leg. 62 n. 11, memorandum, 8 Feb. 1622.
[2] AHN Osuna leg. 899 n. 1, 'advertencias' (1622?).
[3] Jago, 'The Influence of Debt', 222–3.
[4] AHN Osuna leg. 602 n. 15, Oliva v. creditors, 1611.

reached this point was that the peasants either appealed to the royal courts for a sequestration of seigneurial rents so that they could pay off the creditors themselves out of the proceeds (this happened with the Duke of Mandas in 1596), or they would offer a lump sum as a sort of equitable payment which would absolve them from all further responsibility (this occurred in 1606 when the inhabitants of the Gandía and Oliva estates offered to buy out 71,186 *lliures* of ducal debts, about an eighth of the total).[1] The Valencian situation – even allowing for these compromises, which were usually ratified by the royal courts – was clearly more iniquitous and unfair to the peasantry than the state of affairs in Castile, and in 1614 the Crown specifically forbade the resettlements to contract any debts on behalf of their senyors, a partial measure of relief in a kingdom where (in the government's words), 'the lords are very domineering and their vassals very cowed and submissive to them'.[2] But it left the old-established areas still at the mercy of their masters, and when a Duke of Gandía wanted to borrow as late as the 1690s, he simply told his towns of Gandía, Oliva and Pego to do it for him.[3]

Borrowing, then, seems to have been somewhat easier for the 'domineering' Valencians than for their Castilian cousins. Thus the funded debts of some of the Castilian houses studied by Jago tended to consume from a quarter to a third of gross revenues; a consumption of one-half of the revenues was approached only in the worst cases, whereas one-half seems to have been the base line for the eastern magnates. It is surprising that these people found anyone willing to lend to them in the first place. That they did so was because of the stoutly aristocratic social structure of Valencia. Ex-merchants, rich peasants and *ciutadans*, lacking alternative investments in trade or agriculture, sought to put their money in rents – which, even if it was not altogether profitable, procured them the social status they could get in no other way. In England or France a rising bourgeoisie could invest its savings in the purchase of noble estates; in Spain,

---

[1] AHN Osuna leg. 748 n. 2/13 (1596); leg. 1027 n. 8 (1606).
[2] ACA CA leg. 607 n. 49/1, consulta of Audiencia (1610?); cf. chapter 27 of *asiento general* of 1614, in Boronat, *Moriscos*, II, 628–9.
[3] AHN Osuna leg. 4082, record of borrowing, Nov. 1692 to Jan. 1699.

Table 14. *Owners of the censals lying against the estates of the Duke of Gandía in 1624*

	Amount (in lliures)	Percentage
Upper nobility	219,374	43
Hospitals and clergy	75,951	15
Lower nobility and commoners	209,184	42
Total	504,509	100

There are no figures for Turís.

because of the exceptional rigidity of the perpetual entail, few noble estates ever came on the market. For the same reason, those that did were prohibitively expensive, and cost around 40 times the annual rental – as against only 16 to 20 times the rental in Elizabethan England, for example.[1] Thus the baronies of Albalat, Turís and Chella, worth 2,328 *lliures* a year, went for 106,000 *lliures* in 1664; Benavites, renting 750, fetched 32,000 around the time of the expulsion of the Moriscos; while Planes, a big estate worth 6,500, was sold for 300,000 in 1592.[2] It would have taken a combination of luck and desperation in Habsburg Valencia to buy a fief at a return of 2½ per cent on capital, when the money could be loaned in perpetuity to the existing senyor at 6⅔ per cent. It was the latter development, of course, which took place. Wealthy merchants and younger sons of the senyors themselves, excluded from land, came to constitute an alternative aristocracy – an urban nobility or patriciate, based on possession of the *censals*. It comes as little surprise to find, for example, that 13 of the 18 creditors of the Count of Real, and 27 of the 68 creditors of the Marquis of Guadalest were themselves nobles, or that the upper nobility (those with the title *don* before their name) held 43 per cent of the capital of the Borja debts (see table 14).[3]

The *censals* themselves became, like land, a subject of entail.

[1] Stone, *Crisis of the Aristocracy*, 245.
[2] AHN Osuna leg. 696 n. 54; ADM Cocentaina leg. 6 n. 49; ACA CA leg. 646 n. 2/2. It is interesting that all three sales were to old seigneurial families – Marrades, Belvís, and the Duke of Maqueda respectively.
[3] ARV Diversorum 385 fols. 92v–112v; Clero leg. 404, *concordia*, 1619; AHN Osuna leg. 895 n. 19.

We find aspiring lawyers like Juan Bautista Sapena (who was soon to found a noble dynasty), or old-established families like that of don Francisco Bou, handing on these bonds to their heirs as an inalienable trust which was to be passed to their descendants in perpetuity, observing the rule of male primogeniture at each generation. If the bonds were ever redeemed (an eventuality which lay at the discretion of the borrower), the money was to be immediately reinvested in the same way.[1] Valencia had, in effect, two aristocracies by 1609: the 157 senyors and their eldest sons, and several hundred (perhaps 500, according to the lists available for the Cortes) cadets or ennobled persons of lesser origin, who fused into a single 'urban nobility' living mainly off the annuities payable by the senyors.

But to see the situation in terms of two fundamentally antagonistic groups would surely be misleading, for some of the senyors had considerable bond-holdings of their own. Don Francisco Roca, lord of the community of Adzuvia, held 50,000 ducats worth of credits against his fellow fief-holders and became the leading spokesman of the creditors' lobby after the expulsion of the Moriscos.[2] Don Ramón Sanz was lord of Guadasequies, but more than half of his income must have come from 15,000 ducats worth of bonds and from his salary as an Audiencia judge.[3] Don Josep Sanz was a man in the middle: as lord of San Juan he drew rents of 1,400 *lliures* (cut to 500 *lliures* by the expulsion of the Moriscos); he was by his own account 'heavily in debt' and tended to identify with the hard-pressed senyors; but he also inherited quite a few *censals* of his own which would be damaged by any fall in interest rates.[4] Especially at the lower level, there was a fair amount of intermarriage between the landed nobility and the bond-holding patricians. Don Galcerán Mercader, brother of the first Count of Buñol, walked off with the heiress to Pedro de Caspe's fortune, while around the same time don Vicente Villaragut, brother of the first Count of Olocau, married the daughter of one of the big financiers of the day, doña Madalena Rovira.[5]

[1] ARV Clero leg. 400, testament of J. B. Sapena, 19 July 1616; ACA CA leg. 707, Bou-Sanz marriage contract, 15 Nov. 1622.
[2] ACA CA leg. 1357, consulta of the Junta de las Cortes, 16 April 1626.
[3] ACA CA leg. 871, petition (1626?).
[4] ACA CA leg. 655, consulta of the Junta de Materias de Valencia, 16 April 1626.
[5] *Coses evengudes*, II, para. 2900; ACA CA leg. 881, petition of don Vicente Villaragut, 20 June 1640, and ARV B *arrendamientos*, 13 Oct. 1637.

Of course, ties of blood would not always cancel financial rivalry, and we find another of the Mercader brothers, don Baltasar, emerging as a leading spokesman of the Duke of Gandía's creditors, and demanding the break-up and sale of the Borja estates, even though the head of his own family, the Count of Buñol, had no hope of paying his own debts.[1] The point to bear in mind is that debtors and creditors were not two distinct and bitterly opposed classes. To see the problem in terms of a rivalry between a decadent feudal aristocracy and a nascent bourgeoisie is at best an oversimplification. Ties of blood, marriage and common life-styles helped blunt the sharp edge of the conflict, and enable us to understand how the senyors could go on piling up such huge debts with so little security, and – more important – how they could avoid ruin in the process.

There was a variety of reasons for the senyors getting themselves into debt in the first place. Personal extravagance was perhaps the least of them. The Council of Aragon reckoned that the Duke of Gandía could live decently on 8,400 *lliures* a year just before the expulsion – no mean sum when one considers that judges of the Audiencia earned 1,200 *lliures* at most.[2] This sum represents about an eighth of his gross revenues at the time. Unfortunately no household budget has come to light for the period before 1609; but we know that in 1636 the eighth Duke reckoned to spend 8,359 *lliures* on what might be termed his own needs as against those of the estate – that is, on clothes, food, and wages for the palace servants (see appendix 3). At the time he employed about 24 people directly in the palace as stewards, lackeys, cooks, ladies-in-waiting and the like. By 1671 household expenditure had risen somewhat as the period of financial stringency following the expulsion of the Moriscos came to an end. In that year some 10,021 *lliures* were being spent on the household, with an expanded establishment of 41 servants, including now three slaves (a new item, this).[3] By the 1690s, when the tenth Duke went to live at court, his needs rose dramatically, to the sum

[1] AHN Osuna leg. 899 n. 1, petitions of don Baltasar Mercader (1623?).
[2] AHN Osuna leg. 895 n. 10, king to viceroy, 25 Nov. 1608.
[3] AHN Osuna leg. 4083, accounts, 1670–7. The Duke of Béjar, with about three times Gandía's income in the 1630s, was spending about 28,053 ducats (29,455 *lliures*) on the household; cf. Jago, 'Aristocracy, War and Finance', 224 and 229.

of 14,356 *lliures* a year (appendix 3). But even in these exceptional circumstances, the duke was only spending about a third
of his gross receipts on himself.

It is difficult to get figures for any other Valencian house
– especially since most of the other magnates lived outside the
kingdom. But before 1575 the Dukes of Segorbe were resident
there. In 1569 the third Duke had an income of 23,000 *lliures*
from Valencia, Catalonia and royal pensions.[1] We do not know
how this money was spent, but a decade earlier in 1553 and
1556 the detailed accounts of the Valencian patrimony show
an average expenditure of 6,013 *lliures* a year on food, clothes,
silverware, and general household maintenance.[2] It seems likely,
therefore, that the first nobleman of Valencia was able to live
quite comfortably on one-quarter of his gross rentals.

From the details of licences granted for the mortgage of the
mayorazgos in Castile, it has been estimated that service to the
Crown was the biggest single cause of noble indebtedness.
Ostensibly at least, 58.1 per cent of official aristocratic borrowing
there was laid out on court ceremonial, embassies abroad, levies
of troops for the king, and the like.[3] The information is much
less systematic for Valencia, where the nobility did not require
royal authorization to borrow. However, the *censals* assumed
by the seventh Duke of Gandía, amounting to 111,595 *lliures*,
went (according to his own story at least) 'almost all to serve
His Majesty in the journey to Germany', when he along with
other great nobles escorted Philip III's bride, Margaret of
Austria, back to Spain in 1599.[4] The sum constituted about a
fifth of the total *censal* burden of the Borjas by the time of the
expulsion of the Moriscos, then running at 541,493 *lliures*. The
fourth Marquis of Guadalest, similarly, was alleged to have run
through 100,000 ducats of his own money while serving as
ambassador of Philip III to the court of the Archdukes in
Flanders (1604–16). This sum was equivalent to about one-third
of his total *censal* commitments at the later date.[5]

---

[1] ARV MR 10187, revenues of the Duke of Segorbe, 1569.
[2] ADM Segorbe leg. 14 n. 10, accounts of 1553 and 1556.
[3] Jago, 'The Influence of Debt', 224.
[4] AHN Osuna leg. 899 n. 1, 'por los acreedores censalistas', and annotation by Duke's
    agent (1623?). But in fact 75,000 ducats of this sum may be accounted for by the
    funding of loose debts of his father, the sixth Duke; cf. above, p. 130.
[5] ACA CA leg. 654, consulta, 28 March 1622.

Of course, there were salaries attached to office. But the Duke of Gandía as viceroy of Sardinia between 1612 and 1618 was simply unable to manage on his official allowance of 6,000 *lliures*, when his ordinary household needs in Valencia ('where he can live less ostentatiously...than a viceroy can be expected to') were 8,400.[1] In the same way the subsequent rewards of service, in the form of royal pensions, were frequently illusory, as the Habsburgs were as bankrupt as their nobility, 'and often take years rather than months in finding the money'.[2] Yet the Valencian nobility, except those of the first rank, were not drawn into royal service as frequently as the Castilian. Even among the magnates – at least the indigenous ones, like Gandía or Guadalest – the king's business seems only to account for about a third of their debts, as against a proportion of nearer two-thirds in the case of the Castilians.

Left to itself, the Valencian nobility dissipated its energy and money in fierce internecine feuds – in family quarrels and litigation. Something like 215,978 *lliures* – around 40 per cent of the Borja obligations – had been borrowed during the period of the great litigation to defend the family's claims to the county of Oliva against the Centelles clan between 1569 and 1597.[3] The defence of the *mayorazgo* led the first Count of Carlet to saddle himself with 13,800 *lliures* on top of existing *censals* of about 6,000 after 1587.[4] Litigation was, of course, a feature of the age – a relief from boredom for a domesticated warrior class, as Lawrence Stone has described it, but also a soul-destroying tread-mill. The fight for Oliva cost the fifth Duke of Gandía 'far and away the best years of his life', as he ruefully confessed before it was half over.[5] If so many Valencian nobles, nevertheless, found themselves drawn into the trap, it was surely because of the rigidity of the entail system as it had developed from the later Middle Ages.

One tends to assume that entail and primogeniture created a strong and stable aristocracy in western Europe in early modern times. In a political sense undoubtedly it did, and this

[1] AHN Osuna leg. 899 n. 1, 'advertencias' (1623?).
[2] AHN Osuna leg. 900 n. 2, sequestration petition, 11 Sept. 1604.
[3] AHN Osuna leg. 1033 n. 75, list of *censals*.
[4] ARV Procesos de Madrid P 751, 1623.
[5] AHN Osuna leg. 600 n. 6, *concordia*, 20 Aug. 1577.

is one of the features which distinguishes the much weaker
absolute monarchies of France and Spain, for example, from
an autocracy like that of Russia, where an independent nobility
was slow in developing. But there was a concealed cost to be
paid for the strength of the *mayorazgos* – their financial commitments to younger brothers and sisters, their involvement in
litigation with collateral branches. Debts increased, the more
rigid the entail became: this seems to have been the case in
eighteenth-century England, and it was certainly true of Habsburg Spain. Don Francisco Milán had twelve other children
to provide for as well as his heir; the third Count of Real had
ten others.[1] Their claims had to be met, in one way or another,
out of the resources of the *mayorazgo*. The Dukes of Gandía
had regularly nine or ten children each during the Habsburg
period (with the single exception of the seventh Duke –
1597–1632 – who was said to 'have no other thought' but his
crippling debts, and who had just one son).[2] The seventh Duke
was paying out around 5,400 *lliures* a year in annuities to
younger brothers and sisters, and another 5,250 to his widowed
mother – in all, about a sixth of his gross receipts. The tenth
Duke, with about half his ancestor's income, had to find 4,271
lliures for similar purposes – plus another 2,844 to maintain his
eldest son, who had recently come of age, in a separate
household. Of course these claims varied from generation to
generation and indeed according to the age and circumstances
of the cadets themselves. The eighth Duke, though, with no
brothers or sisters, and no grown-up heir, was in an exceptionally favourable position in 1636.[3]

The Borja cadets virtually never married – except for Pedro,
the second son of the fifth Duke, who was fortunate enough
to acquire a piece of the Centelles inheritance in the shape of
the barony of Cofrentes. The destination of most of them was
the army, but above all the church. They staffed the universities,
cathedral chapters and bishoprics of Spain.[4] Of the Borja girls,

[1] ACA CA leg. 886, petition of don Francisco Milán, 22 Aug. 1644; leg. 709, king to
Marquis of Los Vélez, 20 April 1644.
[2] Alberto and Arturo García Caraffa, *Diccionario Heráldico y Genealógico de Apellidos
Españoles* (70 vols., Madrid 1919–52), 'Borja'. The quotation comes from AHN Osuna
leg. 745 n. 2, Fray Borja to Duke of Gandía, 10 Oct. 1614.
[3] Cf. appendix 3.
[4] Cf. R. L. Kagan, *Students and Society in Early Modern Spain* (Baltimore and London
1974), 183.

most went into convents (sometimes before adolescence, and usually into Santa Clara in their home town of Gandía).[1] The pressures here were obvious: they were perhaps most clearly spelled out by the ninth Count of Cocentaina when he offered his younger daughter Guiomar 20,000 ducats if she married, 2,000 (and an annuity of 500) if she became a nun.[2] Usually two of the Borja daughters (on whom our information is fullest) would marry in each generation. They struck the cruellest blow at the *mayorazgo* – for whereas nuns, priests and soldiers only required an annuity until they were established in life, married daughters took away large capital sums permanently from the main line.

The swelling dowries of Habsburg Spain (they seem roughly to have doubled in Valencia during the late sixteenth century before stabilizing in the seventeenth)[3] reflected partly the movement of prices and partly the desire of the nobility to mobilize assets which were increasingly frozen by the extension of entail. For a Duke of Gandía his most ready access to cash was to marry – for then he would touch 100,000 ducats (the figure at which the Borja dowries were finally stabilized after 1593). Unfortunately the process also worked in reverse: when his daughters came to marry they required 100,000 ducats each for their partners, the grandees of Castile. Since each duke (except for the seventh) could reckon on marrying two of his daughters, he had to mobilize during his lifetime 200,000 ducats, or about three or four times his gross annual revenues. The only way the money could be raised was by borrowing. Alternatively the obligation could be funded directly and paid as an annuity. Of the 35,546 *lliures* interest payable by the seventh Duke of Gandía, a ninth (4,090 *lliures*) represented annuities to the Duke of Lerma and the Count of Lemos in respect of old dowries.[4] Similarly, of the 10,696 *lliures* interest payable by

[1] León Amorós, 'El monasterio de Santa Clara de Gandía y la familia ducal de los Borja', Archivo Ibero-Americano, xx-xxi (1960–1).

[2] ADM Cocentaina leg. 11 n. 9, *testamento*, 4 Jan. 1623.

[3] 60,000 ducats for the last Count of Oliva in 1562, AHN Osuna leg. 600 n. 33, and 100,000 for his grand-nephew and heir, the seventh Duke of Gandía in 1593; ARV ME 1632 n. 6/53 fols. 25–37; 16,000 for the Count of Cocentaina in 1547, and 60,000 for his successor, the seventh Count, in 1601; ADM Cocentaina leg. 21 n. 49 & leg. 10 n. 50. For the subsequent stabilization at these figures in both cases, cf. Cocentaina leg. 9 n. 35 (1615), and Osuna leg. 127 n. 2 (1637) and 4082 (1695).

[4] AHN Osuna leg. 846 n. 2, memorial of Cristóbal Monterde, 1613.

the eleventh Duke about the year 1720, roughly a third (3,300 *lliures*) represented annuities to the Count of Benavente and the Duke of Béjar who had married two of his aunts.[1]

Compared with the claims of family and creditors, the other standing charges on the *mayorazgos* appear small. Religious patronage ate up around 2,000 *lliures* before the expulsion of the Moriscos, and expenditure on administration of the estates was running at about 6,000. The only economy the royal authorities could suggest when the Borjas went bankrupt in 1604 was to prune the size and the cost of the administrative establishment (lawyers, bailiffs etc) from 41 people earning about 2,236 *lliures* to 23 earning 990 *lliures*.[2] But one cannot help feeling that this was merely tinkering with the problem of Borja commitments.

Perhaps something could have been saved by a tighter practice of accounting. The dukes spent until there was no more to spend, and it is never clear whether they realized the seriousness of their situation until it was too late. The Dukes of Gandía had their *contador*, those of Segorbe their *tesorero*, who was supposed to keep an eye on expenditure and receipts. Occasionally these men drew up a provisional estimate (*tanteo*) of what money was needed for the year ahead and where it would come from. 'The estate of Pego owes 300 *lliures* at St John's Day', noted the accountant of the Borjas in 1635; but St John's Day came and went, and so did All Saints', 'and nothing has come'.[3] The bad weather of the summer of 1635 ruined the harvest and spoiled the calculations of the ducal treasury. The more remote the estates, the more difficult to make any forward provision. The Centelles patrimony in Sardinia, which came to the Borjas in 1597, could never be relied upon – there was a 15 per cent premium payable to the financiers who worked the exchanges with the mainland, and the money came to Valencia slowly and irregularly.[4] In the slow-moving agrarian civilization of the age, there seemed little hope of fitting expenditure exactly to income. Most of the accounts of the houses of Gandía and Segorbe, and of the lesser nobles, were a series of statements forwarded from the various officials in charge of revenue

[1] AHN Osuna leg. 4082, *censos antiguos* (1720?).
[2] AHN Osuna leg. 895 n. 10, king to viceroy, 25 Nov. 1608.
[3] AHN Osuna leg. 806, 'tanteo para la casa del duque mi señor para este año 1635'.
[4] ACA CA leg. 874, consulta, 14 Dec. 1627.

The bankruptcy of the senyors

collection of what they had actually received and what they had paid out or forwarded to the central treasury. Running deficits were a normal feature of these accounts, to be made up out of future receipts.[1] The job of the *contador* or *tesorero* (or royal judge, in the case of lesser houses, whose accounting system is only known to us through the records of the court of sequestration) was simply to saddle with recurring expenditure – interest on debts, annuities – those receipts which he thought could take the strain. The fullest accounts we have are those of Pedro Dolz del Castellar for the tenth Duke of Gandía between and 1670 and 1677.[2] This doctor of medicine, turned chief accountant, actually received and accounted for, on average, 7,112 *lliures* a year during his tenure of the treasury – a mere quarter of the effective receipts of the Borjas (and a mere ninth of their nominal income). The *contador*, like his master, would find it impossible to know what the overall financial situation was. So long as the local receipts continued to honour their commitments, by spreading local deficits forward if necessary into future revenue, then the cumbersome machine would be made to work somehow.

The expulsion of the Moriscos, however, threw the whole system out of gear. With the fall in seigneurial revenues after 1609 even small obligations sometimes became unpayable. By 1614 some 75 senyors had demanded relief for their debts, and they were joined by a further 17 by 1625.[3] In all, well over half of the lay senyors of the kingdom found difficulty paying their creditors by the time of Philip IV's accession, provoking one of the biggest political storms in Valencian history and creating a painful dilemma for the Crown. For what the creditors now began demanding was the break-up and sale of at least the most bankrupt *mayorazgos* to enable them to get their money back – otherwise it would be tantamount to 'stripping the creditors of their entire fortune, just as if they had been in league with the Moriscos'.[4]

[1] See, for example, AHN Osuna leg. 805 n. 54, accounts of 1631–2.
[2] AHN Osuna leg. 4083, 'thessorería quenta del dr Pedro Dolz', 1670–7.
[3] Boronat, *Moriscos*, II, 637–57; ACA CA leg. 886, petition of Jaime Pascual, senyor of Negrals, 20 March 1645; ARV R 698, memorial of mossèn Bartolomé Sebastián (1613?).
[4] AHN Osuna leg. 899 n. 1, 'por los acreedores censalistas (del duque de Gandía)', 1622/23.

At the outset it must be recognized that the senyors held many of the best cards. The Duke of Gandía was second cousin to the great Duke of Lerma, favourite of Philip III and virtually in control of the destinies of Spain at the time of the expulsion. For the Borja party at court Lerma was the benevolent 'uncle' (*el tío*), the man who 'has promised to work miracles for us...In his hands lies everything.' When it came to deciding policy in Valencia, the next most influential voice in the Council of State was that of the Duke of Infantado, baron of the community of Alberique. Infantado's interests lay very clearly with the indebted senyors, for though he had few *censals* lying against his own Valencian estates, he was worried about the fate of the bankrupt and childless Duke of Mandas to whom he was heir. Mandas was actually in receipt of allowances from his patron at this time, and the bonds between the two men were, as Mandas put it, very close, 'for we both grew up together in the house of the lord marquis of Mondéjar, his father and my uncle'.[2]

But in the end whatever help Lerma or Infantado could give to their hard-pressed Valencian cousins would be ground very fine indeed as it passed through the mill of the impersonal Spanish bureaucracy. For the responsibility for domestic policy lay largely in the hands of committees of lawyers. The real decision about how much relief to give to the bankrupt senyors came from the Valencian Audiencia and the Council of Aragon. Whether Lerma did much to influence their deliberations is doubtful. A man with a sensitive if somewhat irregular conscience he appears to have given no countenance to the 'unreasonable and unchristian' attitude of those who were hoping for a general annulment of debts as a result of the expulsion.[3] The political situation in Valencia anyway ruled out overgenerous concessions to the senyors. For, after all, these men were only a minority of the nobility as a whole, and it was their creditors, not they, who dominated the political institutions of the kingdom. It was the assembly of the nobility, the Estament Militar, which protested in 1617 against general reductions of

---

[1] AHN Osuna leg. 745 n. 2, Fray Borja to Duke of Gandía, 1 Sept. 1614.
[2] AHN Osuna leg. 764 n. 23, extract from Mandas testament, 10 March 1615. For the *censals* of Infantado – 2,116 *lliures* a year against receipts of 10,830 after the expulsion – *ibid.*, leg. 3146 n. 2.
[3] ACA CA leg. 607 n. 46/1, don Diego Clavero to Duke of Lerma, 9 Jan. 1610.

interest on the *censals*, and which went on in 1623 to denounce the failure of the senyors to pay their debts.[1] It would have been politicially dangerous to have ignored this powerful counter-lobby in Valencia. The protest of 1623, which led to the despatch of an envoy of the Estates to Madrid in 1624, coincided rather awkwardly with Olivares' attempt about this time to approach the nobles and communities of the Crown of Aragon for grants of money. To appease the creditors, who were recognized to be in an ugly mood, the king ordered an enquiry into the failure of the senyors to pay their debts in the summer of 1625.[2]

In fact, the only general measure of relief which came the way of the Valencian senyors was a reduction of interest, mostly to 5 per cent, granted to some 62 houses in 1614 by the *asientos* of that year – a rate which was made universal by 1622.[3] This drop from 6⅔ to 5 per cent or thereabouts (which of course only nudged the backward eastern kingdom a bit nearer Castile, where the lower rate had been adopted from 1607) no doubt helped some. But it left a large group of families whose debts were so heavy and/or whose post-expulsion revenues had sunk so low that the change made little material difference. Moreover the government only gave reductions in 1614 to those lords who would assume the liabilities of the old Morisco communities – at 5 per cent where there was common land to pay the bill, at 2½ per cent where the senyor had to dip into his own pocket.

The result in the case of the Duke of Gandía, for example, was to saddle him with another 21,693 *lliures* capital of debt, pushing his interest charges up to 36,421 *lliures* a year. Lerma's 'miracle' of 1614 brought this total down to 22,154 – a sum which would have absorbed virtually all Gandía's Valencian revenues at the time, and forced him to call on his royal pension (unpaid and unpayable) and on a subsidy from his peasants in order to make ends meet.[4] The Count of Cocentaina more cleverly

[1] ARV R 529 fol. 19, and 530 fols. 116 and 305. Cf. AHN Osuna leg. 899 n. 1.
[2] ACA CA leg. 1353, consulta de la junta de los Regentes de Valencia, 17 Jan. 1625; leg. 871, king to viceroy, 13 June 1625.
[3] Boronat, *Moriscos*, II, 611–57; AMV Churat 1635 n. 105.
[4] AHN Osuna leg. 1037 n. 40, 'tanteo hecho de las fuerças de los estados de Gandía, Oliva, Lombay y varonías a ellos adjacentes conforme los arrendamientos hechos desde el anyo 1613 hasta él de 1618 inclusive'.

got his new settlers to pay part of his debts. Whereas his interest charges had been 12,056 *lliures* against revenues of 21,000 before the expulsion, after the resettlement they were somewhere around (the exact figure is uncertain) 9,202 against rents of 16,117.[1] This manoeuvring, however, earned the Count a royal reprimand and exclusion from the reductions of 1614. It also turned out to be counterproductive, as the debts proved too heavy, the people of Cocentaina took to their heels, and the Count's rents came tumbling down to 9,000 *lliures* by 1623.

Whatever the methods adopted in each case, therefore, bankruptcy seemed inevitable. The traditional method of relief for nobles who could not pay their way was what was known in Valencia as *secuestro y alimentos*. The estates were put into the hands of a receiver appointed by the Crown, and the senyor was assigned an allowance appropriate to his rank as a first charge on the revenues, with the rest going to pay endowments, costs of administration and debts, in that order. The system was parallel to devices used in Castile and Sicily to bail out noble bankrupts. In both countries it led to a tightening of the bonds of dependence between throne and feudatories in the seventeenth century, and the social and economic cost of propping up a financially crippled but immovable aristocracy was probably very high.[2]

Fourteen houses were put under sequestration in Valencia in 1614, and a further 42 claimed either sequestration or massive reductions of interest by 1625. In all, though figures are unfortunately lacking, it is possible that around 50 or 60 of the 157 lay senyors of Valencia were eventually placed on an allowance at some time during Philip IV's reign (1621–65). The great advantage of the system from the point of view of the senyors was that their peasants were now protected against distraint, and the slide in their revenues halted. They themselves continued to reside on their estates and exercise ordinary rights

[1] ADM Cocentaina leg. 2 n. 15, *carta puebla*, 23 April 1611; ACA CA leg. 657, report of don Baltasar Sanz (1630?); ARV Real Cancillería libro 390 fols. 148–82, *concordia* with creditors, 11 Dec. 1619. I am grateful to Pau Ferrer of the Universitat Autònoma of Barcelona for drawing my attention to the document of 1619 and providing me with photocopies of it. When his own study of the debts of the Valencian senyors is finished, we shall have a much fuller understanding of many points only touched on in this chapter.

[2] Jago, 'Influence of Debt', 229–30; Tricoli, *Deputazione degli Stati*, *passim*.

of jurisdiction. The powers of the sequestrators were limited to arranging a farm of the revenues and apportioning the money which came in. But it proved extremely difficult for any tax farmer to operate in the area unless he came to an understanding with the local senyor. The frauds inherent in sequestrations were well outlined by the envoy of the Estates in Madrid in 1624:

The senyors are paid very high allowances, and whatever is left over is divided proportionately among the creditors, which means that they get nothing at all. The reason is that the senyors can go into their estates freely and continue to exercise jurisdiction there and control the officials, so that they can take whatever share of the rents they want to. The sequestrator cannot stop them doing this because it is just not possible for him to check what is coming into another man's house with that man living there. And anyway he will not want to cross the senyor, who is often his patron.[1]

It emerged, for example, that the Count of Anna set up fictitious creditors who competed with the real ones, and who kept back what money they got for the Anna family.[2] Others simply returned statements to the distant sequestrators in the city of Valencia that there was no money available that year, that it had all gone in indispensable administrative costs – when the truth is, complained the embittered spokesman of the Estates, 'in the old days they could never be bothered so much as to put a tile on a roof'.[3] Apart from these illicit clawbacks, the creditors objected to the whole way in which allowances were assessed for debtors. The estate of Torres Torres, for example, had standing charges and interest dues lying against it of 3,934 *lliures* when it only rented 2,500. It was put under sequestration, and the senyor given an allowance of 833 *lliures* a year. But he was also senyor of Canet which fetched him 350 *lliures* a year, and he had a house, a couple of *censals* of his own, and the profits of jurisdiction in both Canet and Torres Torres. When he applied for a bigger allowance from Torres Torres at the expense of his creditors, the Council of Aragon had to refuse.[4] But too often, the creditors believed, the senyors were given

[1] ACA CA leg. 869, petition of don Francisco Roca, 23 Oct. 1624.
[2] ARV ME 4/33/29, testimony of Alonso Yañez, 1634.
[3] ACA CA leg. 869, petition of don Francisco Roca, 1624.
[4] ACA CA leg. 872, consulta of Audiencia, 14 Dec. 1627, and endorsement.

allowances which were far too high, no account being taken of their other sources of income.

Sequestrations often proved to be just a half-way house on the road to an agreement or *concordia* between the two parties by which the senyors offered to provide a guaranteed sum every year for interest payments, and in return received back full financial control of the estates. Thus in 1622 the Duke of Gandía managed to persuade his creditors that they had no hope of getting 22,154 *lliures* a year in interest, and he got them to accept an annual deposit of 10,000 instead, of which 7,000 should go to redeeming capital. Likewise in 1628 the Duke of Segorbe persuaded his creditors in Benaguacil to reduce interest from 5 to 3¾ per cent, to cancel half the arrears which had built up, to accept a deposit of 1,000 *lliures* a year to pay the rest of the arrears, and 500 to redeem capital.[2] The Count of Real drew 2,000 of the 2,700 *lliures* which his estates rented as an allowance, leaving only 700 for his creditors. He recovered control of his patrimony in 1615 by promising to provide a guaranteed deposit of 3,000 *lliures* a year for his creditors, of which 2,000 was to go on redemption of capital.[3] The Marquis of Guadalest drew 2,775 of the 8,325 *lliures* which his estates rented as an allowance, leaving the balance to satisfy interest payments of 21,000. In 1619 the dowager marchioness recovered control of the property on promise of payment of 4,600 a year, of which 3,000 was to redeem capital.[4] The Marquis of La Casta, under sequestration, had an allowance of 1,600 *lliures* a year – more even than his estates actually rented. Three-quarters of his debts were anyway in the name of his vassals, and he managed to persuade these unfortunate peasants to take over the burden (much as the Count of Cocentaina had done earlier). The other quarter he offered to pay at 3¾ instead of 5 per cent, but a quarter of the arrears were to be cancelled and the rest payable at just under 1¼ per cent. This *concordia* was made in 1633, and revised as regards the *censals* against part of the estates in 1647, when all arrears were annulled, and current interest was also brought down to under 1¼ per cent.[5]

[1] AHN Osuna legs. 895 n. 19, and 899 n. 1.
[2] ADM Segorbe leg. 42 n. 5, *concordia*, 1 April 1628.
[3] ARV Diversorum 385 fols. 92v–112v, *concordia*, 1615.
[4] ARV Clero leg. 404, *concordia*, 13 Sept. 1619.
[5] ARV Alacuás *expedientes* n. 118 (1633) and n. 43 (1647).

How did the senyors get away with it? The bait was, of course, the guaranteed deposits – the prospect of at least some money rather than perhaps no money at all. The deposits themselves, indeed, are interesting testimony to the real financial strength of the noble houses, many of whose assets lay simply beyond the touch of creditors and courts. The seventh Duke of Gandía was able to call on the 100,000 *lliures* dowry which had just come to his son and heir around 1617, with the latter's marriage to the Princess Doria. He was also helped out by a promise from his vassals to pay off 25,700 *lliures* capital over 25 years.[1] The Count of Real's estates were only worth 2,700 *lliures* a year, yet he gave his creditors 3,000. The explanation is that he himself had income from lands of his own, that his wife and son-in-law were extremely wealthy people in their own right, and that subsequently his grandson, the third Count, contracted an advantageous marriage with the city heiress, doña Ana Maria Mateu. The Counts of Real used the money – on their own terms – to bail out their depopulated and indebted fiefs.[2] Likewise the Marquis of La Casta was able to offer his creditors the income from his own *censals* and urban property if they showed themselves amenable.

The fundamental problem, of course, was that the *censals* were mortgages secured locally. The lawcourts maintained the principle of the separate liability of separate estates for their own debts, even though they both belonged to the same master. There was just no way in which the creditors could get at the total fortune of their victims. At most the courts would take into consideration this total fortune before deciding how much, if anything, to set aside from a sequestrated estate for personal allowances. But even here, in practice, there was much ambiguity, uncertainty and downright fraud. In the circumstances the readiness of the creditors to accept substantial cuts in interest via the *concordias* is easily comprehensible. Their great aim during the seventeenth century was to get back something of their capital, given the collapse of interest payments. 'There is not one of them', the Duke of Gandía's agent told his master,

[1] AHN Osuna leg. 1019 n. 12, king to viceroy, 2 Aug. 1614, and leg. 602 n. 29, petition of Oliva, 5 April 1618. Cf. ACA CA leg. 607 n. 19/2, consulta, 5 June 1614. Double this sum had been offered by the Moriscos before the expulsion; AHN Osuna leg. 1027 n. 8.
[2] ARV B Apéndice 78, *censal* holdings of the Counts of Real, 1682–1705.

'who would not give his *censals* away for much less than they are worth.'[1] In fact in 1664 the eighth Duke managed to buy out 164,328 *lliures* worth of credits for an immediate cash deposit (raised out of the sale of some estates) of 54,776 *lliures* – an effective depreciation of two-thirds.[2]

This was a marked feature of seventeenth-century Valencia – the progressive freeing of at least some of the greater houses of the old *censal* burden of the past. The development is rather different from the situation in Castile or Sicily, where the bankrupt nobility was content to remain under some form of sequestration and just keep up interest payments. The difference in Valencia is no doubt due to the sheer gravity of the financial collapse after the expulsion: interest was simply unpayable out of falling landed rents. In the circumstances it seemed better for both sides to devote what money was available to redeeming capital. Thus by about 1720 all that was left of the old *censals* of the Borjas (over half a million *lliures* in 1609) was a mere 70,452 *lliures*.[3] Thus too between 1628 and 1688 the Dukes of Segorbe managed to redeem 29,268 of the 90,000 or so *lliures* of debts on Benaguacil, Paterna and Pobla, and they bought out 21,341 of the 52,333 *lliures* lying against Vall de Uxó and Sierra de Eslida by 1669.[4]

But it would be misleading to suggest that this was a universal process. A *concordia* had to be maintained, and it could all too easily be sabotaged by maladministration or bad luck. The Marchioness of Guadalest, having offered 3,000 *lliures* a year to buy out her creditors by the agreement of 1619, was complaining within three years that these payments were too heavy. The house of Guadalest appears to have remained crippled with debt for the rest of the Habsburg period.[5] The Count of Anna's *concordia* of 1616 had been dependent on the marriage of his son and heir with a rich city heiress; but his son died unexpectedly without children, forcing his father to repay the dowry, scrap his agreement with the creditors and

1 AHN Osuna leg. 1029 n. 3, 'arbitrio para el desempeño' (1640?).
2 AHN Osuna leg. 696 n. 54, sale of Albalat, Turís and Chella, 7 April 1664.
3 AHN Osuna leg. 4082, 'censos antiguos ympuestos sobre los estados del duque de Gandía mi señor' (1720?).
4 Calculations based on ADM Segorbe legs. 42 n. 7, 61 n. 9 and 62 n. 11.
5 ACA CA leg. 654, consulta, 28 March 1622; leg. 611 n. 38/2, petition of Marchioness of Guadalest, 1674; leg. 612 n. 47/2 & 3, petition and consulta, 4 March 1686.

plead for his estates to be put under sequestration.¹ Inevitably
it was the bigger, more successful families which could actually
afford to keep up redemption payments. For example, the real
solution to the financial distress of the Counts of Cocentaina
came with a lucky series of marriages which brought the
holders of the title into the ranks of the Castilian aristocracy.
Antonia, tenth Countess, married the eighth Count of Santisteban. Her own livelihood secure she was able to make – and
more important maintain – an agreement with her creditors in
1638 reserving most of the rents of Cocentaina for them. Her
descendants continued to live in Castile, forming part of the
court aristocracy, and the twelfth Count could boast in 1701
of the many *censals* he had redeemed.²

Yet in the very same breath, this twelfth Count asked
permission of the king to charge new obligations on his estates.
And between 1692 and 1701 the tenth Duke of Gandía was busy
saddling himself with 49,257 *lliures* worth of new debts, and had
to find another 5,000 a year in instalments on a dowry to his
son-in-law, the Prince of Cariati. By 1720 the total funded debts
of the Borjas were back at 215,139 *lliures*, or nearly half the
old total of Morisco days.³ There could be no escape in the long
run from the traditional pressures of settling daughters and
younger sons in life, serving the king, fighting off litigants, and
all the other scourges of entail. At most the post-expulsion
arrangements bought the senyors a little breathing space.

One can hardly, therefore, speak of a triumph of the feudal
aristocracy in seventeenth-century Valencia without seriously
qualifying the proposition. Their rents remained low; some
managed, with a little help from the Crown, to loose the old
millstone of debt from round their necks, only to find that they
were still hard pressed for money. The problem was aggravated
by the fact that they had to stand on their own feet, financially-
speaking, since the Crown largely failed to live up to its promise

¹ ACA CA leg. 874, petition, 12 Oct. 1627. He eventually made a revised *concordia*,
cf. ARV ME 4/36 fol. 1, 23 Jan. 1630.
² ADM Cocentaina leg. 21 n. 42, agreement to pay the debts of the town of Cocentaina,
30 June 1639; leg. 22 n. 1, farm of Cocentaina by the Count of Santisteban, 1649;
leg. 22 n. 13, 'memoriales dados al Rey por el señor conde don Francisco de
Benavides', 1701. The redemptions specified, however, only related to his Castilian
estates.
³ AHN Osuna leg. 4082 *censos antiguos*; cf. appendix 3.

of compensating them for losses sustained in the expulsion of
the Moriscos. True, some 60 senyors were granted either tracts
of Morisco land on the royal domain, or cash subsidies out of
the proceeds of sale of these properties, or both.[1] The general
level of compensation seems to have worked out at about 7,000
lliures for the hardest hit – men like the Counts of Castellar,
Real and Buñol (though since land was too hastily surveyed,
the actual value of the real estate given away may occasionally
have topped the 7,000 mark). But taking this figure as it stands,
7,000 *lliures* invested at 5 per cent would have fetched a return
of 350 a year – a miserable sum for someone like Castellar, whose
landed revenues had fallen from 13,650 to 1,050 *lliures*. To add
insult to injury the cash was sometimes not forthcoming,
because the land sales conducted by Bayarte and his successors,
from which it was to come, occasionally fell through.[2] The two
biggest families – Segorbe and Gandía – secured, it is true,
exceptional treatment. Segorbe received back his sequestrated
duchy of that name in 1618; Gandía was given the estates of
Villalonga and Villamarchante (recently confiscated from don
Pedro Franqueza) and a cash grant of 30,000 ducats. But, as
always, the Crown promised more than it delivered. The 30,000
ducats were never forthcoming from the bankrupt treasury,
while the Franqueza estates were so depopulated and harassed
by creditors that they only began to have a small surplus for the
Borjas in the latter half of the seventeenth century.[3]

Nor was there a great deal to be hoped for from subsequent
royal benevolence. The history of the Valencian pension list
is eloquent evidence of the fact that the senyors could not hope
to be maintained at the king's expense. In 1619 pensions to
individuals on the royal treasury of Valencia amounted to
34,696 *lliures*; by 1645 with the onset of war and the fall in
receipts, the figure had been cut down to a mere 12,264 *lliures*.[4]
In default of more tangible rewards, there was the promise of

---

[1] For the land grants the fullest source is ARV MR 10113. For the cash subsidies, ACA
CA leg. 593, register of names (1620?).
[2] ACA CA leg. 869, petitions of the senyors of Antella and Alboy, 1624. And cf. leg.
707, king to Deputy Maestre Racional, December 1630.
[3] ARV G 1956 fol. 227 (Segorbe); ACA CA leg. 639 n. 21/3 (Gandía); and cf. leg. 874,
petition of Gandía, 1628.
[4] See the table of royal budgets 1619–85, below, chapter 8.

employment in the king's service held out to 11 senyors in 1613, 'for the natives of that kingdom are so poor and ruined by the expulsion of the Moriscos that they can hardly make ends meet'.[1] But it was a vain hope. 'Where in the world', asked the Duke of Infantado ironically when the proposal was first mooted, 'are we going to find provinces for 400 people to govern, where in all the Military Orders put together do we have the *encomiendas* to keep them happy?'[2] Subsequent events proved him right: the problem of employment for the smaller aristocracy remained to trouble Philip IV and Charles II.

Certainly some of the great families obtained considerable pickings at court. The biggest success story in seventeenth-century Valencia was undoubtedly that of Cardinal Gaspar de Borja (1582–1645), son of the sixth Duke of Gandía, who made a fortune as viceroy of Naples and President of the Council of Aragon. His wealth was apparently colossal. Just before he died he was negotiating the purchase from the Crown of the seaport of Cullera in Valencia, 'being desirous of adding to the patrimony of Gandía' – a deal which he was confident would go through 'in such days as these, when the treasure of the king and the blood of his vassals are just not sufficient to keep the enemy out of Flanders and Milan'.[3] The Duke of Gandía meanwhile was thinking of touching grand-uncle Gaspar for a loan of 100,000 ducats or asking him 'to put in a good word for him with the merchants of Seville' as surety for an equivalent sum.[4] At his death, in fact, the cardinal left a fabulous rent of 28,000 ducats in *juros* or government bonds to the eighth Duke. Had the money actually been paid, it would have doubled the Borja revenues at a stroke. Alas, the Crown was so bankrupt that only a couple of thousand ducats dribbled into Gandía every year, and even these were stopped in 1675, 'for the recovery of sums appropriated by the lord Cardinal Borja in Naples when he was viceroy, over and above what he was entitled to for his salary'.[5] It is perhaps small wonder that the tenth Duke buckled

[1] ACA CA leg. 661, consulta, 17 June 1621.
[2] ACA CA leg. 607 n. 50, copy of consulta of Council of State, 24 March 1610. The 400 refers to the nobles who presented their credentials for the Cortes of 1604.
[3] AHN Osuna leg. 1024, a servant of 'Su Eminencia', to don Francisco de Villamayor, 6 Dec. 1644.
[4] AHN Osuna leg. 1029, 'arbitrio para el desempeño' (1640?).
[5] AHN Osuna leg. 4083, 'thessorería quenta del dr Pedro Dolz', 1670–7.

on his sword two years later and joined Prince Juan José of Austria in toppling the government of the Queen Regent.

The one concrete favour which the Crown proved able to give the senyors in the end was protection against their creditors. The most impressive feature of Habsburg Valencia, in fact, is the sheer stability of the great houses. Of the 61 titles listed in 1707, only 8 belonged to men who had acquired their estates after the expulsion of the Moriscos.[1] And, if we exclude the dukedom of Liria created for the Duke of Berwick, victor of Almansa, most of these were tiny holdings, covering the odd village or hamlet. Though there was some alienation of fiefs by the greater houses – the Duke of Gandía's sale of Albalat, Turís and Chella in 1664 was perhaps the most notable – the dominant trend was rather the other way, towards the amalgamation of estates through intermarriage and the failure of heirs. Thus the sixth Duke of Segorbe succeeded to the *mayorazgo* of the Dukes of Lerma in 1640; and on the death of the seventh Duke in 1670 both houses, with vast possessions in Valencia, passed to the Dukes of Medinaceli. Thus too the tenth Duke of Gandía picked up the marquesate of Quirra in 1675 when his cousin died without heirs. In fact, the 61 titles of 1707 were shared among 49 families, most of them established on their patrimony since at least the fifteenth century.

So the picture we have of the Valencian landed nobility in later Habsburg times is one of consolidation rather than decline. The *mayorazgos* lumbered on majestically into the nineteenth century, plagued by many of the difficulties which they had faced around 1600 – heavy debts, inefficient administration and bad luck. There was no full and final solution to their problems, nor in the nature of things could such a solution have been found. But at least the expulsion of the

---

[1] The list of 1707 is in Domínguez Ortiz, *Sociedad española en el siglo XVII*, I, 358–60; that of 1609 in Boronat, *Moriscos*, I, 428–42. The new men included ex-peasants like the Almunias, Marquises of Ráfol (cf. ARV MR 5522, *tercio diezmo* of Beniganim, 1645), successful financiers like the Miralles, Marquises of La Torre de Carruz (ACA CA leg. 641 n. 17, ennoblement of Pedro Miralles, 10 May 1629), and ex-tradesmen like Crisóstomo Peris, Marquis of Castelfort (whose marquesate was opposed by some ministers as cheapening the dignity, ACA CA leg. 631 n. 58, consulta, 7 Dec. 1689). But these are really only a handful in a solid galaxy of old family names, many of whom had been plain gentry (with the title *don*) in 1609, but still lords of the estates over which they ruled as counts and marquises in 1707.

Moriscos helped relieve some short-term distress, paradoxically enough by bringing it to crisis point. Under cover of the emergency arrangements adopted after 1609 to protect noble bankrupts, the old slate of debts could be partly wiped clean and a fresh beginning made. The whole process, of course, carried with it immense political implications. 'The brightest jewel and stoutest buttress of Your Majesty's throne': those were the words used by the seventh Duke of Gandía to describe the *mayorazgos*, as he urged Philip III not to listen to demands from his creditors for the break-up and sale of his estates.[1] The Habsburgs took the point. Undoubtedly much of the political stability of seventeenth-century Valencia (as of Castile and Sicily) depended on this growing interdependence of monarchical and noble power.

[1] AHN Osuna leg. 846 n. 2, memorial of Cristóbal Monterde, 1613.

7

The eclipse of the Popular Estate

The Third Estate of seventeenth-century Valencia consisted of four cities (Valencia, Alicante, Orihuela and Játiva), and some 29 'royal towns' with representation in the Cortes.[1] These varied in size from the capital with its 12,327 households to the remote mountain community of Castelfabib with a mere 154. Within this spectrum Castellón de la Plana believed itself to be 'very big and populous, having 1,500 households'.[2] In fact, the average size of the nine politically most important towns, excluding the capital, works out at just under 1,300, with the median being 1,350. In social composition they ranged from the metropolis with its '1,500 houses (at very least) belonging to the lords and great men of the kingdom' (according to the exaggerated claim of Antoine de Lalaing) and its churches and convents which (thought Escolano) 'must certainly occupy a third of the superficial area', down to the overgrown village of Villarreal, few of whose 459 families 'can get by without working for a living' and the seaport of Villajoyosa, most of whose 350 families 'are working people, occupied in tilling the soil or fishing'.[3] The royal towns were not, then, a homogeneous social group – any more, indeed, than the senyors. But they formed a clearly defined political and juridical category – the 'voice of the people' as expressed through the Third Estate.

Compared with the multiplicity of works on rural society,

---

[1] Lorenzo Mateu, *Tratado de la celebración de Cortes Generales* (Madrid 1677), 142–4.

[2] ACA CA leg. 710, petition, 1635.

[3] Antoine de Lalaing, in J. García Mercadel, ed., *Viajes de extranjeros por España y Portugal* (Madrid 1952), II, 477; Escolano, *Décadas*, I, 494; AMV Cortes 30, vols. 64v ff., declaration of Villarreal, 18 March 1626; ARV R 519, *acte de cort* 54 of Braç Real, 1626. A fascinating insight into the social structure of early sixteenth-century Valencia is given in R. García Cárcel, 'Notas sobre población y urbanismo en la Valencia del siglo XVI', *Saitabi*, xxv (1975), 133–53.

good urban studies are something of a rarity in early modern European history. Whereas there is at least a crude framework of reference for the aristocracy – crisis and survival – nothing comparable exists for the towns. At most one can argue (although on shaky evidence) that by 1700 the Spanish town was less populous in general, less wealthy, and less powerful than it had been in 1500. But as to the nature or extent of the decline, not a great deal is known.[1] The present chapter is concerned with one main problem: the weakening of the voice of the Third Estate in Valencia. This weakening appears to reflect a loss of confidence by the governments of the royal towns in their role, and that loss of confidence appears to have been heavily influenced by a crisis in municipal finance.

In 1610 the president of the Audiencia warned of the serious situation facing the royal towns which had accumulated debts as bad as those of the senyors.[2] But the full crisis erupted only later in the reign of Philip IV. In 1626 the senior Valencian minister, don Francisco de Castelví, reported that there was no use asking the Third Estate directly for taxes to help the Monarchy: 'such is the state of the city of Valencia, and the other cities, towns and villages in the kingdom that every single one, with not two exceptions, is paying out in recurrent obligations, *censals* and costs of distraint far more than it has in the way of income'.[3] The expenditure of the city of Valencia in the 1620s was put at 194,750 *lliures*, and of this 131,500 represented interest on debt – a truly enormous sum, perhaps equivalent to a half of the liabilities of the whole aristocracy.[4] The budget of Orihuela, the second city in the kingdom, was for 8,959 *lliures* according to a report of 1633, and of this a half – 4,219 *lliures* – was spent merely on servicing the debt.[5] The situation seems to have got worse as the century progressed. The *censals* lying against Jijona amounted to 10,090 *lliures* capital in 1614; by 1649 this had risen to 16,140; by 1693 the

[1] Important exceptions have to be made for sixteenth-century Valladolid, studied by Bartolomé Bennassar, and for Seville; cf. Antonio Domínguez Ortiz and Francisco Aguilar Piñal, *El Barroco y la Ilustración*, Historia de Sevilla, vol. IV (Seville 1976).
[2] ACA CA leg. 607 n. 48, memorandum (1610?).
[3] ACA CA leg. 1372 fols. 109–11, memorandum, 1627.
[4] ACA CA leg. 869, 'balance del patrimonio de la ciudad de Valencia', 30 Oct. 1623.
[5] ACA CA leg. 711, memorial of Dr Jaime Serra, 1633.

figure had doubled to 33,584.[1] The funded debts of Alcira totalled around 30,000 *lliures* in 1614; by 1643 they were put at 47,000 ducats, and by 1693 at 150,00 ducats.[2] In an age when the feudal aristocracy was actually managing to reduce its debts, the performance of the royal towns looks staggeringly inept. What had gone wrong?

Part of the problem, of course, was falling revenue. Overall figures for municipal income tend to be misleading here since they merely reflect higher taxation (a contributory factor itself, no doubt, to the cycle of economic decline). But if we single out the old taxes – the *sises majors* or *sises velles*, as they were often called – which were excises on foodstuffs and which constituted the basis of municipal revenue, we have a fixed measure over time by which to gauge the pressures at work (see table 15). A dramatic decline in Orihuela (where the excises under Charles II were running at well under a half of their old maximum under Philip II) was matched by a more gradual fall in Castellón. In neither town did the expulsion of the Moriscos mark much of a watershed. Instead the key factor appears to have been the size of the local population and its aggregate consumption of goods, on which the excises were indexed. The number of inhabitants in Orihuela was virtually halved between 1609 (2,520 families) and 1692 (1,112), whereas that of Castellón held its own (1,165 and 1,146 families at the terminal dates).[3] In general, the performance of the Valencian towns as a whole is probably closer to that of Orihuela than that of Castellón – a sharp crisis under Philip IV and a certain stabilization under Charles II.

In any case the faster or slower decline of traditional sources of income led to the need for new taxes to stop the rot. Unfortunately it is extremely difficult to reconstruct a budget for any Valencian town. In the first place there were several different treasuries in most of the bigger ones – three or four in Castellón, four or five in Valencia itself – and each had different receipts and separate accounts. Also the accounts were

[1] ACA CA leg. 932, petition, 7 Feb. 1693.
[2] ACA CA leg. 933, 'memorial de los nobles y generosos de Alzira', 20 April 1694; AMA 03/132, 20 Jan. 1614.
[3] According to the official censuses. On the other hand the cadastral surveys of Castellón list 1,276 household heads and property-owners in 1608, 1,827 in 1702.

Table 15. *Evolution of the old excises in two selected Valencian towns: average annual yield (to the nearest lliura)*

	Castellón	Orihuela
1570–9	1,033	
1580–9	1,233	2,695
1590–9	1,278	2,907 (only one quotation, for 1597)
1600–9	1,605	2,952
1610–19	1,350	2,623
1620–9	1,660	1,800
1630–9	1,655	1,615
1640–9	1,515	1,484
1650–9	1,700	1,315
1660–9		1,374
1670–9	1,310	1,242
1680–9	1,235	1,120

A blank in the table indicates that there is no information available.
SOURCES: AMC Llibres de Consignacions 1570–1689; AMO Clavariat 1586–1689.

drawn up in the form of charge and discharge, with the treasurers crediting themselves with nominal receipts and debiting themselves with rents which they had failed to collect. Many of the revenues of any town – up to a third, for example, in the case of Orihuela – would consist of arrears from previous years. Expenditure also is difficult to estimate. Municipal accounts tend to balance beautifully. One admires the unruffled calm of municipal clerks as they totted up the credit and debit sides of the ledger, while the creditors were hammering on the door. There is little sense of crisis or debt – little evidence, indeed, of either – in any municipal account book (except for a few *lliures* which had gone astray, probably having dropped through the lining in the treasurer's pocket). But, of course, the account books are a monumental fraud. Or rather, they are designed to tell a story – that the treasurer had done his job – which was irrelevant in the general debacle of municipal finance. For behind the figures for actual expenditure one has to seek the expenditure which ought to have taken place, had the treasurers received the rents they were supposed to receive. At the beginning of the fiscal year the *jurats* or chief magistrates appropriated certain revenues to meet specified obligations (those recurring items such as salaries and interest payments which could be gauged in advance). In the worse-governed towns – such as Orihuela before 1613 – the treasurer was merely given a list of obligations, not of the revenues on which they were consigned, a sure recipe for trouble. However, even where the appropriations or *consignacions* were clearly known, responsibility for payment tended to rest with the tax-farmers. The treasurer and magistrates were, therefore, working during the fiscal year in relative ignorance of whether the appropriations were actually being met. Going on their own estimates of the nominal balance in the tax-farms, they issued warrants (*mandatos*) for expenditure on ad hoc, non-recurring items (building, alms, festivities), which tended to be honoured before the appropriations. Since so much of the expected revenue anyway was 'loose' (that is, arrears and non-funded credits against previous administrators of city money), the *mandatos* flowed too fast and freely, eating up that part of the ordinary revenues set aside for appropriations. In simple terms, given the absence of double-entry book-keeping, and given that the treasurer and the magistrates never really knew how much money was in hand, they spent first and asked questions afterwards. The system was somewhat tighter in the city of Valencia, where all the revenues had to pass through the main bank or Taula, but the trouble there was that the appropriations were neither clear nor rigorous enough. As the ecclesiastical and noble estates pointed out in 1649, when the Taula went bankrupt through overdrawing by the city treasurers: 'all the sufferings of this commonwealth stem from the fact that there is no separation of receipts, but that all the money is piled up in a heap and spent without rhyme or reason'.[1] Interestingly enough, bankruptcy in Orihuela led to similar reforms in 1650. All the revenue was now to pass through the hands of a paymaster, and the treasurer or magistrates were not to issue *mandatos* until the paymaster had actually met the original appropriations.[2]

In table 16, the evolution of the ordinary revenues of Orihuela (excluding returns from the wheat supply) is set against actual expenditure by the city treasurer. The two columns are not strictly comparable; arrears and loose credits

[1] ACA CA leg. 679, memorial of the Estaments Militar and Eclesiàstic, 1649.
[2] AMO XII/5/39, 'estatuts de clavari i caxer', 20 Dec. 1650.

Table 16. *Income and expenditure in Orihuela*

	Average ordinary revenues per year (in lliures)	Average actual expenditure (in lliures)
1590–9	5,585	5,672
1600–9	6,788	9,079
1610–19	8,667	8,372
1620–9	10,350	8,869
1630–9	9,935	9,087
1640–9	9,350	9,446
1650–9	12,126	11,117
1660–9	11,968	12,847
1670–9	10,397	12,176
1680–9	10,618	13,075
1694	10,460	11,515

SOURCE: AMO Clavariat 1590–1694, *passim*.

would swell the receipts side, while the appropriations which were not met would swell the debits (at least until the reforms of 1650 when the new paymasters had to settle the *consignacions* first, thus making actual expenditure virtually identical with the nominal obligations of the town). At most the table can suggest the relative fluctuation in income and outgoings over a period of time, though no balance of profit or less can be drawn for any one decade.

The apparent expansion in Orihuela's income was achieved by heavier taxation. New imposts on meat and flour under Philip III came near to doubling revenue over this reign. A second spate of taxation followed in the 1640s as Orihuela, like all Valencian municipalities, had to find extra money for subsidies to Philip IV. The levy of 1646, for example, was reckoned to cost Orihuela 26,000 *reals* – about 2,600 *lliures*, or over a quarter of the ordinary revenues of the town.[1] New taxes were again laid on meat and flour, and a monopoly of tobacco and soap was instituted. After this, taxation stabilized. The reign of Charles II passed in Orihuela – and in Castellón, and probably most other Valencian towns – with scarcely a single new tax.[2] The old war taxes of the 1640s were kept going. But in fact

[1] AMO III/1/4, 20 Feb. 1646.
[2] Except for a temporary impost on meat in Orihuela to pay for the plague of 1678, AMO III/4/30, 22 April 1684.

Table 17. *Nominal obligations of the town of Orihuela (before the reforms of 1650)*

	lliures		lliures
1597	8,285	1626	9,013
1604	12,229	1628	8,725
1608	10,502	1631	11,499
1611	9,727	1633	10,383

the period saw a gradual fall in the income of the municipality. The golden days of King Charles were not only days of cheap bread in Valencia but of low taxation also.

The movement of expenditure is less clear-cut. The figures for the first half of the century are somewhat illusory, since they fell short of the appropriations. Only for a few years in the late 1620s – after a royal commission of reform in 1624 which succeeded for a time in getting appropriations honoured first – did actual expenditure conform to nominal obligations (see table 17). Inevitably there was some fluctuation (the *visita* of 1624 clearly succeeded in its avowed aim of eliminating 'useless' expenditure, at least for a time). Nevertheless one is more liable to be impressed by the comparative stability of the figures – Orihuela was spending (or was obliged to spend, rather) almost as much under Philip III as under Charles II. Deficits were catastrophic under both kings, though the failure to collect rents on time and the adding of arrears on to current revenue, would require a laborious reconstruction of the figures in order to determine what the deficit actually was. It was difficult for the men of those times, in fact, to draw up a proper budget at all. One of the magistrates of Orihuela waxed indignant in 1625 'that the present city has no clear idea and no list of the debts which it has contracted, paid off or now owes'.[1] And another councillor denied that new taxes were needed; rather there should be a special commissioner 'to determine if there really is a surplus or a deficit in the accounts of this city'.[2]

Inadequate accounting no doubt explains much of the chaos in municipal finance, but royal commissions of enquiry tended to blame peculation on the part of the magistrates – 'the truth

[1] AMO IIB/2/47, 15 Nov. 1625.   [2] AMO IIB/2/46, 19 May 1624.

is', noted the president of the Audiencia in 1610, 'that in some towns the money has found its way into private purses'.[1] In the city of Valencia the commission of 1625 uncovered some 300,000 *escudos* (about 390,000 *lliures*, or two years' revenue) illegally appropriated;[2] in Orihuela the commission of 1624 turned up 11,000 *lliures*, that of 1650 some 51,997 (equivalent to four years' revenue).[3] But these figures have to be handled with caution. Pure embezzlement seems to have been comparatively rare. Rather the chief charge against the culprits was that they had received advances of municipal money (sometimes quite legally in order to buy wheat, meat or other supplies) but had not paid it all back. One of the administrators of the meat supply for Valencia owed 13,000 *lliures* in 1686; the Council of Aragon decided that it was not his fault, 'because some friends, seeing him with money in his hands, had asked him for a few loans which he had not been able to resist, and so he is worthy of compassion'.[4] Slackness in collecting rents or pursuing arrears (which tended to build up in the tight economic circumstances of the black seventeenth century) testify to the humaneness of the age, and probably account for most of the actual corruption in municipal government.

More substantial, perhaps, was the charge often levelled by viceroys that the Valencian municipalities lived beyond their means. The pride with which the chronicler Bendicho wrote of his native Alicante that 'she is so generous, open-handed and free with her money that though her income is huge her expenditure is huger still', was not shared by government commissions which recommended the suppression of the municipal 'dancer' as being a 'very superfluous item', and the ending of the 400 *lliures* of sweetmeats given to the magistrates on public holidays.[5] To read some government reports, one might come away with the impression that the Valencian municipalities were destroying themselves in an orgy of bread and circuses. In table 18 I have attempted to group expenditure by three selected

[1] ACA CA leg. 607 n. 48, 'expediente y traza', 1610.
[2] ACA CA leg. 869, Francisco Miguel Pueyo to king, 4 March 1625.
[3] ACA CA leg. 615 n. 57, Onofre Bartolomé Ginart to don Nicolás Mensa, 17 June 1625; leg. 616 n. 23, don Antonio Juan de Centelles to king, 27 March 1651.
[4] ACA CA leg. 606 n. 12/53, consulta, 12 Feb. 1687.
[5] RAH 9.26.5.D.107, Bendicho, 'Crónica de Alicante', fol. 124v; ACA CA leg. 706, viceroy to king, 31 Jan. 1612.

Table 18. *Municipal expenditure (excluding the municipal granary and supply fund)*

	Orihuela (1600)		Castellón (1604/5)		Alcira (1607/8)	
	lliures	Per-centage	lliures	Per-centage	lliures	Per-centage
Ordinary administration (Official salaries, paperwork, mail, equipment of town hall)	1,351	18	742	13	385	8
Litigation and embassies	771	10	273	5	571	12
Policing	485	7	75	1	20	1
Welfare	510	7	320	6	53	1
Education	180	2	118	2	120	2
Public works	1,041	14	1,066	19	415	8
Festivities	372	5	249	4	468	9
Religion	229	3	165	3	327	6
Defence (militia)	237	3	141	2	6	1
State taxes (king and Diputació)	219	3	509	9	8	1
Debts	2,045	28	1,752	30	(2,500)	51
Costs of deputy to Cortes of 1604	Nil		348	6	Nil	
Totals	7,440	100	5,758	100	4,933	100

SOURCES: AMO XII/1/8; AMC 'Rebudes i dades del Clavariat' 1604–5; AMA 03/131.

towns at the beginning of Philip III's reign in order to determine where the money was going. This table should be treated with caution. The budget for Alcira is not strictly comparable with the others since it is based mostly on the *mandatos* of the *jurats*. Had we access to the appropriations, we would have more accurate figures for debt payments (which have had to be estimated from other sources), and almost certainly the figure for 'ordinary administration' would be swelled (since so many official salaries were consigned directly on the tax-farms and did not enter the treasury). As they stand, the Alcira figures tend to place too much weight on incidental, non-recurring expenses such as festivities. Nevertheless it is interesting to note that even here expenditure which might be called 'superfluous' – bullfights, sweetmeats, alms to mona-steries, the rounding up of 'the ladies of the brothel' for exhortatory sermons in Holy Week – does not account for more than about 15 per cent of the budget. The percentage is much less elsewhere – 8 per cent in Orihuela and 7 per cent in Castellón (the aggregate for the two categories labelled 'festivities' and 'religion' in table 18).

Essentially – if we leave aside the servicing of the debt for the moment – the municipal budgets appear to have been devoted overwhelmingly to administration and welfare. Education is everywhere the Cinderella of the story – there were two secondary teachers and one primary teacher in Castellón (population 1,165 families), exactly the same establishment in Orihuela (population 2,520) and one secondary teacher and his assistant in Alcira (population 800 families). Welfare is a comprehensive category, but includes four main items – medical and sanitary expenditure (such as the maintenance of hospitals, and wages to doctors and grave-diggers); the doling out of bread, meat and cash to the indigent poor (often in one lump grant at Christmas); the reform of prostitution (subsidies to ex-prostitutes while they looked for a husband or another job, and in one case the grant of 8 *lliures* to the widow of a magistrate of Orihuela 'because she is a young woman and extremely pretty, and need is often the enemy of virtue'); and finally bounties for the killing of wolves (there were no fewer than sixteen taken in Orihuela in just one year) – roughly in that order. In so much of their daily lives the ordinary people obviously looked more to their town councils than to the distant king who taxed them and spent their money on remote battlefields.

But in order to get a real idea of the pervasive nature of this 'little commonwealth' one has to include the whole supply policy, separately administered and kept apart from the main accounts. The city of Valencia had been buying wheat for its citizens probably since the Middle Ages. The new feature of the Habsburg period is the extension of the idea of municipal granaries to the other towns of the kingdom, perhaps starting with Villarreal as early as 1564.[1] In Orihuela the crucial decision appears to date from 1600, as a measure specifically designed to counter scarcity and rising prices: 'the price of wheat is in such a state with the needy selling off their stocks at the beginning of the year to bakers who store it and hoard, waiting

---

[1] Viciana, *Crónica*, III, fol. 142.

Table 19. *Budget of the granary of Castellón de la Plana*

	1604–5			1680–1		
	lliures	sous	diners	lliures	sous	diners
Gross turnover/receipts of the sale of grain	32,561	6	10	2,140	16	1
Cost of purchase (including transport etc.)	30,208	6	1	1,979	9	2

for the poor to get rid of all their grain...that it keeps going up and up.'[1] Unlike the Castilians, the Valencians generally had no *tasa*, no fixed ceiling for grain. Instead each municipality began to buy enough reserves after the harvest and to sell them off at cost price in order to hold the price steady through the winter and spring. Exceptionally in Orihuela after the plague of 1648 the decision was taken to sell below cost in order to alleviate hardship.[2] A separate study would really need to be made of the granary accounts in order to see how the fund was actually administered. Figures from Castellón – separating out debt payments and miscellaneous obligations laid on the fund – indicate the situation shown in table 19. If one includes an advance of 2,000 *lliures* to contractors for the supply of meat in 1604–5, and 1,502 for the same purpose in 1680–1, the total budgetary expenditure of Castellón from the three main treasuries of the town (excluding some smaller ones such as the fund for the construction of a bell-tower) amounts to 38,027 *lliures* 19 *sous* 6 *diners* in 1604–5, falling to 13,259 *lliures* 17 *sous* 7 *diners* in 1680–1. One can see from the figures (which should be compared with the non-supply expenditure in table 18) that more than three-quarters of the town's money in 1604–5 was going on the purchase of grain, only about a sixth of it in 1680–1. The management of the bread supply was perhaps the most vital function performed by the Valencian municipalities in the early seventeenth century. The steep drop of around two-thirds in the budgetary provisions of Castellón between 1604–5 and 1680–1 is due to the virtual abdication of this role. Times had changed. The Valencia of Charles II saw

[1] AMO II/5/31, 25 June 1600.   [2] AMO III/1/5, 9 May 1648.

a fall in grain prices and a cheapening of bread: the old welfare policy, devised in the harsher inflationary age of Philip II and Philip III had become redundant.

For the community of Valldigna in 1700 municipal granaries were costly and useless – 'the reason why so many towns have gone on the rocks'.[1] The figure from Castellón would hardly support such a sweeping statement. The municipality actually recorded a small surplus on its grain transactions, and in Orihuela we find the main treasury having to be helped out in 1640 from the surplus in the granary. The real problem is more subtle. Given the inadequate accounting methods of the age, the bigger the budget the bigger the risk of confusion. The granaries were anyway kept separate from the main receipts, but the sheer scale of turnover magnified all the problems of administration faced by the ordinary treasurers – a lack of knowledge of what money was available at any one time and a consequent tendency to spend first and ask questions afterwards. If and when things did go wrong with the granaries, they went catastrophically wrong: and insofar as the granaries shrank in scale under Charles II, all municipalities must have had an easier time. The initial funding of the granaries – and their maintenance in hard times – explains much of the borrowing in which municipalities indulged. But it does not explain it all. For, as we have seen, Alcira and Jijona (and Castellón too) went on increasing their debts into the late seventeenth century, when the grain policy was a thing of the past. The persistent deficits in the ordinary budget, the inability of taxation to keep pace with expenditure, and the easier credit of Charles II's reign, all made borrowing inevitable. Tentatively one can reckon that anything up to three-quarters of municipal expenditure in the early seventeenth century was on the purchase of grain; anything up to one-half of the rest went on servicing debts; and the bulk of what was left over provided a minimal level of sanitation and comfort in a depressed and cheerless existence. The granary should probably be disregarded since it was self financing. For the rest, can one simply attribute the financial embarrassments of the Valencian towns to the sheer poverty of the tax base (rather than to 'extravagant'

[1] ARV Clero leg. 781, *concordia*, 18 March 1700.

or 'superfluous' expenditure), and secondarily to an accounting system which foxed contemporaries as much as it can still fox historians of today?

Almost inevitably the financial crisis in the towns led to political conflict, inasmuch as Philip IV and Olivares began from the 1620s to implement the Union of Arms, a programme designed to make the peripheral areas of the Monarchy like Valencia relieve an exhausted Castile of part of her military and tax burden.[1] The most serious clash came in 1646 when the viceroy, the Count of Oropesa, finding that the capital city was heading for its third bankruptcy in a generation and lacked the will to raise more taxes for the war in Catalonia, abolished the autonomous system of government under which the magistrates were elected and gave the Crown back its old power of directly nominating to these offices.[2] This recourse to direct rule, instead of producing the expected funds, led to a near-revolutionary situation, with an unholy alliance of oligarchs and democrats (ex-magistrates and assemblymen) successfully blocking all business. At Christmas 1646 Valencia seemed poised to go the way of Catalonia. That it did not was partly due to an immediate retreat by Oropesa, followed reluctantly at some months' interval by the central government. Oropesa, declaring that he would avoid at all costs the setting up of a *democracia* in Valencia, wooed the old oligarchy by offering to restore all their privileges. The crisis was over by July 1647, although, because of the interruption caused by the plague of that year, the oligarchy was not formally set up in business again until the spring of 1648. The disturbances had cast a fascinating light on the structure of power within Valencia. More than anything, they showed that the political tranquillity of the city rested squarely on an entente between an exclusive ruling elite and the monarchy, neither of whom would be well advised to push the other too hard.

As in Catalonia, most towns in Valencia were governed by the so-called *insaculació* – that is, the placing in a sack of a restricted list of names which were then drawn at random for

---

[1] Cf. J. H. Elliott, *The Revolt of the Catalans* (Cambridge 1963), 182–214.
[2] J. Casey, 'La Crisi General del segle XVII a València 1646–48', *Boletín de la Sociedad Castellonense de Cultura* (1970).

vacant offices.[1] The system had developed in the latter Middle Ages as a reaction against the supposed violence and corruption inherent in open, popular elections. 'Happy indeed are those communities which are ruled by knowledgeable persons', declared the council of Castellón in 1476, 'by people wise and experienced in matters of government'.[2] This simple platitude became the official excuse for reserving all official positions to a handful of men picked for life by their colleagues, a system first introduced into Játiva in 1427 and finally set up in Valencia itself in 1633.

The actual rules laid down in these grants of *insaculació*, which always emanated from the Crown, varied a good deal. In Valencia new candidates were admitted to the sacks for office every four years, and in Orihuela every three years. In both Valencia and Orihuela it was the magistrates who happened to be in office at the time who had the responsibility for sponsoring prospective entrants; but the names had to be approved by a panel of existing *insaculats* in Orihuela, and by the king and the Council of Aragon in the case of Valencia. The reserve power held by the Crown in the capital city partly reflects the much greater control which it had always exercised there – directly nominating, in the days before the grant of 1633, the twelve candidates who would draw lots for the six offices of *jurat* or chief magistrate.[3] It also reflects a tightening of royal control in municipal government generally, as the Habsburg period advanced. The *insaculacions* conceded by Philip II – for example, that to Carcagente in 1589 – no longer left the locality free to make its own lists of candidates but reserved confirmation to the Crown.[4] The reign of Philip III marks something of an interruption, though, for the Cortes of 1604 abolished all these reserve controls. Valencia's own *insaculació* came too late, in 1633, to profit by the benevolence of this weak monarch. But even where the king's confirmatory power was given up, in practice royal intervention was a fairly important factor throughout the seventeenth century. In particular the Crown

[1] Elliott, *Revolt of the Catalans*, 140–2.
[2] AMC Llibre de Insaculacions, 10 May 1476.
[3] For the details, see Casey, 'Crisi General', 97–104.
[4] Mariano Madramany y Calatayud, *Tratado de la nobleza de la corona de Aragón* (Valencia 1788), 303.

could simply impose its own candidates ad hoc – as in Alcira in 1616 when a certain Vicente Prexech was foisted onto the reluctant magistrates with the warning: 'where there are orders from His Majesty all must give way'.[1] More frequently, at the regular triennial or quadrennial elections of candidates, the municipal councils were so hamstrung by factional disputes that the viceroy and Audiencia had to be called in to make the nominations instead.[2]

More controversial was the king's right to eject someone from the lists once he had been elected, for the position carried life tenure. This sort of security, the Count of Oropesa believed, lay at the root of bad government in the city of Valencia, 'for the certitude which these men have of being able to run for office big and small, year in year out, gives the craftier ones the idea that they can make a living that way at the expense of the commonwealth'.[3] His attempt to remedy the situation in 1646 came spectacularly unstuck. Admittedly the king always retained the right to dismiss anyone convicted of corruption in the courts, but this power was more theoretical than real. As one of Oropesa's predecessors had pointed out at the time of the original grant of *insaculació* to Valencia, 'usually the behaviour of these men is not of a kind to lead to judicial exclusion, but it would make anyone think twice before letting them run for office in the first place'.[4]

In practice, therefore, the municipal governments of seventeenth-century Valencia were mostly self-recruiting. The *insaculats*, nominated for life by their fellows, saw their names put into a barber's basin every year, and waited for a young child to draw at random the slips of paper on which these names were written. This annual lottery determined (as in Catalonia) which office went to whom. In a few towns – Morella, Onteniente and Beniganim – the royal bailiffs still had an old right to select one of three names drawn by lot for certain principal offices. But this power was reckoned so insignificant that Philip IV gave it up without protest in the Cortes of 1645.[5] What really interested the Crown was control of the principal financial office

---

[1] AMA 03/133, 9 Sept. 1616.   [2] ACA CA leg. 704, viceroy to king, 19 June 1612.
[3] ACA CA leg. 673, viceroy to king, 4 April 1646.
[4] ACA CA leg. 678, viceroy to king, 23 Sept. 1633.
[5] ACA CA leg. 1355, memorial of don Cristóbal Crespí, 25 Jan. 1646.

– the *racional* or treasurer, once described by the Council of Aragon as 'the helmsman and captain' of the city of Valencia.[1] In the city, in fact, this office remained to a certain extent in the king's gift, though he was supposed to appoint from three names drawn by lot from among the *insaculats*. In the handful of other big royal towns where the finances were complicated enough to warrant a separate treasurer – Alicante and Játiva – the office also seems to have been in the appointment of the king, although selected from the indispensable *terna* of three oligarchs submitted by the local magistrates.[2]

Paradoxically enough, the very security of the oligarchies from royal interference, which led to a narrowing of the recruitment base in the seventeenth century, also provided the opportunity for the royal authorities to intervene increasingly on an ad hoc basis in appointments to office. What tended to happen at election time was that the candidates were often disqualified from serving in the post for which they had been drawn, because they had held office in the previous year, or had been selected already for another office, or did not meet the property qualifications, or (a growing phenomenon, this, with municipal bankruptcies) refused to take on the more unpopular jobs in the accounts department.[3] These so-called *impediments* had to be pointed out on election day by one of the magistrates, and either rejected or confirmed by their colleagues. One suspects that the balance of decision swayed according to political favouritism. In Alicante, despite laws against relatives holding office in the same year, the Pascuals monopolized the top posts in 1617 and again in 1630, blocking the rise of the Briones, who appealed to the Crown.[4] Growing factionalism within the ranks of the oligarchy (itself a reflection of a narrowing of the recruitment base) led, inevitably, to growing interference by the Crown. In Orihuela one finds the viceroys having to step in at almost every election, exempting favoured candidates from their disqualifications. But in 1650 the headstrong Count of Oropesa overstepped the mark by going outside the *insaculació* lists altogether and nominating a

[1] ACA CA leg. 653, consulta, 18 June 1614.
[2] *Ibid.*, consulta, 31 March 1613.
[3] Information from the *Actas* series of the municipal archive of Orihuela.
[4] ACA CA leg. 874, petition, 30 May 1631.

certain Tomás Ruiz as *jurat*, since the other candidates were disqualified. This led to a near-riot in the town, and the experiment seems not to have been repeated.[1] Valencian municipal government under the Habsburgs rested on a delicate interdependence between king and oligarchy: neither side was entirely free to go its own way.

The cornerstone of this alliance was the assumption that the people were unsuited to rule. Opposing the demand of the artisan guilds of Castellón for seats in the local assembly (Consell General), the Council of Aragon noted: 'Your Majesty has seen how in Aragon the towns which were most opposed to voting a subsidy in the Cortes were those where the ordinary people had a voice in government, because, having less experience and talent in public business, they do not look to the general good but only to getting out of the obligation to pay taxes.'[2] The general trend of the age was towards excluding the 'mob' from political responsibility. In Castellón and Orihuela the assemblies were somewhat muted anyway since they were recruited largely from the magisterial class. Elections here simply consisted of a drawing of names every year from the lists of *insaculats*. Indeed there were so few names on the lists in Orihuela that the *jurats* in most years had to make up numbers in the forty-man assembly out of their own nominees – a privilege exercised by the viceroy in an occasional year where there were more than thirteen places to be filled.[3] In the smaller towns where a more open assembly seems to have survived, there were demands in the Cortes of 1626 and 1645 by the local oligarchies for a reduction in size – demands which the minister in charge in the latter year urged the Crown to accept: 'these concessions appear not only painless but appropriate, given that the fewer people you call together in these times, the more quietly you can get through your business'.[4] The one exception to the rule was the capital city herself, where a large assembly survived outside the *insaculació* to the end of the Habsburg period. There were over 140 individuals here at full strength, comprising the ex-magistrates of the preceding

[1] ACA CA leg. 617, don Antonio Juan de Centelles to king, 23 Aug. 1650.
[2] ACA CA leg. 628, consulta, 28 July 1626.   [3] AMO II/5/31, 24 Dec. 1601.
[4] ACA CA leg. 1355, memorial of don Cristóbal Crespí, 25 Jan. 1646.

year, four lawyers, twelve notaries and four petty nobles, all appointed directly by the *jurats*, and four 'worthy men' from each of the twelve parishes of the city, selected by the *jurats* again from a list of eight forwarded by each parish. It is not known, unfortunately, how the parishes actually chose the original eight, though most of the names in the seventeenth century are those of merchants or artisans. Finally, the balance of the assembly was made up by the guilds. These originally had the right to elect four members each, of which the *jurats* would select two, but by the seventeenth century the *jurats* had acquired the right of nominating ten representatives of all the guilds at their discretion, and with these ten proceeded to elect any guildsmen they fancied.[1]

Despite these institutional safeguards, the tameness of the Valencian assemblies could ultimately only be guaranteed as long as there were no controversial issues to stir up popular feeling. But the bankruptcy of one royal town after another in the seventeenth century, and the demand for more taxes to cover deficits challenged a fundamental assumption on which the towns were ruled. It meant, in effect, that the ruling oligarchy had to humble itself and go cap in hand to the assembly for money. Like the battle over taxation which was being fought in all the monarchies and empires of Western Europe, the request for an extra penny on a pound of goat's meat roused the most surprising passions. Everywhere the assemblies threw up their hands in horror when the *jurats* came to them with such requests. In Alcira in 1608 'many persons are not content, and say that it is not good that another excise be placed on merchandise, for it would only drive away trade, while a direct tax is a most odious thing'.[2] In Algemesí the council could not bring itself to impose a mere 150 *lliures* in direct taxes to meet the cost of a levy of troops in 1643, 'since that kind of tax is so odious to collect'. It tried to borrow the money instead.[3] Summing up the situation, the Council of Aragon mused on the danger of asking the city of Valencia for money to refloat the bankrupt Taula in 1649: 'experience shows the resentment of the populace in days past and present

[1] Casey, 'Crisi General', 105.   [2] AMA 03/131, 16 Jan. 1608.
[3] Archivo Municipal de Algemesí, Actas dels Jurats 86, 15 April 1643.

at any mention of *gabelas*'.[1] The first bankruptcy of the Taula (1614) and the third (1649) mark the limits of a critical period in which this issue came to the fore in unprecedented fashion.

Inevitably the financial question became mixed up with the way in which the *jurats* managed the supply of bread to the municipal granary, because this was the biggest item in the whole budget. The assembly of Valencia bitterly attacked in 1614 the nine privileged interests which had secured exclusive rights of selling wheat in the granary: 'these men are in league with hoarders and speculators, people who have huge stocks of wheat in Castile, Aragon and Valencia itself and who are the leeches of any community. When there is much wheat in the granary, they send word that no more be sent until further notice, so allowing them to force the price up to its present high level.'[2] As a move against corruption in the management of the bread supply, the assembly refused to grant the magistrates the usual right of buying wheat at the price and on the terms the latter would fix, demanding a voice for their own spokesmen in drawing up the contracts. They broadened their offensive into an attack on the idleness and incompetence of the oligarchy as a whole: men who 'to get into office give up their trade, put their money into *censals* and set up as men of leisure...letting foreigners in to steal away our wealth'.[3]

But the repeated refusals of the assembly to allow the *jurats* to buy grain at their discretion, and their opposition to new taxes in 1612, 1633 and 1645 merely reinforced the alliance of oligarchy and Crown, as the magistrates appealed to the king to overrule the popular voice.[4] 'The *jurats* would apparently like to be absolute', sneered the assembly of 1614, 'for we see them running to His Majesty and The Supreme Council for total and unfettered power of buying bread.'[5] The diagnosis was accurate enough, but there was little the popular leaders could do to remedy the evil. For, not surprisingly, the king

[1] ACA CA leg. 679, consulta, 9 March 1649. The incredible hatred which the magic word *gabelles* aroused in France at the time is well brought out by Yves-Marie Bercé, *Histoire des Croquants* (Geneva 1974), 620–2.

[2] ACA CA leg. 719, memorial of the Consell General, 15 April 1614.

[3] Quoted in Carreres, *Taula de Cambis*, 41.

[4] AMV CM 58, *jurats* to king, 9 April 1611; ACA CA leg. 882, viceroy to king, 13 Dec. 1633; AMV MC 174, 15 Feb. 1646.

[5] ACA CA leg. 719, memorial of the Consell General, 15 April 1614.

invariably gave the *jurats* what they wanted – except in 1646. In that year, faced with yet another clash between assembly and *jurats* which was holding up the grant of taxes for the war in Catalonia, the viceroy decided that the oligarchy was more of a liability than an asset to the Crown and tried to break its hold on government. This gave the Consell General its first chance since the Germanias of 1519 to seize power. It failed, partly because neither the viceroy nor the Council of Aragon wholly trusted it anyway, and partly because of a notable lack of political ideology or sense of direction on the part of the popular leaders.

We are 'mere assemblymen, not lawyers or knowledgeable people like that'; we are 'not versed in public business but only interested in working for a living' – such were the phrases used time after time as a screen to protect rebellious assemblymen from the wrath of the king.[1] The claim was somewhat disingenuous, as evidence goes to show that a sizeable minority of the assembly made something of a career out of sitting on its benches – nearly a half, for example, of the members in 1645 had been elected before.[2] Also, the popular leaders were not quite so innocent as they liked to make out. Luis Feliperia, a rabble-rouser in 1646, was a lawyer, with a fine collection of 147 lawbooks at home (including the Laws of Valencia, from which he could quote chapter and verse).[3] Pere Torner, described innocuously enough as a tanner, had been one of the farmers of the royal customs dues of the kingdom in 1633, a position which implies either that he was very wealthy or else connected with important financiers who were using his name.[4] The constituency which these men represented was what one might call the 'petty bourgeoisie' of the metropolis – the silk, linen and wool weavers, the butchers, ironsmiths and prosperous peasants. It was mostly through the guilds that the elections were nominally conducted, and it was to the guild masters that the assembly turned at Christmas 1646 when a confrontation with Oropesa and the Crown seemed imminent.[5]

---

[1] *Ibid.*, and AMV CM 59, *jurats* to king, 8 Jan. 1622.   [2] Casey, 'Crisi General', 111.
[3] ARV Clero leg. 745, inventory of Dr Luis Anselmo Phelipperia, 25 Jan. 1658.
[4] ARV B 130, farm of *Peatge*, 27 Aug. 1633.
[5] ACA CA leg. 674, Duke of Medina de las Torres to king, 16 Feb. 1647; leg. 673, viceroy to king, 3 April 1648.

But in the end these master craftsmen proved unwilling to risk their lives and property by a show of force. No more than in 1519 were they really eager to govern for the sake of governing.[1] What they wanted, as good family men, were low taxes, cheap bread, and protection against French silks – interests which they claimed were badly protected by the cabal of idle patricians and racketeers who governed them. But they were also looking nervously over their shoulders at that faceless mob of students, journeymen and vagabonds whose periodic riots (in 1605 for bread, in 1619 to prevent the images of a folk saint from being torn down by the Inquisition) were a menace to all property, and they had no real desire to get their own windows broken in 1646.[2] And besides, their representatives in the assembly – the Luis Feliperias of this world – proved more interested in feathering their own nests than in getting taxes lowered. The most important demand actually put forward by the Consell General of 1646–7 was that its members should be recruited in future from a list of life-tenured *insaculats*, allegedly so as to make them more independent of magisterial influence. This political careerism was hardly likely to win many votes on the streets of Valencia, especially since the personal links between some of the councillors and the magistrates were suspiciously close – Calixto Valladolid was the protégé of the recently disgraced oligarch Gaspar Juan Zapata, and Luis Feliperia himself was allied to Vicente Trilles, one of the *jurats* of the day, who later served as guardian for Feliperia's children. It is clear enough that the assembly only won its influence during 1646 because of the rift between the viceroy and the old ruling elite. Zapata, Trilles and the other oligarchs were merely using the Consell General and the threat of a popular uprising as a stick with which to beat the Count of Oropesa. And all opposition had collapsed by July 1647 when Madrid and the old oligarchy reached agreement on a restoration of the status quo of the days before Oropesa's rule.[3] In general the reign of Charles II, with low bread prices and no increase in taxation, completed the eclipse of popular influence.

[1] R. García Cárcel, *Las Germanías de Valencia* (Barcelona 1975), 240–1.
[2] The authentic voice of the petty bourgeoisie, grumbling at corruption but afraid of the mob, emerges well from the diary of the parish priest of San Martín: Porcar, *Coses evengudes*, I, paras. 772 and 1,603, and II, para. 2679.
[3] For the details, see Casey, 'Crisi General', *passim*.

It left one of the narrowest oligarchies in the Crown of Aragon effectively in control of municipal destinies, and completely loyal to the Monarchy. For there was no parallel, in Catalonia at least, to the sheer isolation of the Valencian ruling elite from the mass of its fellow citizens. In the cities of Valencia and Orihuela only petty nobles (*cavallers*) or rentiers (*ciutadans*) could compete for any of the top offices, whereas in Barcelona, for example, merchants and artisans held two of the five posts of chief magistrate.[1] Admittedly the *ciutadà* class in the eastern kingdom was a lot more open than its Catalan equivalent, which was virtually a cooptive oligarchy of its own. In Valencia anyone could originally become a 'citizen' simply by giving up his trade or profession. A silversmith's son claimed admittance to the *insaculació* since his father 'gave up his trade back in 1608, had his name taken off the guild register in 1611, and lived thereafter with the lustre befitting a distinguished family, driving around in a coach'.[2] By the time this petition was written, however, that easy social mobility – at least in the city of Valencia – was a thing of the past. Laws of 1605, 1624 and 1626 gradually barred from office in the capital ex-tradesmen, and even their children.[3] In the provincial towns lawyers and doctors of medicine were reckoned equivalent to *ciutadans* – though Orihuela began to be more severe in the 1680s, requiring a doctorate in law and not just a mere *licencia*, unless the man happened to be the son of a *ciutadà*.[4] One of the most open systems which I have seen in Valencia was that in force in Castellón (perhaps the proximity to the freer lands of Catalonia had some influence in this northern town). Here the petty nobles held one of the four posts of chief magistrate one year in every two, the *ciutadans* one post every year, the 'artist' guilds (notaries, apothecaries and surgeon barbers) one post, and the 'peasants' either one or two posts, depending on whether the nobles competed or not.[5]

But even in Castellón government was not quite as 'demo-

[1] Elliott, *Revolt of the Catalans*, 165–6. However in Zaragoza tradesmen were also excluded from office after 1561; G. Redondo Veintemillas, 'Cargos municipales y participación artesana en el Concejo zaragozano 1584–1706', *Estudios del Departamento de Historia Moderna*, Facultad de Filosofía y Letras (Zaragoza 1976), 159–90.
[2] ACA CA leg. 875, petition of Tristán del Pinell, 18 Aug. 1631.
[3] ACA CA leg. 710, petition of Simón Colomer, 1631; leg. 720, petition of Pedro Juan, 1641. Cf. *fur* 40 of the Cortes of 1626.
[4] AMO III/4/30, 13 May 1684.   [5] AMC Llibre de Insaculacions, 19 Dec. 1676.

cratic' as it looked, for to get into the *insaculació* lists in the first place one had to be sponsored by the *jurats* of the day and be approved by the assembly, itself recruited from the *insaculats*. Underneath the blanket title of 'peasant' one is probably dealing with a social elite of rich farmers who were on good terms with and intermarried with the ranks of notaries, apothecaries and surgeons. Thus when the artisan guilds of Castellón tried to break into the charmed circle in 1626 – the weavers, tailors, and others – they were unceremoniously repulsed by the Council of Aragon, avowedly so as not to make the government too democratic in character.[1]

The Valencian oligarchies were generally, therefore, small and rather select bands of people. Some 90 individuals competed in the city of Valencia for magisterial office, in a population of at least 10,000 families and – more relevant perhaps – excluded a *ciutadà* population estimated by one contemporary at 500 persons.[2] In Castellón there were nominally 70 people able to hold office, in a population of something under 1,200 families. In Orihuela the *insaculats* numbered about 30 to 40 – counting here the so-called 'lesser citizens' (usually notaries) who were allowed to compete with the *cavallers* and *ciutadans* for seats in the assembly (one-third to each class) – in a population of around 2,500. Inevitably the very exclusive character of government in the Valencian towns – much more exclusive, for example, than in Catalonia – made them easy prey for the monarchy. Generalized resistance to tax demands or unpopular policies was out of the question. Nor was the patrician oligarchy itself strong enough to take an independent stand. Though there were property qualifications for admission to the *insaculació* – 1,000 *lliures* in Alcira, 2,000 in Orihuela after 1625, 400 in the capital after 1648 – these should be seen as efforts to halt the decline in *ciutadà* fortunes rather than as a policy of reserving office for plutocrats.

Received opinion during the early seventeenth century was that the urban oligarchies had no financial backbone. Since they were by definition composed of rentiers, the wreck of the *censals* after the expulsion of the Moriscos affected many of them

[1]   *Ibid.*, 8 Oct. 1626; ACA CA leg. 628, consulta, 28 July 1626.
[2]   ACA CA leg. 710, memorial of Martín de Isaba, 1644.

badly. The magistrates of Játiva emphasized this point when they protested againt a reduction of interest rates to 5 per cent: 'for they have to live mostly off *censals* and credits...and now find themselves greatly straitened, not being able to take jobs but having to make do with their measly rents.'[1] It was the idea, rooted in court circles, that oligarchic 'poverty' was responsible for bad government and municipal bankruptcy that led to the introduction of property qualifications – at least in Orihuela in 1625 and Valencia in 1648. Whether things got any better after these reforms is a moot point. For the whole trend of the age was carrying the wealthier *ciutadans* and *cavallers* into the ranks of the upper nobility through the purchase of the title of *don* – 'now made more attractive by the modern usage of Spain', as one minister commented, deploring the quality of the unfashionable backwoodsmen who dominated government in Orihuela.[2] The dons were excluded from municipal office everywhere in the kingdom; they got a foothold in the city of Valencia only in 1652, in Alicante in 1655, in Orihuela in 1656, and in Játiva in 1671. Demanding *insaculació* in Alcira as late as 1694, the dons pointed to the bankruptcy of the town and the irresponsibility of the governing oligarchy: 'if this town fell in ruins, we nobles would alone feel the hurt'.[3]

It was, of course, during the 1630s that the penniless Philip IV began the practice of selling noble status in Valencia, a practice continued under Charles II. Though there was never a fixed tariff, a *cavaller* could buy full nobility for between 300 and 700 *lliures*, and a simple commoner for 1,300.[4] Given that a rich peasant of Gandía might have 500 or 600 a year and a lawyer somewhere around 1,000, there was some danger that the only people who would be left as *cavallers* and *ciutadans* in later Habsburg Spain were failures who could not afford the price of promotion or cranks who wanted to stay where they were. There is not a great deal of quantitative information available, unfortunately, to chart the supposed decline of the *ciutadà* class. Statistics from Castellón, however, warn us against

---

[1] ACA CA leg. 718, memorial, 1622(?).
[2] ACA CA leg. 617, don Antonio Juan de Centelles to king, 24 Jan. 1651.
[3] ACA CA leg. 933, memorial, 20 April 1694.
[4] ACA CA legs. 655, 656 & 658, 'expedientes que se han beneficiado por la secretaría de Valencia', are full of information on the situation in the 1630s and 1640s.

overemphasizing the rate or extent of decay: the average property of a *ciutadà* here in 1608 was worth 15,925 *sous* (official valuation for tax purposes), and this had gone down to 11,605 *sous* by 1702, bringing the class down from first to second most wealthy section of Castellón society, behind the dons.[1] The figures remind us, in fact, that this group of rentier commoners was always being recruited from below, by new wealthy men, even if it was losing some of that wealth to the nobility. There was some loss of footing by this sector during the seventeenth century, but not a headlong decline.

Perhaps the real problem, ultimately, was that the oligarchy which ruled the towns of Valencia was not even representative of the whole *ciutadà* class. Narrowly based, it relied on the Crown to uphold its privileges. Overwhelmed by the financial problems of the communities it governed, the magisterial group virtually ceased to function in the body politic. The voice of the towns was stilled, and the floor was left to just two sparring partners: the king and the nobility.

[1] AMC Llibres de Vàlues 1608 and 1702.

8

The rule of the judges

In the medieval federation of the Crown of Aragon, Valencia was decidedly the junior partner. Though there had been a Moorish kingdom there before, it was really during the 1230s and 1240s that Valencia acquired its modern form under the stern rule of its great founder Jaime the Conqueror. A frontier territory with a large, infidel population, it owed its continued survival to the power of the king.

The basis of that power was finance. Though the royal demesne was progressively whittled away by alienations to the nobility, it remained substantial enough in Habsburg times. Around two-thirds of the Crown's revenues came from the quit-rents, *regalías* and *tercio diezmos* of the agrarian hinterland. The rest came mainly from a monopoly of salt, and from the customs dues known as the *Peatge* and *Quema* which belonged to it by hereditary right independent of any parliamentary grant.[1] Philip II considerably expanded this patrimony by annexing the mastership of the Military Order of Montesa in 1587, which brought him considerable patronage and increased his revenues by about a sixth. From all these sources the Crown had an income which was the envy of ministers in other parts of the Crown of Aragon, 'such huge sums', according to Escolano in 1610, 'that it can pay all the costs of government and still have enough left over for the salaries of the viceroys and inquisitors of Zaragoza and Barcelona, as well as for pensions to a whole host of people'.[2]

Unfortunately by the time these words were written the royal

---

[1] The rate at which the customs were levied had long been fixed, but there was nothing in theory to prevent the king raising it; ACA CA leg. 1355, the king to the viceroy, 20 Sept. 1626.   [2] *Décadas*, I, 435.

Table 20. *Budgets of the Bailía General of Valencia (in lliures, to the nearest whole unit)*

	1619	1645	1656	1685
Salaries in Valencia				
Viceroy and guards		9,050	9,050	9,050
Audiencia		4,937	4,664	5,376
Fiscal and military establishment		12,608	11,041	11,412
Total	19,083	26,595	24,755	25,838
Salaries outside Valencia				
Council of Aragon	Nil	8,163	9,513	13,500
Viceroys of Aragon and	15,192	14,525	7,325	Nil
Catalonia and guards				
Total	15,192	22,688	16,838	13,500
Incidental costs of administration				
Paperwork, mail, bonuses to	9,500	9,469	9,259	7,873
tax-farmers and festivities				
in Valencia				
Subsidies to the Council of	Nil	5,106	8,417	11,308
Aragon				
Total	9,500	14,575	17,676	19,181
Annuities to individuals: the pension list				
Perpetual annuities	2,000	3,014	3,014	4,815
Discretionary	32,696	9,250	12,054	3,211
Total	34,696	12,264	15,068	8,026
General total	78,471	76,122	74,337	66,545
Income	71,400	64,427	67,305	67,901

SOURCES: ACA CA leg. 1357, consulta, 9 June 1619; leg. 647 n. 26/1, 2 and 4. The treasury of Orihuela rented an additional 8,886 *lliures* in 1619, rising to 17,542 in 1676 with the staggering growth of trade through Alicante; cf. ARV MR 4691. For Montesa add another 13,776 *lliures* in 1619, making a total income of 94,062, or over twice the royal revenue in Catalonia; cf. Elliott, *Revolt of the Catalans*, 96.

For 1619, no separate breakdown of the first three items is available.

fortunes were beginning to decline. The year 1602 was virtually the last in the whole Habsburg period in which the treasury could meet all its commitments, although 1619 is the first year for which a breakdown of the figures is possible. I have shown in table 20 the evolution of income and expenditure for the main Valencian treasury (excluding the autonomous receipts of Orihuela-Alicante and Montesa for which no clear statements are available) between 1619 and 1685. The figures in the table give only a hint of the severe financial embarrassment in which the monarchy found itself in seventeenth-century Valencia. Already by 1619 some 74,212 *lliures* worth of arrears had accumulated – equivalent to one year's revenue. And although the treasury was nominally in surplus under Charles II, extraordinary payments played havoc with the estimates of the royal accountants. In 1627 the government recognized the inevitable, and drew up a schedule of priorities for the disbursement of such money as was available. At no time in the later Habsburg period could the treasury actually meet all its commitments, a point which has to be borne in mind when analysing the table.[1]

The least of the monarchy's problems, perhaps, was falling revenue. The buoyancy of the ports helped counterbalance what ministers were fond of referring to as the 'sterility of the age', the tendency of bad harvests or low prices to depress agrarian rents. In this sense the king emerged from this critical period stronger than his nobility. The real trouble was that expenditure remained obstinately high. When we look at where the money was going, though, we may be more impressed with the strengths rather than the weaknesses of the Valencian government. Interestingly enough the monarchy never became the pawn of its creditors as it did in Naples.[2] When there was not enough money the Valencian treasury stopped payments: it almost never borrowed (though it sometimes anticipated revenue), and it had no formal debt. This tough line is also reflected in the history of the pension list, which was cut savagely from almost a half of the budget under Philip III to a sixth under Philip IV to an eighth under Charles II. The savings were not devoted to administration in Valencia, where the number of officials and the salaries they were paid hardly changed over the seventeenth century.[3] Indeed, if anything, economy was the order of the day here too, with new limits set in the 1640s, and again after the accession of Charles II, on expenditure on building and the postal service. The sur-

---

[1] For example, the revenues of 1645 had actually all been spent in 1643 and 1644, ACA CA leg. 631, Maestre Racional to king, 28 Jan. 1647. And by 1673 magisterial salaries in Valencia had gone unpaid for three years; leg. 640 n. 14/14, consulta, 5 June 1673.

[2] In the Italian province the creditors virtually took over revenue collection; cf. R. Villari, *La rivolta antispagnola a Napoli: le origini 1585–1647* (Bari 1967), 141–52 and 165–6.

[3] The apparent increase between 1619 and 1645 I find inexplicable except in terms of an underestimate of the real salary bill at the earlier date. Most salaries had been fixed as long ago as the fifteenth century; cf. ACA CA leg. 1355, consulta of Junta de Materias de Valencia, 21 Dec. 1645.

pluses built up in this way were in fact lost to the kingdom and transferred to the needs of the Monarchy.

Under Olivares the salaries of the Valencian ministers and secretariat of the Council of Aragon appear to have been offloaded onto the local Valencian receipt. At the same time more warrants were issued than ever before for the transfer of money from Valencia to Madrid under the general heading of subsidies towards the costs of the Council. These included grants for newly appointed ministers to help them set up house in the capital, and for their widows, in due course, when these desired to return to Valencia.[1] The figures also cover the paper, ink and quills required by the secretariat, and, increasingly in the 1640s, reimbursement for the benevolences or loans extracted from the Valencian ministers for the war in Catalonia. The real figure for subsidies in this decade, in fact, was around 12,235 *lliures*, or nearly a fifth of revenue. Table 20 merely gives the nominal ceiling which Philip IV consented to place on such expenditure from 1645 in view of the impossibility of meeting the salary bill within the kingdom if the old, higher level continued.[2] The steep rise in both the salary and subsidy payments to the Council of Aragon under Charles II is illusory, and reflects mainly the insistence of Madrid on being paid in Castilian 'double silver' *reals*, which the Valencian treasury had to buy at a discount of between 10 and 18 per cent. But in any case the overall pattern of expenditure suggests that Olivares scored a permanent triumph with his policy of making Valencia bear a little more of the expenses of the Monarchy. The nobility got less and the government took more of the available resources – though the increasing payments to Madrid had to be met in the end, interestingly enough, by removing the costs of the Catalan and Aragonese viceroys from the overburdened Valencian treasury. Ultimately there was a limit to the amount it could supply. One should note, for example, that the appropriation of 11,000 ducats by the viceroy in 1644 for urgent military commitments on the Catalan frontier made salaries unpayable for that year inside Valencia, and prompted a round condemnation from the Council of Aragon.[3]

---

[1] For the details, ARV MR 282, *Recepta de la Batlia General*, 1686.
[2] ACA CA leg. 631, Receptor to king, 16 Oct. 1646.
[3] *Ibid.*, Junta Patrimonial to king, 18 July 1645.

In general, though the financial situation was never less than shaky, it was perhaps not as bad as in other parts of the Monarchy at the time. This may explain some of the notable resilience of royal government in seventeenth-century Valencia. In particular, there was no generalized abandonment of authority into the hands of the senyors, of the kind which Villari has traced for Naples. Feudal jurisdictions in Valencia had always been more tightly controlled than, for example, in Aragon, where every lord held automatic rights of life and death over his vassals.[1] It was not until 1646 that the Valencian ministers began to contemplate selling off supreme criminal jurisdiction to the fairly sizeable number of Valencian senyors who did not possess already a specific grant of this privilege.[2] And, as far as I can calculate, there were only approximately 15 alienations between 1614 when the practice really started and about 1650 – which represented no great shift of power in a kingdom of over 700 jurisdictional areas.[3] Also these grants were usually hedged about with restrictions; enquiries might be made into the fitness of the claimant to exercise rights of justice, and the new holders were always required in principle to confer with the local royal judge in cases of serious crime.[4]

The problem was, of course, that the Valencian nobility were too desperately poor to contemplate taking on major new responsibilities. The Count of Real had to stagger his payments for a gallows in Catarroja over two years; the senyor of Puebla Larga had to borrow the money.[5] In fact, the striking feature of seventeenth-century Valencia is the way in which, despite the external appearance of power, existing baronial jurisdictions were being robbed of their force. In 1628 the Count of Sinarcas had to call on the king's forces for help against the bandit Juan Zavallos who was active in his territory; the Marquis of Ariza wanted the king's judges to sort out the feuds in his barony of Calpe in 1636; the Duke of Segorbe appealed for a judge to come and audit the accounts of the *jurats* of his ducal stronghold.[6] In trying to keep order or discipline their

[1] Lorenzo Mateu, *De Regimine Regni Valentiae*, 2nd edn (Lyon 1704), 162–3.
[2] ACA CA leg. 718, memorandum of Abogado Patrimonial, 1646.
[3] ACA CA consultas and correspondence 1600–50, *passim*.
[4] ACA CA leg. 655, consulta, 8 Feb. 1635; Mateu, *De Regimine*, 162–3.
[5] ACA CA leg. 718, consulta, 12 Aug. 1631; leg. 1356, don José de Villanueva to king, 5 Nov. 1645.
[6] ACA CA legs. 874, 878 and 886, petitions of Sinarcas, Ariza and Segorbe.

vassals – no longer Morisco serfs, after all, but propertied lawyers and *dons* – the senyors had to rely more and more on the power of the Audiencia.

The government of the king as it had come down from the Middle Ages was a skeletal structure superimposed on the self-running Valencia of *senyorius* and communes. Under the Crown were four governors (Valencia, Játiva, Castellón and Orihuela), the Baile General who collected the king's revenues, the Receptor who stored them, the Tesorero who spent them, and the Maestre Racional who audited the accounts. These fiscal offices had their equivalents in the autonomous receipts of Orihuela and Montesa. They tended to be recruited from among the middle-sized seigneurial families as a rule. It was considered undesirable to allow potentates with private interests of their own to get their hands on the king's money. Thus in 1637 when the Count of Elda tried to have his younger son made Baile General of Orihuela, the Council of Aragon objected, not only because the child was too young but because 'the count has most of his estates in that area'.[1] Occasionally, it is true, the rule was breached – as when the Marquis of Guadalest was promoted Baile General of Valencia as a wedding present from a bankrupt Philip IV who had no other means of payment.[2] But in general these major offices of state were kept out of the hands of the magnates, and used as a reward for that section of the nobility which was close enough to the throne to be visible but not powerful enough to be dangerous. Forty senyors, with revenues not over 20,000 but not under 3,000 *lliures* a year, together with leading members of their families, chased after a dozen or so top posts. It was with an eye to this imbalance that some ministers of the Council of Aragon argued in 1624 against letting the then Maestre Racional hand on his office to his son:

It is very upsetting for those who serve Your Majesty to find the door closed on their hopes in this way . . . The promise of just one vacancy hooks many people, stimulating and encouraging them to do good service to Your Majesty with the hope of eventual reward. This is a well-known maxim of government the world over, but especially

[1] ACA CA leg. 630, consulta, 19 Sept. 1637.
[2] ACA CA leg. 886, petition, 22 April 1644.

in the kingdom of Valencia and the Crown of Aragon where the resources at our disposal are so limited.[1]

And the same argument was trotted out again by the Council in 1642 when it refused don Basilio de Castelví's request for a reversion to the governorship of Valencia.[2] The interesting thing, however, is that eventually both men got what they wanted. In practice the consideration that one was related to the existing holder was a decisive factor in appointment to office in Habsburg Valencia – but the door was always left just a little ajar to encourage political obedience.

Below the level of the great offices of state, there were over thirty posts of bailiff in charge of revenue collection in the local royal towns. Inevitably most of these were of little value – like that of Villfamés, 'which carries no salary nor emoluments, nor any privilege but the name and the right to receive Holy Communion before anyone else in the local church'.[3] For village *caciques* such prizes were tempting, but hardly for outsiders. There were, it is true, all sorts of pickings to be made from handling the king's money in the bigger towns. But the Crown was careful enough to reserve that sort of post to local men of capital who had something to give in return. Opposing the demand of don Felipe de Cardona for the job of bailiff of Burriana, the senior Valencian minister commented: 'give Cardona a tercio or a castle in Flanders or Italy when one falls vacant, but not Burriana where he will not reside and which is only worth 15 *lliures* a year in salary'.[4] If they could not get themselves appointed bailiff, the nobles could always turn to the dozen or so castles which lay scattered across the kingdom; some of them (such as Peñíscola and Guardamar) carried posts of considerable responsibility, while others (like Biar) were now useless, from a military point of view, with their guns trained aimlessly on Castile. But the profits of command were everywhere small. When the second Count of Real asked that his son be made warden of the fortress of Penáguila, the Council of Aragon sighed that the post was hardly worthy of the family,

[1] ACA CA leg. 656, consulta, 21 May 1624.
[2] ACA CA leg. 633, consulta, 21 Feb. 1642.
[3] ACA CA leg. 885, petition of Francisco Mas, 15 Jan. 1643.
[4] ACA CA leg. 872, don Francisco de Castelví to don Nicolás Mensa, 29 June 1627.

renting only 50 *lliures* a year.[1] Completing the list of offices suitable for the aristocracy were the ten regiments of the militia set up in 1597, which again carried more prestige than remuneration or duties.

But outside the world of the senyors the Crown had a quite considerable patronage at its disposal in Valencia – a myriad petty posts of clerk, janitor, police inspector and so forth. And a fair proportion of the time of the Council of Aragon was spent in sorting through the applications. Do we really need to bother the king, wondered the viceroy in 1641, with a list of candidates for the treasureship of the dam of Alicante, which is only worth 25 *lliures* a year?[2] In fact, it was below that limit of 25 *lliures* – a quarter of what a wage-labourer could earn in a year – that applications had no need to be forwarded to Madrid but could be decided by the viceroy. Sale of office along the lines which proved so profitable to the kings of France had never been widely practised in Valencia, as it had in Castile.[3] Nor on the other hand had it been totally unknown. As early as 1588 Matías Chorrieta, warden of the great Gate of Quart in Valencia city, had been allowed by the Council of Aragon to dispose of his office 'so that with the proceeds he may put one of his four daughters to be a nun'.[4] But it was really only in the last days of Olivares, when the Crown was casting around wildly for money from any source, that the practice became at all systematic. It was in 1641 that the Protonotario informed the authorities in Valencia that the Crown would expect candidates for non-judicial office to offer something in cash. But the size of the purse was to be only one factor involved in reaching a decision: 'applicants are to be told that this door is open, but the fact is not to be broadcast publicly'.[5] Certainly it was during this period that the practice of sale gathered momentum. The most amazingly underpaid posts fetched three or four times their annual value. Dr Verdier paid 220 ducats for a reversion to the Inspectorate of Prisons (emoluments 70 ducats a year);

---

1 ACA CA leg. 654, consulta, 31 May 1623.
2 ACA CA leg. 721, viceroy to king, 19 Feb. 1641.
3 It was chiefly municipal office which was sold in Castile; cf. K. W. Swart, *Sale of Offices in the 17th Century* (Martinus Nijhoff 1949), 20–39.
4 BL Add.MSS., fol. 141, consulta, 5 June 1588.
5 ACA CA leg. 720, don Cristóbal Crespí to Protonotario, 24 Dec. 1641.

Ana Francisca Rodina paid 100 *lliures* for her dead husband's office of Royal Weigher of Raisins and Figs (emoluments 35 to 40 *lliures* a year).[1] The pervasive nature of this royal patronage in Valencian society is evident enough – as is the need of some of the bourgeoisie for royal office in order to get by (which was so in the case of Ana Rodina).

The process of sale soon met its limits. Antonio García de Padilla had bought the enormously responsible post of co-adjutor of the Maestre Racional in charge of accounts in 1647. He died a few years later, and his widow pleaded that his infant son take over in view of the large sum (600 *lliures*) paid out. The Council of Aragon advised against acceptance: 'offices which involve the administration of finance or justice should be appointed uniquely on merit, taking no account of offers of money, for fear of the consequences'.[2] The Habsburgs, in fact, proved curiously half-hearted in the pursuit of a policy which was bringing in such revenues to their Bourbon cousins. Outside the judicial bureaucracy (which in its higher ranks required men with university degrees and should be considered separately), the really responsible positions in the king's bureaucracy were those concerned with revenue collection – the bailiffs in the rural hinterland, the Deputy Maestre Racional and his two coadjutors who audited the accounts. And if there is one principle of recruitment clearly detectable in this sector it is that of appointing the nearest competent relative of deceased incumbents, with offers of money or, very often, without.[3] Urging that Baltasar Roser Gil should be granted his request to have his sixteen-year-old son as joint coadjutor with reversion after his death, the viceroy wrote:

since I have been here, it has been my experience that the posts in the accounts office absolutely require someone versed in paperwork, who picks up the business as he goes along...and this skill can best be acquired by a father coaching his son to take over from him when he dies than appointing an outsider when a vacancy occurs.[4]

[1] ACA CA leg. 655, king to Cardinal Borja, 8 April 1642 and 12 Feb. 1643.
[2] ACA CA leg. 627, consulta, 26 March 1651.
[3] For example, the disposal of the *batllias* of Villajoyosa and Monforte, ACA CA leg. 882, petition of Joachim Pujalt, 30 May 1637.
[4] ACA CA leg. 727, viceroy to king, 28 Sept. 1649. Cf. leg. 660, petition of Roser Gil, 30 Aug. 1647.

Things were admittedly never so simple. Roser Gil had to offer to place thirty soldiers in the fortress of Tortosa in the black days of the Catalan Revolt before his request was even considered, and it was only when gout in his hand began to affect his work that matters were speeded up. The hereditary principle, unencumbered by considerations of venality, was more in evidence in the case of the Deputy Maestre Racional. This key post virtually revolved round the dynasty of the Gil Polo in the early seventeenth century – first Gaspar, then his son Julián (ennobled in 1626), then Julián's brother Juan, then Juan's son Basilio, and then Julián's son José. The Council of Aragon was always careful enough to scrutinize the claims of each Gil Polo before making the appointment, passing over a son, for example, in favour of an uncle with greater experience. Nevertheless the very security of the family's position led to trouble. Juan was condemned as old and unfit in 1634, and recommended for retirement, but he refused to step aside voluntarily, alleging that he needed the 300 *lliures* a year salary, and the Council of Aragon shrank from the prospect of dismissing him.[1]

Given that the king's servants tended to think of their offices as a benefice, revenue collection did not always function efficiently. A government enquiry of 1635 found that the accounts of some bailiffs from the 1590s had still not been closed. Inevitably there was a limit to what the handful of coadjutors in the Maestre Racional's office could do to hurry them on. The Crown occasionally preferred to solve the problem by inventing a figure, charging the revenue collectors with paying it, and waiting for them to come forward with a compromise offer. The senyor of Almácera was suddenly presented with a bill for 52,226 *lliures* in 1647, the sum for which his ancestors had gone bail in 1580 for a bankrupt farmer of the *Peatge*.[2] In 1645 the baron of Alcácer secured that there should be no more enquiries into the accounts of his father and grand-father, Treasurers of the Kingdom, by offering 2,000 *escudos* to the Crown.[3]

The fiscal system in Valencia no doubt worked slowly. But it was not plagued by the wholesale corruption and inefficiency

[1] ACA CA leg. 714, don Martín Funes to king, 19 Sept. and 24 Oct. 1634. For part of the Gil Polo saga, leg. 632, consulta, 10 Feb. 1634.
[2] ACA CA leg. 726, Dr Miguel Jerónimo Querol to king, 12 Feb. 1647.
[3] ACA CA leg. 1356, consulta of Junta de Materias de Valencia, 16 Nov. 1645.

which were such a marked feature of municipal government at the time. The records of the Maestre Racional – tome upon tome of carefully checked censuses, cadastral surveys, receipts and disbursements – are in their own way a tribute to the control which the Crown was able to keep over its servants in Valencia, even in the worst days of economic decline. At most Julián Gil Polo would use the king's writing paper to arrange the purchase of two oxen for his private herd in the course of correspondence with the bailiff of Corbera on the *tercio diezmo*; at most the bailiff of Bocairente, when forwarding his accounts, would slip in a word about his nephew who was hoping for a place in one of the city colleges.[1] The great enquiry of 1634–5 into the functioning of royal government in Valencia turned up little evidence of active corruption or maladministration – a mere 3,702 *lliures* were imposed in fines on eight bailiffs and others who had defrauded the royal treasury.[2] But, of course, the figures in the budgets speak for themselves: in spite of all the difficulties, the king was in somewhat better financial shape than his nobles or his towns.

But the collection of money was not (at least in theory) an end in itself. Resisting the renewal of a pension to the dukes of Segorbe in 1646 the viceroy reminded the king: 'the administration of justice is a binding obligation on Your Majesty, and the reason why kingdoms pay taxes at all'.[3] The king was first and foremost the giver and upholder of law, the father of his people. As late as 1645 the *jurats* of Valencia pinned their hopes of avoiding bankruptcy on Philip IV's physical presence in the city, 'for relief is at hand when the prince can see and hear for himself the tears of his subjects'.[4] But since the Habsburgs rarely visited Valencia, government devolved in practice on their ministers – the viceroy (usually a great Castilian noble appointed for three years at a time), his council of advisers (the judges of the high court of the Audiencia), and the king's own advisers in Madrid, the Regents of the Council of Aragon, who were themselves largely recruited from the Audiencias of Valencia, Catalonia and Aragon.

The outstanding feature of Valencian political history under

[1] ARV MR 5673 and 5598.
[2] ACA CA leg. 713, 'memorial de condenaciones hechas' (1636?).
[3] ACA CA leg. 612, consulta, 18 Aug. 1646.
[4] ACA CA leg. 1355, petition of the *jurats*, 26 Nov. 1645.

the Habsburgs was the growth of the power and prestige of the king's government – a development spearheaded by the lawyers who surrounded the viceroy. Set up officially in 1543 and reaching its maximum extension of thirteen magistrates (including eleven judges, a prosecutor and the *canciller*, an arbiter in disputes with the church courts) in 1585, the Audiencia quietly built up its authority under Philip II.[1] Its rise marked clearly the new professional character of the government and challenged the old influence of the barons. By its growing interference in the relations between lord and peasant after 1580 it helped break up the common front against outsiders presented by the Moriscos and their masters, which had defeated so many campaigns of evangelization by the Catholic Church. In this sense it may be said to have paved the way for the neutrality of the senyors at the time of the expulsion. The nobility also began to lose their traditional freedom in other ways too. In 1616, after the imprisonment of some of its members for lawlessness, the assembly of the nobility declared angrily: 'it is quite obvious that the minds of the judges are not well disposed towards us'.[2]

Traditional interpretations of the growth of absolute monarchy in Europe, of course, tend to associate it with the aspirations of a rising bourgeoisie, among whom it found its most slavish supporters in the task of curbing aristocratic freedoms. A Spanish writer of the time, don Diego Hurtado de Mendoza, may have done as much as anyone to foster this potent image. For him it was the *gente media*, promoted into government from the days of the Catholic Kings, who effectively ruled Spain.[3] And in Valencia the nobility tended to associate the Audiencia with much the same class of people, men who owed everything to the Crown and who therefore had little interest in maintaining the traditional liberties of the kingdom – which they (naturally enough) tended to identify with their own privileges. The Duke of Arcos, viceroy between 1642 and 1645 and related by marriage to the Borjas, 'believes the

[1] There is no good study of the rise of the Audiencia, but the chronology can be pieced together from AMV Churat 1634 vol. I, *pragmáticas* of 1543 and 1607.
[2] ARV R 528 fol. 486.   [3] *Guerra de Granada* (1627), 2nd edn (Barcelona 1842), 8.

aristocracy have a case when they complain about having too few of their own kind as magistrates'.[1]

The origins of the judges are not the easiest thing in the world to track down, since it was never regular practice to include details of birth on the dossiers for promotion; this is significant enough in its own way of what the nobility were complaining about. Certainly many judges and ministers seem to have come from Mendoza's 'middle class', like Carlos del Mor, son of a wealthy merchant, or Pedro Rejaule, whose father was a university professor, or Juan Polo, son of a doctor of medicine.[2] Inevitably though, as the Audiencia grew older and more settled in its ways, a certain tendency towards inbreeding became apparent, with judges related by blood or marriage to their predecessors. Nothing equivalent to the French robe nobility ever developed in Valencia, since judgeships were not hereditary and not for sale. Nevertheless, since promotion depended to a large extent on the recommendations made to the Crown by the judges themselves (and their senior colleagues, the Regents of the Council of Aragon), cousins or sons-in-law stood a better chance of success, other things being equal, than rank outsiders. In the course of time, the bench became increasingly aristocratic in its composition. True, ex-judges were not accorded automatic ennoblement – in the case of Honorato Pascual in 1616, for example, it was a point in his favour that his brother was already a noble.[3] It was only after about 1630, with the sale of titles under Philip IV, that the phenomenon of noble judges became at all common. But from then on, the normal recruiting ground for the Audiencia came to be this vastly expanded nobility, which now included families with a legal tradition. Already in 1646, despite the warnings of the Duke of Arcos two years before, no less than five of the twelve judges were in fact nobles.[4] But this shows not so much that the aristocracy had captured the bench as that the lawyers had captured the aristocracy.

[1] ACA CA leg. 623, consulta, 9 March 1644.
[2] ARV Clero leg. 743, marriage contract of Carlos del Mor, 1632; Vicente Ximeno, *Escritores del Reino de Valencia* (2 vols., Valencia 1747–9), I, 264 and II, 2.
[3] ACA CA leg. 623, consulta, 21 Aug. 1616.
[4] ACA CA leg. 1355, signatories to petition of Audiencia, 14 Jan. 1646.

Of course there were genuine members of the old sword nobility who found their way into the law too. The baron of Alcalalí had been educated as a lawyer, 'being the second son of our family'.[1] But there was perhaps a certain prejudice in this social milieu towards the world of the long robe, with its hair-splitting, pettifogging activities. Don Cristóbal Crespí, grandson of the baron of Sumacárcel, records in his diary how strong an aversion his mother had to his becoming a lawyer at all: 'I heard her once say that if she had twenty sons she would not put one of them in for the law, reckoning it dangerous for one's salvation.'[2] It was poverty which eventually drove Crespí, as it must have driven other young nobles, into the law schools.

When it came to senior promotions, gentle birth unquestionably played some part. The composition of the Council of Aragon, for example, always seems to have been a little more aristocratic than that of the Audiencia. Of the seven ministers appointed to this body from Valencia between 1618 and 1645, three came of old seigneurial families – don Francisco de Castelví, of a junior branch of the Counts of Carlet, don Cristóbal Crespí, and don Andrés Sanz of the line of the senyors of Ayacor. A fourth, don Pedro de Villacampa, had sword connections, but his family had only been ennobled in 1622. Finally the other three were commoners in origin – don Melchor Sisternes, the son of a judge who had been ennobled in 1612, Francisco Jerónimo León, the son of a secretary in the fiscal office in Valencia, and Gregorio Mingot, the cousin of the royal bailiff of Alicante.[3]

At all times, however, the first criterion in promotion was a man's ability as a lawyer. Rejecting the claims of don Miguel Vives for a post in the Audiencia, the viceroy noted: 'he is well born, but an ignoramus and good for nothing'.[4] Refusing to consider don Carlos Coloma, son of the Count of Elda, for a judgeship, the Council of Aragon commented: 'he has neither

---

[1] ACA CA leg. 726, petition of don Luis Ruiz de Liori, 3 Dec. 1645.
[2] BN 5742, 'Diario del Vicecanciller Crespí', fol. 195.
[3] Biographical details in ACA CA legs. 624, 633, 640, 870 and 1351. On the Crespís, cf. Gonzalo Vidal Tur, *Un obispado español: el de Orihuela-Alicante* (2 vols., Alicante 1961), I, 204–6, with information on Cristóbal's brother Luis, bishop of Orihuela 1652–8.
[4] ACA CA leg. 623, consulta, 27 Nov. 1641.

practised as a lawyer for the legally required time, nor had three years as a college fellow'.[1] At the base of the system were merit and learning, and since Valencia had its own laws the basic legal training had to be local. After the expulsion of the Moriscos, financial considerations may have joined those of a political nature in keeping Valencians at home in their own university. The three additional chairs of law set up in 1613 would, it was hoped, 'ease the straits in which this city and kingdom now find themselves, with many well born and distinguished people no longer able to afford to send their sons to Salamanca or elsewhere'.[2] There were a number of exceptions – Crespí was educated at Salamanca, and so were Juan de Centelles and don Carlos Coloma, while other judges we know had been to the universities of Huesca and Lérida. But Crespí, Juan de Centelles and Coloma belonged to important seigneurial families, with connections at court and in Castile. For their colleagues the cultural horizon did not stretch so far.[3] Essentially, from a political point of view, this was a closed society – closed because all the judges had to be Valencians anyway, and because the laws they applied were local laws.

Inevitably the king's servants had to be men of independent means since low salaries were common from top to bottom of the hierarchy – 1,500 *lliures* for a Regent of the Council of Aragon, 1,200 for a senior magistrate of the Audiencia (falling to 1,000 after the expulsion), 733 for his junior colleagues in the criminal chamber, 500 for the assessor to the governor of Valencia, and a bare 160 for the assessor of the Baile General of Orihuela (whose responsibilities extended to judging all litigation connected with the recovery of the king's revenue in the Alicante area). These figures should be set against the 1,000 to 3,000 *lliures* which lawyers were often earning in private practice before they accepted office.[4] To add insult to injury the salaries increasingly went unpaid in the black days of the

[1] ACA CA leg. 625 n. 1/8, consulta, 3 March 1663. It is only fair to add that both Coloma and Vives were eventually promoted anyway – Coloma directly by the king, overruling the Council, *ibid.* n. 1/9, consulta, 24 Oct. 1666.
[2] AMV CM 58, *jurats* to king, 15 Oct. 1613.
[3] For the dearth of Valencians attending the universities of Castile, see Kagan, *Students and Society*, 114–23 and 204–10.
[4] ACA CA leg. 883, petition of Miguel Jerónimo Sanz 1641; leg. 874, petition of Francisco Jerónimo León, 1627.

wars against Richelieu, Mazarin and Louis XIV.[1] The consequent embarrassment of the magistrates was aggravated by the contemporaneous collapse of the *censal* on which so many of them depended (two-thirds of the judges had to be excluded from handling the debts of the Duke of Gandía after the expulsion because they were interested parties).[2] By 1647 the Council of Aragon learned with dismay that 'the ministers of the Audiencia are reported to be going around in an undignified way on foot without any attendants'.[3]

Surprisingly enough in these circumstances, there was no shortage of candidates wanting to be a judge, probably because the top posts were comparatively few. Don Francisco de Castelví, 35 years old in 1598, was already 'one of the lawyers of greatest fame in the city and kingdom', but he had to wait another three years before getting a foothold on the ladder of promotion – on the bottom rung as assessor to the Baile General of Valencia. Josep Ferriol spent 43 years as assessor to one bailiff and governor after another, only managing at the ripe age of 68 to get a place in the viceroy's council as Advocate Fiscal (at a salary of a mere 600 *lliures* a year).[4] It is interesting to compare this situation with that in France under the Ancien Régime: there the magistrates of the Parlements, who all bought or inherited their offices, tended to be young men in their twenties when appointed.[5] Valencia gives the impression of having been ruled by a gerontocracy – somnolent by comparison with the independent, spirited magistrates who defied the French king at the time of the Fronde and who were to cause such trouble to Louis XV and Louis XVI. Given that the best jobs in Valencia were always directly in the king's gift, there was a queue of candidates, pressing its way up through the miserably paid *asesorías*. Fortunately for the stability of the system, the relatively

---

[1] ACA CA legs. 640, 645, 725 and 875, consultas and correspondence, 1633, 1645, 1673 and 1694. Salaries were officially cut in 1633 and 1644 by one-eleventh, and in 1694 by a third for those years; but arrears continued to pile up, with the judges receiving nothing at all in 1645 and between 1670 and 1673.

[2] ACA CA leg. 709, memorandum (1620?).

[3] ACA CA leg. 660, memorandum of the Council, 13 May 1647.

[4] ACA CA leg. 624, consulta, 6 March 1598 (Castelví); leg. 639, viceroy to king, 25 April 1645 (Ferriol).

[5] Cf. John Hurt, 'The Parliament of Britanny and the Crown 1665–75', in R. Kierstead, ed., *State and Society in 17th Century France* (New York 1975), 55.

advanced age of those who managed eventually to attain high
office led to frequent vacancies through death or resignation.[1]

This peculiar career pattern encouraged a breathtaking rate
of turnover within the ranks of the judiciary. In 1617, the year
in which judge Castelví was promoted to the Council of Aragon,
and in which two of his senior colleagues died or retired, the
entire criminal bench was elevated en bloc to the vacant civil
posts.[2] Don Cristóbal Crespí was successively assessor of the
governor of Valencia in 1629, then public prosecutor in 1631,
then a junior judge in 1632, and then a judge of the civil bench
in 1635, before obtaining his promotion to the Council of
Aragon in 1642 (he was rejected in 1638, at the age of 39,
because he was too young).[3] Don Antonio Juan de Centelles,
appointed to the criminal bench in 1643, was the senior member
there by 1645.[4] And in that year, as it happened, he was made
a civil judge in succession to Gregorio Mingot who had gone
to Madrid. Mingot's own career was meteoric – he was assessor
of the Baile General of Orihuela in 1638 and public prosecutor
in 1640 (?); promoted to the civil bench in 1641, and the Council
of Aragon in 1644, he was dead six months later.[5] Small wonder
that Judge Bono should have demanded a patent of nobility
to avoid the discredit of having been four years on the criminal
bench without promotion![6] The main problem facing the
Valencian judiciary was that its lower, but enormously responsible posts were ill paid and filled too late in life: this created
unease, dissatisfaction and heavy pressure on the senior magi-
stracies. The Council of Aragon recognized the danger in 1673
when it took the revolutionary step of nominating a cleric, Fray
Hipólito Sempere, as assessor of the Baile General for the
specific reason that 'he will not want promotion'.[7]

The other disadvantage of the system was that the judges
of the civil bench – and the Regents of the Council of Aragon
– were often old men, prepared to settle back and enjoy the

[1] See on this point J. M. Batista, foreword to H. G. Koenigsberger, *The Government of Sicily under Philip II of Spain* (London 1951), 32.
[2] ACA CA leg. 623, consulta, 1617.
[3] ACA CA legs. 633 and 722, consultas of 1629, 1638 and 1642.
[4] ACA CA leg. 623, consulta, 28 Jan. 1645.
[5] ACA CA legs. 632 and 623, consultas of 1638, 1641 and 1645.
[6] ACA CA leg. 658, petition (1640?).
[7] ACA CA leg. 640 n. 14/14, consulta, 5 June 1673.

rewards of the long struggle to get where they were. The great enquiry of 1635 noted this slowness as one of the great defects of the senior magistracy. Judge Blasco was always 'splitting hairs'; Judge Mora was doddering; Judges Sanz and Gamir 'do not get things done'.[1] Audiencia suits could indeed be notoriously lengthy, dragging on for generations. Complaining of the delay in despatching its business in 1644, the town of Alcira noted that 'the judges are old, always ill and have too much work to do'.[2] For the chronicler Escolano, the lawcourts were 'the cemetery of the living'.[3]

Overworked and underpaid, it is perhaps not surprising that the judicial bureaucracy appeared to function inefficiently. From the latter years of Philip II to those of Charles II it came in for some very severe criticism, even within its own ranks. In 1597 the criminal bench 'had no good judges'; in 1610 the whole Audiencia was 'bare in the extreme...of useful or competent servants'; in 1638 all three judges on the criminal bench had to be suspended on suspicion of corruption or faction; in 1679 the Audiencia was still said to be 'poorly staffed'.[4] These reports cannot always be believed. Indeed part of the trouble was the inadequacy of information on which promotions or dismissals were sometimes made. To viceroy Borja in 1638 Judge Miguel Jerónimo Sanz was 'not an ignoramus in the law admittedly, but an unpractical man, with no gift for getting things done'; to viceroy Medinaceli in 1641 he was 'a man of learning, devoted to Your Majesty's service'. In 1638 Sanz was dimissed and then reinstated, before being shot dead in the garden of his country house by some men he had offended on the bench.[5] The twist to the story is that in April 1638 viceroy Borja had recommended Sanz (then public prosecutor) for promotion to the criminal bench, and only in October wrote his damning report. This appears not to represent a change of mind. Borja said he had known in April that Sanz was useless, but thought that he would do less harm as a judge than

[1] ACA CA leg. 713, don Martín Funes to king, 13 March 1635.
[2] ACA CA leg. 885, petition, 11 Aug. 1643.   [3] *Décadas*, 1, 398.
[4] ACA CA legs. 624, 625, 640 and 715, consultas of 1597, 1610, 1638 and 1679.
[5] ACA CA leg. 717, don Fernando de Borja to king, 12 Oct. 1638; leg. 623, consulta, 27 Nov. 1641. For his suspension, leg. 715, consulta, 10 Dec. 1638; and for his murder, leg. 721, viceroy to king, 19 Aug. 1642.

as a prosecutor. Faced with such a machiavellian approach in its chief representative, the Council of Aragon resolved that when Borja submitted his next recommendations, 'the members of this Council will try to find out themselves who are the candidates best suited'.[1]

Apart from the idiosyncratic behaviour of don Fernando de Borja (who was afflicted with the ague), there was a long-standing problem concerning the exercise of judicial patronage. In principle the Audiencia was supposed to vote on all recommendations for legal office – much to the dismay of some viceroys like the Marquis of Pobar who said that this was to play into the hands of those with 'private aims and ambitions'.[2] But the instinctive sympathy of the Council of Aragon lay with the Audiencia – in 1593 it had laid down a rule that the viceroy was not to comment on any judge who was up for promotion, 'since all of them are worthy men' by mere virtue of their position.[3] We know that it was routine for ministers who were related to candidates to intervene in the discussions in the Council of Aragon even though they did not vote. Since only Valencian lawyers could hold office in Valencia, who better to give information than the Valencian ministers, even though they were inevitably fathers-in-law or cousins or uncles of the candidates? 'Otherwise', claimed the Council, 'the viceroys would have absolute control of patronage.'[4]

In fact it was precisely against this closed world of patronage that Olivares began to act in the great reforming years of the 1620s. Between 7 March 1622 and 15 October 1633 a whole series of *decretos* began to issue from the king's own secretariat, aimed at tightening up procedure in the Council of Aragon by instituting secret voting for appointments, encouraging those who were outvoted to make separate recommendations, prohibiting relatives up to the fourth degree to be present, and so forth.[5] Actually Olivares was merely making systematic a policy which had already been adopted under the lax Philip III – that of trying to prise patronage out of the hands of the Council

[1] ACA CA legs. 717, consultas, April 1638 & 12 Oct. 1638; leg. 715, consulta, 10 Dec. 1638.　　[2] ACA CA leg. 623, viceroy to king, 21 Oct. 1625.
[3] ACA CA leg. 625, consulta, 1593.
[4] ACA CA leg. 661, consulta, 26 Aug. 1624.
[5] ACA CA leg. 654 and 656, *decretos*, 1622–33.

of Aragon and place it in those of the king himself. In 1617 Philip III rapped the knuckles of the councillors when they refused to send on the reports of the viceroy on judges who were up for promotion: 'I have listened to what you have to say, but you will observe the custom that the viceroys send in their own recommendations.'[1] After Olivares' fall, secret voting on appointments was abandoned; the change came at least as early as February 1644.[2] However the latent struggle continued between Philip IV, uneasy at relatives intervening in the exercise of patronage, and the Council of Aragon, determined to preserve the insulated and isolated worlds of the separate little kingdoms, with their individual promotion systems.

Although the main influence on appointments was always, one may suspect, internal – that is, the Valencian ministers of the Council of Aragon decided which of their junior colleagues in Valencia should move up the ladder – it was never watertight. Miguel Jerónimo Sanz, the *bête noire* of viceroy Borja, had been appointed originally as public prosecutor in 1636 by the king on his own initiative, disregarding the recommendations of the Council. The reason appears to have been that he had married the daughter of a retired judge, 'almost without a dowry' (as he cheerfully noted in his petition to the Crown) in the expectation of a reward for the old man's services.[3] Though the Crown was always very careful not to sell major judicial offices, the temptation during the terrible war years of 1635–59 was to use them in lieu of pensions. Doña Teresa Giner was promised in 1636 that anyone who married her would get the job of assessor of the governor of Valencia at the next vacancy; the lucky man turned out to be ineffectual, 'so devoid of talent', in the eyes of one viceroy, 'that he will never be anything other than an assessor'.[4] Doña Teresa's sister tried a similar ploy on behalf of her prospective suitor. To the angry remonstrances of the Council of Aragon, Philip IV returned a bland reply: 'I know the prime consideration in these appointments should be the administration of justice. But I am sure one can meet

[1] ACA CA leg. 623, consultas, 1 and 29 Oct. 1617.
[2] ACA CA leg. 639, consulta, 29 Feb. 1644.
[3] ACA CA leg. 623, petition (1626?), and leg. 624, consulta, 29 Oct. 1636.
[4] ACA CA leg. 623, consulta, 25 April 1649.

this need while at the same time rewarding some of those who have earned our gratitude by their services. One should bear this form of reward in mind, given that the treasury is bare.'[1]

On the whole this sort of fiscal attitude to judicial appointments was not at all common in Valencia. But there were other, perhaps equally sinister forces at work, bypassing the normal sifting process of the Council of Aragon and the Audiencia itself. Don Pedro de Villacampa, for example, was made a Regent of the Council of Aragon in 1645, though neither the Council nor the viceroy had recommended him. Villacampa got his job, it appears, because he was a favourite of the venerable and enormously influential Isidoro de Aliaga, archbishop of Valencia.[2] The influence of the magnates on promotions was undoubtedly also considerable. Judge Marcos Antonio Sisternes had been a protégé of the Duke of Segorbe; his son, don Melchor, who rose to become Regent of the Council of Aragon, was closely identified with the Duke of Infantado.[3] Judge Bono had been assessor of the estates of the Duke of Gandía before getting into the Audiencia in 1639. In 1644 the viceroy, the Duke of Arcos, promised the Duke of Gandía (to whom he was related by a recent marriage) that he would recommend Bono for promotion as a special favour – even though his predecessor a couple of years before had excluded Bono as being 'a very mediocre lawyer indeed'.[4] Don Pedro de Villacampa, as well as being a protégé of the archbishop, was in the pay of the Dukes of Villahermosa – to avoid scandal, he had to be ordered to quit the Duke's big Valencian house where he lived rent free.[5]

And yet it was this interpenetration with the most powerful elements in Valencian society which gave the Audiencia and the Council of Aragon their power to command. Though servants of the king, the judges and the Regents were closely identified with their native homeland, and it was the balance which they were able to strike between the two interests which

1   *Ibid.*, consulta, 20 May 1649.
2   ACA CA leg. 882, petition of Laura Pascual, 9 Oct. 1641; leg. 1354, consulta, Dec. 1645.
3   ADM Segorbe leg. 62 n. 6, memorandum of the Duke, 1 May 1613; ACA CA leg. 869, petition of the *síndic* of Castalla, 8 Dec. 1621.
4   AHN Osuna leg. 9 n. 11, Arcos to Gandía, 5 Jan. 1644; ACA CA leg. 623, consulta, 27 Nov. 1641.   5   ACA CA leg. 721, viceroy to king, 11 Dec. 1640.

ensured the political tranquillity of Valencia. Don Francisco de Castelví had fomented the opposition of the Estament Militar in 1615 against Adrián Bayarte's commission to sell Morisco lands on the grounds that Bayarte was a 'foreigner' and could not exercise jurisdiction in Valencia; don Cristóbal Crespí had led the opposition of the estates in 1626 against Olivares' attempt to hold the Cortes of Valencia outside the limits of the kingdom (an activity which held up his promotion to the Audiencia for a couple of years).[1] And while these two powerful men were in Madrid during their subsequent careers as Regents of the Council of Aragon, they always remained closely in touch with local affairs. Sixty-five years old in 1629, Castelví pleaded to be allowed to retire as president of the Audiencia in his native Valencia, 'because the air is fresher there and the climate more temperate' than in Madrid – a request which the viceroy of the time strongly opposed 'because of the many kinsmen and connections he has here, who are locked in feuds with their enemies'.[2] Castelví struggled on in Madrid until his death in 1638 and lived long enough to oppose the policy of forced conscription which Olivares began to introduce after the outbreak of war with France in 1635. Don Cristóbal Crespí – a much more sober figure altogether – received the embassy of the city of Valencia which had come to congratulate him on his appointment as Vice-Chancellor of the Council in 1652 with the courtesy due to grandees, 'because Valencia was acting as my mother, and I could not but treat her like my mother'.[3]

But there was another side to Crespí, which comes through in his diary – the punctilious servant of the king, whose authority in Valencia must be maintained in every point of detail. Time after time he clashed with the estates (whose champion he had once been) on what perhaps seem trivial points of precedence, but which reflected a more fundamental disagreement about the limits of government. The Valencians never really forgave him after the Cortes of 1645 when he insisted on receiving their representatives 'seated, with his hat on, while they stood with their hats off' – a symptom of the hard line he

[1] ACA CA leg. 705, Bayarte to king, 8 June 1615 and 2 June 1615; leg. 640, consulta, 14 April 1628; Diego José Dormer, *Anales de Aragón en el reinado de Felipe el Grande*, RAH MS. 9/490, fols. 198v–9.
[2] ACA CA leg. 625, petition, 29 April 1629.   [3] *Diario*, fol. 4v–5.

was to take towards their petitions.[1] Lions under the throne
some judges and ministers certainly believed themselves to be.
In the preservation of law and order they frequently fell foul
of the most powerful elements in Valencian society – and the
rumbling discontent of the Estament Militar suddenly exploded
in 1616 with the decision of that body to exclude four over-zealous
judges and all their descendants from ever sitting in its august
ranks.[2]

But fortunately for the whole structure of government in
Valencia such headlong clashes were comparatively rare. The
threads of personal dependence ran across the divide and
prevented the development of any clean split between governors
and governed. From the Duke of Infantado or the Duke of
Villahermosa in Madrid a chain of patronage passed through
both the bureaucracy and the native aristocracy. And the
bureaucrats themselves were caught up in the trammels of local
society by their marriages, their birth or their personal interests.
Rejaule, the professor's son, was married to the daughter of
one of the most powerful and wealthy city patricians, Navarro
de Gasca; Castelví's wife and the governor of Valencia were
godparents at the baptism of one of his children in 1627 – a
baptism attended by 'a numerous throng of noblemen and their
ladies' and more splendid than that of any viceroy, 'which
caused people to snigger and murmur'.[3] Such hobnobbing
between the king's servants and the old elite (which was not,
of course, peculiar to Valencia) could have more serious
repercussions on government policy. Marcos Antonio Bisse
blamed his failure to implement the *almirantazgo* programme
in Alicante on sabotage by ministers of the Audiencia. The case
against him was presented by Pau Salafranca, deputy of
Alicante, 'a man with a hand in the smuggling, and a son-in-law
of the public prosecutor of the Royal Audiencia of Valencia,
who is himself also a native of Alicante' (he meant Gregorio
Mingot, who within a few years was to become Regent of the
Council of Aragon).[4] Mingot was by all accounts an unsavoury
character, and deeply embroiled in Alicante politics. He was

[1] ACA CA leg. 1357, petition of the ambassador don Josef Sanz, 1647.
[2] ARV R 528 fols. 381–81v.   [3] Porcar, *Coses evengudes*, II, cap. 3019.
[4] ACA CA leg. 882, petition of Bisse, 28 May 1641.

suspected of the murder of Melchor Fernández de Mesa, another of the potentates of the great trading mecca of the Valencian south.[1]

Men like Mingot had the power to indulge their personal animosities and favour their friends, for the judicial bureaucracy was mainly self-recruiting and self-regulating. The attempts to weed out corruption from time to time by means of formal inquests (*visitas*) failed because they were too few and far between. One such enquiry was held shortly after the Cortes of 1604, and though by law they had to be renewed every six years, there was no money to pay for another until 1634.[2] Certainly Canon Funes, who conducted the latter, found little evidence of malpractice in the Audiencia. But one may wonder whether the investigations were followed up with sufficient zeal. The Council of Aragon, which supervised the whole *visita* anyway, was somewhat chary about undermining the authority of its junior colleagues in the Audiencia. Serious accusations against Judge Ginart, for example, were hushed up: 'let the viceroy call Ginart to himself secretly and without formal process...and find out what he has to say to each of the charges, and send all the documents [to Madrid]'.[3] The Council of Aragon did not produce the papers, and nothing more was heard of the affair.

For the majority of judges, no doubt – as Funes said – their sins were those of omission rather than commission. The government of Valencia had an inbuilt system of checks and balances which led to appalling slowness at all levels, and which served to maintain the status quo. The Council of Aragon, staffed by lawyers like the Audiencia itself, was poorly equipped to initiate reforms or pursue any active policy in the eastern kingdom. The ministers remained at heart judges, enmeshed in the minutiae and routine of administration and loving it. The diary of don Cristóbal Crespí is notable for its lack of interest in general questions of policy and its obsessive concern with personal detail and rights of precedence. The highlight of Crespí's political career, to judge from the amount of space he

[1] ACA CA leg. 633, consulta, 20 May 1633.
[2] The records of this *visita* are in ACA CA legs. 713 and 714, correspondence of Canon Martín de Funes, Vicente Gregorio, the bishop of Petra and others, 1634–6.
[3] ACA CA leg. 714, Funes to king, 1 Aug. 1634, and endorsement.

devotes to it, was the seating arrangements for Philip IV's funeral. And yet in a sense such attitudes on the part of the governors were just what was required to bring a traditionally independent and prickly body of the governed into dependence on the throne. It was no accident that one of the demands of the Cortes of 1626 was to have all litigation dealt with exclusively by the Council of Aragon, since Valencians 'who have business at Your Majesty's court are ill-treated by the ministers of Castile who have no knowledge of them'.[1] As long as the government of Valencia remained primarily in the hands of lawyers, who considered their real business to be the adjudication of conflicts of interest between parties, then the nobility, drawn like flies to a honey-pot, could be kept in dependence.

But of course to treat the government of Valencia primarily in these terms would leave out of account the very forceful alternative which did exist and which seemed for a time under Olivares to be in the ascendant – the formulation of policy nearer the throne and the bypassing if necessary of the normal channels of execution. After all, the right arm of the king was not the Council of Aragon or the Audiencia at all, but the viceroy. Of all the offices of government connected with Valencia this was perhaps the one which stood closest to the throne, for it was really a personal delegation of authority from the king himself. The Council of Aragon might offer its suggestions as to who should be made viceroy, but the king often enough took soundings in other quarters, as in 1618 when Philip III nominated the Márquis of Tavara, telling the Council: 'though you did not recommend him, I think he is suitable'.[2] At the end of the century, Charles II prolonged the triennium of the Marquis of Castel Rodrigo, without asking the opinion of the Council.[3]

Inevitably the viceroys had enormous power because of their direct access to the king, and also on a personal level because not all of them came to Valencia as total strangers. The Duke

[1] ARV R 519, *fur* 179 of 1626.
[2] ACA CA leg. 867, consulta, 1618. He proved to be an exceptionally tough and unpopular viceroy, clashing with the Estates and part of the Audiencia on the execution of a turbulent noble; leg. 707, Tavara to king, 11 May 1622.
[3] ACA CA leg. 932, consulta, 16 Nov. 1693. The Council condemned Castel Rodrigo as unsuitable, 'for he has earned the dislike of the natives, particularly the nobility'.

of Arcos (1642–5) was related by marriage to the Duke of Gandía; the Count of Oropesa (1645–50) was related to the Count of Sinarcas.[1] Most of them were men of political experience: Oropesa came from the viceroyalty of Navarre and don Fernando de Borja (1635–40) from that of Aragon.[2] Valencia was an intermediate stage in their careers, followed by a more lucrative Italian viceroyalty (Naples for the Duke of Arcos, Sicily for the Marquis of Tavara), or by a posting in Madrid itself (the presidency of the Council of Orders for the Marquis of Caracena, and for the Marquis of Pobar).[3]

Though Valencia was only a couple of days' ride from Madrid, a viceroy could arrogate considerable independence to himself. A notorious example of this is the political revolution engineered in the city of Valencia on 22 March 1646, when the Count of Oropesa got the Consell General to petition for an abolition of the *insaculació*. Though Oropesa was in communication with Regent Crespí, then in Valencia, he did not report what had been going on to the Council of Aragon until 4 April. And it was not until 13 April that the Council actually got round to giving its advice on the matter to the king.[4] A similar situation developed at the time of the Second Germania of 1693. The viceroy told the secretary of the Council of Aragon on 14 July 1693 that he was sending the militia against the rebels, though he had no instructions as yet to do so. On the 17th he reported the successful battle which had taken place south of Játiva. On the 21st a surprised Council of Aragon demanded more information. And it was not until 27 July – over two weeks after events had been set in motion – that the Council drafted its report to the Crown, in which a majority of Regents deplored the battle as an unnecessary waste of life.[5]

An independent viceroy was not the only danger which the Council of Aragon had to guard against. Interference with its monopoly of power could also come from ministers or grandees

[1] AHN Osuna leg. 127 n. 2, marriage contract Borja-Ponce de León, 27 March 1637; ACA CA leg. 659, Count of Oropesa to king, 17 Aug. 1647.

[2] ACA CA leg. 1354, consulta, 27 June 1646; leg. 612, consulta, 24 July 1632.

[3] Porcar, *Coses evengudes*, I, chapter 1169, and II, chapter 2510; Diego de Vich, *Dietario valenciano 1619–32*, ed. Francisco Almarche Vázquez (Valencia 1921), entry of 8 Nov. 1627; Villari, *La rivolta antispagnola a Napoli*, 153 and 228.

[4] ACA CA leg. 673, viceroy to king, 4 April 1646, and consulta, 13 April 1646.

[5] ACA CA leg. 580 n. 2/5, and n. 5/8, 19 and 32.

at court. The sixth Duke of Infantado, in the very year he died, made a vindictive attempt to hold up the despatch of a title to don Pedro de Belvís. His wife summoned don Nicolás Mensa, the Valencian secretary, to her house in Madrid the afternoon following a discussion of the title in the Council of Aragon and asked him to hold back the papers. Mensa, in fact, refused; but the incident sheds a curious (and rare) light on the secret pressures at work in Madrid.[1] More serious were conflicts of competence between the Council of Aragon and the Council of State on matters of policy. During the heroic days of Olivares' ministry something approaching a general policy for the Monarchy as a whole began to the be elaborated. Starting with the needs of defence, it extended to the regulation of contacts between the peripheral provinces and outsiders. In 1622 there began the attempt to break the illegal spice trade through Alicante. The Council of Aragon's sympathy throughout was with the men of Alicante. Protesting against the remitting of jurisdiction over the condemned merchants to the Council of War, it pointed out:

this contravenes a *fuero* sworn in the Cortes of Valencia in the year 1604, which is still valid and which reserves such cases to this Council, not that of War. Your Majesty (saving your royal grace) is obliged to observe this and the other laws which you will have to swear when you are pleased to favour the kingdom with your royal presence.[2]

The Council of Aragon was never fully master in its own house. And yet it was sufficiently in control for the potential conflict between Valencia and Madrid never to develop. The weakening and then the collapse of all interference with the Alicante spice smugglers, and the subsequent demise of Marcos Antonio Bisse and the *almirantazgo*, all testify to the frustrating inability of the Crown to make any sizeable dent in well-protected local privilege. It was the sheer force of inertia built into the government of Valencia which was the firmest guarantee of the political tranquillity of the region.

[1] ACA CA leg. 654, memorandum of Mensa, 13 Jan. 1624.
[2] ACA CA leg. 603, consulta, 27 March 1623. For a similar conflict of competence over the sale of judicial pardons, leg. 881, consulta de la Junta de Vestir la Casa, 18 Sept. 1639.

9

Outlaws and rebels

There is a seeming paradox in the general picture of political tranquillity which Valencia presented in the later Habsburg period. On the one hand, as the spokesman of the Estates declared proudly to Charles II, 'in more than 400 years which have elapsed since the conquest, not one noble has ever been convicted of treason or disloyalty'. On the other hand, as he went on to say, the problem of lawlessness was worse in Valencia than in any other part of Spain, such that people lived 'under a common misapprehension that the feuds and banditry in Valencia were something to do with the area, and came from the climate or the stars'.[1] Of course the phenomenon of banditry was a general one throughout the Mediterranean states in the early modern period. Its sheer scale has impressed some historians, who have tended to see it as an authentic movement of mass revolt – the revolt of the nobility against the centralizing tendency of the successors of St Peter in the Papal States or the protest of a wretched peasantry against the seigneurial reaction in seventeenth-century Naples.[2] In Valencia it is perhaps more difficult to see any such coherent direction in the random but repeated acts of violence which stain the judicial records of the age. One bandit gang freed two conscripts in an unpopular levy of 1643, another broke up a chain-gang on its way to the galleys, but these are isolated incidents which confirm the general rule that Valencian bandits rarely attacked the Crown or the government.[3] A more serious case could be

[1] AMV Churat 1634 vol. III n. 115, petition of the Marquis of Albaida (1690?).
[2] Villari, *La rivolta antispagnola a Napoli*, 58–88; J. Delumeau, *Vie économique et sociale de Rome dans la deuxieme moitie du XVIᵉ siècle* (2 vols., Paris 1957–9), II, 543.
[3] ACA CA leg. 617, Antonio Juan de Centelles to king, 3 March 1651; leg. 580 n. 28/6, consulta, 9 Feb. 1611. There is a fine recent study of the phenomenon by Henry

made out for associating banditry with an attack on the senyors, especially since the great peasant revolt of 1693, the Second Germania, broke out in archetypal bandit country. However the outlaws, though perhaps helping to create a climate of violence, played no prominent role in the movement itself. More often, indeed, they are to be found in the pay of the senyors – as in the year of the Second Germania, when the gang of Pedro Cortes was used to 'incline the minds' of the peasants of Olocau to a takeover by the Carroz family, or in the 1660s when the famous Josep Artús was used to fight a cattle war between two local potentates in the mountains towards Aragon.[1] In other words, the phenomenon of banditry, which is such a marked feature of Valencian society in the seventeenth century, seems to me to have attained its critical level because it enjoyed the support of the most powerful elements in the land. If Valencia was so remarkably free from social or political upheaval, it was precisely because the lawless breed were in the pay of the most conservative and reactionary forces in the kingdom, who were using the violence against one another, or in order to consolidate their positions of power in the local community. The nearest parallel to this situation is the Mafia in Sicily – another case of violence being used to shore up the position of local potentates. Recent theses, suggesting that the Mafia represents a transitional stage of social development – the self-help practised by ambitious men in a society no longer controlled by feudal barons yet not adequately regulated by the bureaucratic state – probably hold the key to understanding lawlessness in seventeenth-century Valencia.[2]

Of course the private feuds of the barons had drenched Valencia in blood in their own day. But the sort of pitched battles which could take place in the early fifteenth century were no longer feasible in the Habsburg period. Instead the power of the barons declined, and, as it did so, left a sort of vacuum, and led to an unregulated struggle for influence among a host

Kamen, 'Public Authority and Popular Crime: Banditry in Valencia 1660–1714', *Journal of European Economic History*, III (1974), 654–87.
[1] ACA CA leg. 932, viceroy to don Josep de Molina, 24 Nov. 1693; leg. 582, consulta, 26 Sept. 1665.
[2] Henner Hess, *Mafia and Mafiosi: The Structure of Power* (Saxon House 1973); Anton Blok, *The Mafia of a Sicilian Village 1860–1960* (Harper and Row 1974).

of lesser men. As late as 1564 the castle of the Duke of Gandía was a formidable enough affair, with 'its arsenal from which 50 men at arms and 600 arquebusiers could be fitted out in a trice', while his cousin of Segorbe barred the highway to Aragon with his stout fortress, bristling 'with an imposing array of cannon, arms and shot', and the Marquis of Guadalest boasted that he could put 100 armed men in the field at a moment's notice.[1] But in the next half-century this world disappeared for ever. A turning point was perhaps the disarmament of the Moriscos in 1563, which deprived the senyors of their main source of retainers. In 1597 the setting up of a militia under officers nominated by the king marked the decisive shift of military power into the hands of the Crown.[2] Though all of these measures would require more detailed research, they surely reflect the financial weakness of some of the greater houses in this period. They also suffered a run of biological ill-luck. The bigger houses were becoming fewer through extinction of the male line – Segorbe in 1575, Guadalest in 1583, Mandas in 1617, Cocentaina in 1623, Lerma in 1640, and Segorbe again in 1670. The amalgamation and rearrangement of inheritances meant that of the eight magnates who dominated the kingdom by the weight of their territorial possessions, only two – Gandía and Guadalest – were resident after 1623, and only Gandía still continued to live on his estates. The smaller men who tried to keep up private armies were easily crushed by the Crown. When the son of the Count of Buñol tried to assemble 70 horsemen for exercise in a meadow outside the city of Valencia in 1614, the viceroy intervened to prohibit the demonstration; when the son of the Count of Carlet escorted his bride from Catalonia the following year with 40 retainers, he was ordered to disband them once he had got through the bandit-infested hills of the Maestrazgo.[3] These are among the last references that can be found to seigneurial armies in Valencia.

Unquestionably the Crown was very successful during this

[1] Viciana, *Crónica*, II, fols. 12v and 38v, and cf. AHN Osuna leg. 1026 n. 6, inventory of the Duke of Gandía, 1572. For Guadalest, ARV Clero leg. 397, *capítulos matrimoniales*, 8 Nov. 1613.

[2] M. Danvila, 'Desarme de los moriscos en 1563', *Boletín de la Real Academia de Historia*, x (1887), 275–306; AMV Churat 1634 vol. 1 n. 29, decree of 1597. By the 1630s the Duke of Gandía had to borrow his arms from the Diputació; ARV G 1958, fol. 156.

[3] ACA CA leg. 703, viceroy to king, 20 May 1614, and governor to king, 24 Nov. 1615.

period in bringing the overmighty subject to heel. Against the traditional independence and irresponsibility of the old sword nobility the royal courts mounted their most sustained and ultimately most telling attacks. Executing don Juan Vich for murder in 1622, the viceroy officially stated the Crown's position: 'let everyone know that a man's blood or status do not excuse him from behaving properly, but rather lay him under a greater obligation in this respect, and that punishments were not devised for the weak but for those who deserve them'.[1] Brave words, which conceal, however, the fact that the authorities generally shied away from such direct confrontations with the nobility. Instead their preferred (but no less effective) method was to harass the victim. It proved impossible to hang the Count of Anna for murder, but he was made to cool his heels on the other side of the frontier, in lonely exile in Castile, for a few years.[2] The Count of Carlet, arrested in 1625 on suspicion of harbouring outlaws, was loaded with humiliation – escorted in public through the streets under guard, thrown into a dungeon for a fortnight, and then released without any charges being preferred.[3] After a generation of this sort of pressure, under Philip III and Philip IV, the senyors began to learn who was master. By the rein of Charles II the transformation was virtually complete, and the viceroy could write to Madrid: 'the nobility generally abhor the bandit'.[4]

But in a sense, perhaps, this triumph of Habsburg policy was counterproductive, in the same way as the dismantling of the feudal jurisdictions in nineteenth-century Sicily actually led to an extension of disorder. For in the countryside the maintenance of public order (such as it was) depended on the barons rather than the skeletal royal bureaucracy. In 1563, when their Moriscos had been disarmed, the barons warned the king: 'we ride out to right wrongs with these people, which we cannot do if the Moriscos are disarmed'.[5] And a few years later the Council of Aragon actually suggested a limited re-arming in

[1] ACA CA leg. 707, viceroy to king, 11 May 1622.
[2] ACA CA leg. 704, viceroy to king, 23 Oct. 1612.
[3] ARV R 519, *contrafur* 12 of 1626.
[4] ARV R 593 fols. 158–64, viceroy to king, 19 April 1689.
[5] Quoted in Halperin Donghi, 'Moriscos y cristianos viejos', *Cuadernos de Historia de España*, XXIII-IV, 66 n. 50.

order to combat the growing problem of lawlessness.[1] The fact of the matter was that the king's servants never had the resources at any time in the Habsburg period to replace effectively the old peace-keeping methods. In 1663 it was noted that banditry was worst in those parts of the Játiva district 'where few lords are in residence, and in the village of Manuel where the owner has little authority over his vassals'.[2] In 1690 the Audiencia invited the Duke of Gandía to chase the Palacios gang into the hills of Alcalalí in the hinterland of his own estates, 'in view of the remoteness of the place and the ruggedness of the terrain'.[3] The only problem here was that the Duke had not the forces to do the job very effectively, nor was he an easy colleague to cooperate with; twelve years earlier he had assassinated a royal bailiff who had issued a summons in Gandía without asking the ducal permission.[4] Senyors and royal judges were both weak, and spent more time sparring with each other than with the outlaws. 'These nobles must realize that their officers have less resources than ours', commented one viceroy, 'and without doubt the bandits would be easier to chase and punish if there were not so many private jurisdictions'.[5] The latter Habsburg period could be caricatured as a still from an old movie, in which two bumbling police officers have just collided with each other, allowing the criminal to get away.

In part what was happening as the senyors relaxed their grip on the countryside was a renascence of kin feuding among their vassals. 'You are hereby advised', the Duke of Gandía told his newly appointed bailiff of Albalat in 1594, 'that it is most urgent to stamp out an evil custom which has developed of late, whereby people who fall out with each other settle the matter with their arquebuses'.[6] Fifteen years later the same area round Albalat was the scene of bloody gang warfare between the Timors and the Talens, 'who go around killing anyone they know or think is their enemy or a friend of their rivals, even though they have done them no wrong'.[7]

[1] ACA CA leg. 582 n. 17/1, consulta (1580?).
[2] ACA CA leg. 580 n. 1/14, viceroy to king, 24 July 1663.
[3] ARV R 593, fol. 136, viceroy to king, 27 June 1690.
[4] ACA CA leg. 645 n. 84/25, viceroy to king, 29 Nov. 1678.
[5] ACA CA leg. 1357, viceroy to king, 21 March 1647.
[6] AHN Osuna leg. 696 n. 33, instructions for the *baile*, 24 Nov. 1594.
[7] ACA CA leg. 704, decree of 1609.

The phenomenon of the kin feud took root in a peasant world whose horizons were very narrow, and where there were ready-formed gangs, so to speak, in the rambling networks of cousins. Out of 492 marriages celebrated in Pedralba and Bugarra between 1610 and 1714, 2 were between first cousins, 17 between second or third cousins, and 29 between the children of third cousins. Virtually all of these occurred after the resettlement had come of age, after the new immigrants of 1610 had been there for about two generations. A fairer measure of the pressure towards consanguineous marriages might be to take the period 1670–1714. In this case approximately one marriage in five, as against one marriage in ten over the century as a whole, took place within the 'prohibited degrees' of the Catholic Church.[1] As well as the habit of marrying cousins, there was the rooted habit of marrying within a limited geographical area. If we take the period after 1630, by which time the bulk of the immigrants had arrived, we find that 106 of the 440 women who married, and 84 of the 418 men in the same category, chose partners from outside the parish. Nearly half the womenfolk married men from the next village – 47 of them married peasants from Gestalgar and Villamarchante, between 10 and 15 kilometres up and down stream respectively. Another 31 unions fall within a 20 to 25 kilometre radius, the distance to the next village but one. More of the men tended to stray farther afield, particularly to the city of Valencia where a quarter of those who married outside the parish found their brides. But the great majority confined their attention to the women of Gestalgar, Villamarchante or Chulilla. Symptomatic of the isolation in which these small communities seem often to have lived is the fairly high degree of rural illiteracy. Until a more systematic study has been made – impossible to make from the parish registers, which are rarely signed – the actual scale of the problem must remain unknown. The material for such an investigation exists in the judicial records, where witnesses were required to append their signature. From the few such documents which I have seen, I am tempted to conclude that nobody in the Valencian villages could do other than make a mark, except for the notary, the barber

[1] Archivo Parroquial de Pedralba, books of marriages, and banns for marriage outside the parish, 1610–1714.

and perhaps one or two wealthier peasants.[1] In other words, one seems to be dealing with a world which is in great measure closed in on itself, whose physical and mental horizons are extremely limited. It was in these conditions that the kin feud flourished in seventeenth-century Valencia once the restraining hand of the senyor was removed.

But the problem of banditry was not limited to the feud. Inevitably men who had been put under the ban of the law for this offence had to branch out into highway robbery in order to keep themselves fed. Already in 1586 the Morisco Solaya, who had a price on his head for feuding, 'since he attracted to himself a lot of assassins and youthful desperadoes, made it impossible for anyone to travel without fear of being robbed or murdered'.[2] A hundred years later, the viceroy of the day dismissed kin feuding as no longer significant. These outlaws, he told Madrid, are nothing but 'bands of thieves, highwaymen, murderers, and criminals of every kind...who spare neither the life nor the purse of the traveller, nor the horse which the peasant uses to plough'.[3] A document of the middle years of the century, called, appropriately enough, 'case histories of atrocious crimes', shows these freely available gunmen helping a shady notary to secure an official appointment, a tax-farmer to frighten off a rival bidder, a jealous husband to get even with his wife's lover.[4] 'As soon as night falls', noted the French traveller Joly in 1603, 'you cannot go out without a buckler and a coat of mail in Valencia, for there is no town in all Spain where so many murders are committed, and every morning they find someone in the gutter'.[5] One cannot, therefore, blame the generalized lawlessness of Habsburg Valencia on blood feuds, either among the nobility or among the peasantry. Nor will it do to put the phenomenon down to petty thievery. The fact that the bandits survived so long on such a wide scale points, as with the Mafia, to protectors in high places.

[1] AHN Osuna leg. 1026 nos. 4–5, leg. 816 (Lombay 1667), and leg. 746 nos. 30–41; ARV MR 10087, 10089, 10098 and 10101. And cf. ARV R 683 where the townsmen of Alcira dismissed the inhabitants of Alberique, one of the biggest and most developed villages in the kingdom: 'you will hardly find a person there who can read or write' (1618). [2] Escolano, *Décadas*, II, 767.
[3] ARV R 593 fols. 158–64, viceroy to king, 19 April 1689.
[4] ACA CA leg. 582, 'exemplares de delitos atrozes' (1650?).
[5] Joly, 'Voyage en Espagne', *Revue Hispanique*, xx (1909), 518.

The sheer size of the gangs, at least in the early seventeenth century, is the first clue which we have to go on. The bands roaming the Júcar Valley 'have occasionally numbered over 100 men, most of them on horseback, and so overbearing that they do not shrink from entering big towns to execute their evil designs and exact their revenge'.[1] The equipment involved – one viceroy paid out 1,900 *lliures* for the horses taken from one amnestied gang in 1647 – suggests that these were not petty desperadoes, but the private armies of local potentates.[2] Where the names are given, it is possible to identify many of the bandit leaders as powerful individuals in their community. The Ayz and Gisbert in Alcoy belonged to two families which both held the post of royal bailiff in the town; the Linares of Villajoyosa must have been related to the Jaime Linares who was deputy for the town in the Cortes of 1645; the Palacios, who were the scourge of Alcalalí in the 1680s, were also big tithe-farmers in the area in the 1690s; the famous bandit Monreal of Alcira was pardoned in 1636 when he agreed to enlist in Captain Monreal's company of soldiers; the outlawed Vicente Escrivá of Carlet was chief justice of the town; his associates, the Talens of Carcagente, were royal bailiffs of that town; and finally the gangsters of the city of Valencia itself, the Anglesolas, Minuartes, Escales, Adells, Zapatas, Sanz and the rest, were among the most powerful financiers and politicians of Philip IV's reign.[3]

Not many of these men, of course, shed blood with their own hands. They had their hatchet-men for that – generally under the command of some unemployed cleric in minor orders, who had what was known evocatively as a 'perch', a benefice which effectively put him outside the reach of the king's courts and left him to be tried only by his ecclesiastical superiors.[4] For added protection, their patrons, the Anglesolas and others, often

---

[1] ACA CA leg. 725, viceroy to king, 21 May 1647.

[2] ACA CA leg. 726, consulta, 25 Feb. 1647.

[3] I have pieced together the biographical details from ARV MR 5534-49, *tercio diezmo* of Alcoy; ACA CA leg. 1356, petition of Jaime Linares 1645; ACV *arriendo de diezmos* 4397, 1697-1700; ACA CA leg. 712, 16 Dec. 1636 (Monreal); leg. 704, dr. Vaziero to viceroy, 6 Aug. 1611 (from Carlet); ARV MR 5628-33, *tercio diezmo* of Carcagente. On the feuds in Valencia city, Casey, 'Crisi General', *passim*.

[4] ACA CA legs. 707, viceroy to king, 11 May 1611; leg. 725, viceroy and archbishop to king, 13 Aug. 1647; leg. 727, consulta of Audiencia, 27 March 1649; and leg. 589, consulta of Council on this report, 28 July 1649.

secured a post as Familiar of the Inquisition, a job as spy which was open to laymen and which exempted them in most criminal proceedings from the royal courts. For the Council of Aragon in 1632 there was no doubt that 'the administration of justice in the kingdom of Valencia suffers from the great number of people who are under the protection of the Holy Office, every viceroy having pointed this out as the biggest single source of trouble'.[1] One wonders if they were right – or if the real problem was that the bandit leaders or patrons anyway worked in the shadows, like authentic Mafia bosses, and rarely got themselves mixed up in crimes.

The ramifications of banditry were very extensive throughout the higher levels of this society, penetrating even into ministerial cricles. Judge Rejaule 'is proud of the many connections and friends he has', wrote one viceroy, 'and I am afraid these friendships rule him'.[2] Judge Sancho was an open enemy of the Anglesola faction; his colleague Judge Sanz was a declared friend of the Anglesolas.[3] Eventually in 1638 Rejaule and Sancho were dismissed; Sanz was suspended, investigated, reinstated and then shot dead as he was taking the air in his garden one hot summer evening of 1642.[4] The Anglesolas had patrons too in the high aristocracy, in the fifth Marquis of Guadalest, while their enemies the Minuartes found sanctuary not only with the archbishop but with the Treasurer General of the Crown of Aragon and ex-viceroy of Naples, the first Duke of Medina de las Torres, resident in Valencia in the later 1640s.[5] The Anglesola connection extended to the Pascual family of Alicante, who provided several judges during the seventeenth century, and who were struggling to establish their ascendancy in the south against the wealthy Palavecinos. Naturally the Palavecinos had their hired killers, and their shadowy protectors, the Minuartes, the archbishop and the archbishop's client don Pedro de Villacampa, who was appointed Regent of the

[1] ACA CA leg. 685, consulta, 21 July 1632. There were 180 Familiars in the city of Valencia alone, as against only 50 each in Granada and Seville, cf. leg. 648, viceroy to king, 7 March 1634.
[2] ACA CA leg. 717, viceroy to king, 12 Oct. 1638.
[3] ACA CA leg. 716, viceroy to king, 19 Dec. 1638.
[4] ACA CA leg. 715, consulta, 10 Dec. 1638; leg. 721, viceroy to king, 19 Aug. 1642.
[5] ACA CA leg. 660, consulta, 14 Aug. 1647; leg. 721, viceroy to king, 16 Nov. 1641.

Council of Aragon in 1645.[1] The bandit Jaime Lloret, who
terrorized the Júcar Valley, was alleged to find shelter with the
Count of Carlet, who was at daggers drawn with don Pablo
Zanoguera, Treasurer of the kingdom. And, of course, the
Count of Carlet was believed to be under the protection of his
cousin, don Francisco de Castelví, Regent of the Council of
Aragon from 1617 until his death in 1638.[2] And so the list reads
on. Many of the Valencian Regents of Philip IV's reign –
Castelví, Villacampa, Mingot and Sisternes – had bandit connections or a violent past. One can, indeed, think of only two
– at least up to 1650 – against whom no breath of scandal was
ever recorded: that earnest, small-time lawyer, Francisco Jerónimo León, and the dour don Cristóbal Crespí (the man who
never went to bullfights until his promotion as Vice-chancellor,
'for then it seemed I should go out of official duty'[3]). But the
others were the colourful products of a faction-rent society.

There were, then, three tiers to the bandit – or perhaps we
should call it the Mafia – phenomenon. There were the common
criminals who did most of the dirty work – the thieves and
murderers on the fringes of the gangs, whom the viceroy urged
to be excluded from the amnesty of 1642.[4] Then there came
the 'employers', who seem to have belonged to what one may
loosely call a middle class – wealthy peasants, royal bailiffs,
ciutadans and *cavallers*. These people were very hard to convict
through the courts either because they were respectable citizens,
like the big mill-owner don Francisco de Villacampa (probably
a descendant of the Regent), who actually built up his following
by pretending to reform bandits, or because they held ecclesiastical immunity.[5] And, fading even further into the shadows,
there were the prominent public figures – the great aristocrats,
the king's judges, the ministers of the Council of Aragon, who
often found some advantage, or recognized some obligation of
kinship, in helping their dependants.

The violence was attributed to various causes. The French
traveller, Joly, thought it was due to the temperament of the

[1] ACA CA leg. 882, petition of Laura Pascual, 9 Oct. 1641.
[2] ACA CA leg. 703, Count of Carlet to king, 8 Nov. 1611; leg. 867, petition of Countess
of Carlet (1618?); leg. 625, consulta, 29 April 1629.
[3] *Diario*, fol. 5, 1 July 1652. [4] ACA CA leg. 722, viceroy to king, 7 Nov. 1642.
[5] ARV R 593 fols. 143 ff., viceroy to king, 6 Dec. 1689.

Valencians: 'they are quick-tempered, drawing their sword for the merest trifle'. Most of their killings, he went on, 'are caused by women, who have the reputation of being very passionate because of the climate'.[1] The government tended more prosaically to blame the technological revolution represented by the invention of the flintlock, which was placing deadly firepower at the disposal of the ordinary citizen for the first time in the seventeenth century. Defending their right to fire-arms, the assembly of the nobility noted: 'they are often carried by our youngsters without the least intention of causing bodily harm'.[2] Perhaps – but bloodshed was all too common among a class so punctilious on a point of honour. That honour could, of course, be compromised most grievously by the behaviour of the female members of the family. Apart from the question of emotional outrage, there was the very rational consideration that a wayward wife or sister could bring financial loss, for the women carried the property which bound two families together, and it was to the formation of their dowries that most of the disposal assets of a household were pledged. Aping the manners of Boccaccio's Florentine patricians, the brothers don Juan and don Francisco Sanz shot and killed their sister for attempting to marry someone of whom they disapproved.[3] When don Jerónimo Ferrer slept with doña Juana Carroz in 1591 he sparked off a row between their two families which had the Council of Aragon seriously worried for a while, 'since the two clans comprise the greater part of the nobility of the realm'.[4] The Count of Buñol hired a gang of thugs to beat up his brother-in-law, the Marquis of Quirra, who had stolen a march on him by marrying the daughter of the Count of Real, whom Buñol had intended for his own son.[5] Meanwhile a long feud raged in the far south of the kingdom between the senyor of Agres and the family of his estranged wife, doña Leonor de Pallás, with first the murder of a Pallás in 1612, and then the shooting dead of the lord of Agres himself.[6]

[1] 'Voyage en Espagne', 518.   [2] *Fur* 29 of the Cortes of 1626.
[3] ACA CA leg. 655, consulta, 12 July 1632.
[4] BL Add. MSS. 28,375 fol. 206, consulta, 1591.
[5] ACA CA leg. 653, consulta, 30 Oct. 1608.
[6] ACA CA leg. 704, correspondence of viceroy, 11 Aug. 1611 and 30 Oct. 1612, and leg. 640, consulta, 29 April 1623.

But women were often just pawns in a game of influence between impoverished and power-hungry local potentates, whether at the level of the village or the region. The Anglesola feud, for example, involved 'a woman of few obligations', but it developed political overtones as the Anglesolas helped the viceroy, the Count of Oropesa, dispose of the *jurats* in office in 1646, who were linked with the old Minuarte gang – only to turn against Oropesa at a later stage when he tried to break their hold on city government.[1] At a lower level, the Talens of Carcagente had more in mind than the defence of family honour when they recruited their gunmen. Josep Talens was bailiff of Carcagente under Philip IV, and as such was entrusted with supervising the draw for the *insaculació* every year. But 'when he had to read out the names of those drawn as *justicias* or *jurats* he paid no heed to what was written on the ballot papers, which he was the only one to see, but called out the names of his friends instead'.[2] One of his opponents protested and was shot dead, and subsequently two of the Talens faction were murdered in retaliation. No doubt this sort of power struggle was nothing new. It may, however, have developed a greater intensity in the seventeenth century as the urban elites became narrower and more exclusive. The wreck of the *censals* after the expulsion of the Moriscos must also have sharpened their appetite for the profits of office.

Violence bolstered the power of the local elites, and it also strengthened their economic position. The Talens of Carcagente were prominent in the silk trade of the area. With mulberry becoming scarcer in the reign of Philip III, they and their like sent 'bands of men, six, eight, ten and twelve strong, all on horseback and armed with pistols, to take all the leaf they need, under the nose of the crestfallen owner, who cannot and dare not open his mouth'.[3] The silk thus acquired was then smuggled out to Toledo without paying duty, the gangs 'armed with shotguns, crossbows and the like, riding by night or at other unwonted times along unfrequented paths'.[4] Much later, in the reign of Charles II, one of the factious Pascuals (then a royal

[1] ACA CA leg. 623, viceroy to king, 1 Feb. 1649.
[2] ACA CA leg. 632, governor of Valencia to king, 9 Nov. 1627.
[3] ACA CA leg. 726, petition of the city of Valencia (1621?).
[4] ACA CA leg. 714, *pragmática de la seda*, 1623.

minister) denounced his fellow citizens of Alicante for smuggling in wool from Castile for embarkation, 'the convoys staying clear of the roads, and escorted by gangs of armed men'.[1] It is inevitably difficult to quantify the sort of damage done to the Valencian economy by this channelling of entrepreneurial talents into commercial rackets rather than into the production of more mulberry or more wool. The *Mafiosi* are the characteristic product of underdevelopment, but they then contribute powerfully to the maintenance of the status quo.

Is it arguable whether the bandits of seventeenth-century Valencia were outlaws or rebels? They seem to have had no potential at all for revolution, because they were manipulated by those who held power within the existing structure. Such banditry is perhaps best defined as a struggle of persons and groups for power in a society no longer controlled by the old feudal nobility. The private armies of the senyors had disappeared, but the government had neither the cohesiveness nor the force to impose more orderly, competitive norms on this society. 'There is no doubt, Sire', the Marquis of Castelnovo told Charles II, 'that the soil of Valencia throws up criminals in the same way that it sprouts wheat or barley, for their seed is virtually impossible to root out in that whole area'. Nevertheless, he went on, 'when those in government are as diligent as they ought to be, the damage can be contained'.[2] Underlying the whole problem seemed to be the softness or incompetence of Habsburg rule.

A basic obstacle here was the inadequacy of the forces at the disposal of the viceroy and Audiencia – 14 *alguaciles* (each of whom was supposed to provide his own horse and an assistant or slave), plus an ill-trained ceremonial guard of 50.[3] Against bandit gangs 100 strong special measures were sometimes taken. The least frequent of these was the calling out of the militia, for the simple reason (pointed out by one minister) that most of the militiamen would be kinsmen or friends of the bandits.[4]

[1] ACA CA leg. 607 n. 38/28, don Francisco Pascual de Ibarra to viceroy, 11 Sept. 1687.
[2] ACA CA leg. 581, consulta, 29 Aug. 1692.
[3] ACA CA leg. 879, memorandum on the post of *alguacil*; ARV R 593 fols. 158–64, viceroy to king, 19 April 1689, on the inadequacies of the ceremonial guard.
[4] ACA CA leg. 703, viceroy to king, 22 July 1615.

Instead the viceroys tended to rely on a specially sworn posse (*batallón*), sent into an affected area under an *alguacil* or a judge of the Audiencia. A first step here was to threaten the local authorities in the hope that they would bestir themselves – as in 1615 when the town council of Alcira, faced with the arrival of Judge Gil from Valencia 'who says he will bring in soldiers at our expense', resolved that its own magistrates should round up a posse of 25 men to sweep the territory.[1] In fact, the *batallón* was only used as a last resort because of the amount it cost the royal treasury – nearly 1,200 *lliures* for a 15-day campaign. Though this expense was usually reimbursed by fines levied on the troubled communities, the bankruptcy of the Valencian towns counselled moderation here, and both the Cortes of 1626 and 1645 secured promises from Philip IV that only he and not the viceroy could authorize such campaigns.[2]

Inevitably the government had to adopt alternative methods. The most popular, perhaps, was that of setting a thief to catch a thief, by commissioning one faction to pursue its enemies. But these *comisiones* often went wrong – as when young Vicente Morell, out to catch his uncle's murderers, was himself ambushed and killed by a gang which had now swollen to 60.[3] As one viceroy pointed out: 'if the parties so commissioned actually catch anyone (a rare enough event in itself), they only conjure up another half-dozen delinquents, kinsmen or friends of the man who was captured, who are fired with resentment at falling victim to private hatreds rather than to the forces of law and order'.[4] Unable to get to grips directly with the outlaws, the authorities tried to harass those who gave them shelter. By an edict of 1586 all the family, including cousins, of wanted men were threatened with expulsion from the kingdom after one month if they did not hand over their guilty relatives. Measures of this type were used at intervals thereafter, but they were not at all common. As the Council of Aragon declared from the outset: 'it is a thing so repugnant to our sense of fairness,

[1] AMA 03/132, deliberation of 18 July 1615.
[2] ACA CA leg. 659, viceroy to king, 19 March 1647; *fur* 17 of 1626, and article 154 of Braç Real, 1645.   [3] ACA CA leg. 710, viceroy to king, 21 Aug. 1635.
[4] ARV R 593 fols. 158–64, viceroy to king, 19 April 1689.

and anyway it goes against the laws of the kingdom'. And in the Cortes of 1604 Philip III promised not to adopt this method again.[1]

To solve the problem, the government was tempted at regular intervals to offer amnesties to the warring factions. There had always been an idea anyway that violence was primarily an affair of the kinship group rather than of society at large. Thus Vicente Ayz was allowed to purchase his pardon from the death sentence in 1625 because he obtained the forgiveness of the widow of the man he murdered, and a similar pardon was sold to Blas Ruiz because his victim was a Frenchman with no kin.[2] Faced with generalized lawlessness, the ministers of Philip IV recognized the need for total amnesties, if only because 'the guilty are so numerous that you cannot hang them all without tremendous bloodshed'.[3] The conditions conformed to a general pattern under Philip IV and Charles II, that the outlaws should enlist in the army for service in Naples or Milan. As a short-term expedient it was probably one of the most successful means ever devised for getting rid of troublemakers. The only problem was that it had no permanence: within a few years the bandits filtered back and renewed their activities.

But at least it solved the difficulty, not only of how to catch a bandit, but (perhaps more important) how to convict him. 'The laws of Valencia', noted the Council of Aragon in 1623, 'leave little room for the sort of diligence in prosecuting crime characteristic of these kingdoms [of Castile], nor do the penalties match the gravity of the offence'.[4] Justice in old-world Valencia was above all popular justice. The courts of first instance – those of the municipal *justicias* – operated according to a jury system in the case of serious crimes. The local citizen assembly alone had the power of conviction or acquittal, by majority vote, and official observers found it incredibly primitive 'that a collection of peasants, inevitably in smaller communities kinsmen or

---

[1] ACA CA leg. 582 n. 17/1, consulta (1580?); AMV Churat 1634 vol. 1 n. 11, decree of 1586; *contrafur* 2 of Cortes of 1604. For the continued use of this method after 1604, ARV Comunes 944, 20 May 1622.

[2] ACA CA leg. 658, consulta, 25 March 1625; leg. 885, petition of Blas Ruiz, 26 Nov. 1642.   [3] ACA CA leg. 725, viceroy to king, 23 June 1647.

[4] ACA CA leg. 1357, consulta, 11 March 1623.

friends of the accused, should have absolute authority as judges, without even having to explain their verdict'. It was no surprise, therefore, that 'there are so many atrocious crimes committed in this kingdom...The only wonder is that there are not more of them, given that the perpetrators get off so lightly'.[1] Even if the public prosecutor appealed to the Audiencia against an acquittal (as he had the right to do), the law intervened at every stage to protect the accused. A man could not be held for more than two days without charges being preferred; he had to be brought to trial within five days, or within forty in the case of a capital offence, 'otherwise he goes free from gaol'. Torture was limited to 'the glove, the rope and the weights' (excluding fire), and could not be applied to minors under the age of eighteen.[2] But the main obstacle to conviction, even before the professional judges of the Audiencia, was the need for witnesses. Because of the disturbed nature of this society, the church had apparently allowed people called to testify the privilege of telling half-truths (*amphibologías*) in order to protect themselves against retaliation.[3] In true Mafia fashion, the big Valencian trials ended in the acquittal of the bandit chiefs for lack of evidence.

When things got out of hand, however, the government had to take a sterner line. With people who overreached themselves, the viceroy or the Council of Aragon would be compelled to invoke the *poder económico* – the king's 'reserve power' of detaining or exiling his subjects in the interests of public safety. This milder equivalent of the notorious *lettre de cachet* of the French monarchy could be as much or as little of a menace as the government of the day chose. In general, the Council of Aragon was too unsure of its own moral authority in the matter to employ the device too frequently. In 1662 it drew up a list of 31 prominent Valencians whom it would be desirable to remove from the kingdom as patrons of bandits. They included the Marquis of Guadalest, three canons, the son of the Maestre Racional, the son of one of the wealthiest Italian financiers, Constantino Cernesio, and a host of nobles. The

[1] ACA CA leg. 713, *Visitador* don Martín Funes to king, 3 July 1635.
[2] Information scattered through ARV R 537 fol. 40 and 538 fol. 52, ACA CA leg. 589, *memorial de contrafurs* (1647?), and cf. *contrafur* 112 of 1626.
[3] ACA CA leg. 720, viceroy to king, 22 July 1641.

prospective purge seems to have unnerved the Council, which shrank from 'ordering out so many people all at once' and duly shelved the report.[1]

Such laxness invariably dismayed Castilian viceroys, who were tempted to take the law into their own hands from time to time, stringing up the odd Mafia boss without trial.[2] 'It has been well said', affirmed the Marquis of Castel Rodrigo, 'that as long as there are *fueros*, there will be bandits'.[3] There was a threat here, never realized, that only when Valencian society and government was remodelled along Castilian lines would the problem of disorder be solved. The Estaments and the Cortes were fully aware of the danger. The *batallones*, the *poder económico*, arbitrary arrest, harassment of kin, the growth of the number of *alguaciles* – every single item in the government's anti-bandit paraphernalia came under attack at some time or other in the seventeenth century as unconstitutional and a menace to the liberty of the subject. There were the makings of political conflict here. But fortunately for the loyalty of the kingdom, there were buffers which absorbed most of the shock. The Audiencia and the Council of Aragon itself were too closely identified with the fears and aspirations of the Valencian elite to countenance any major infringement of the constitution. Instead, Valencia played its own game of tearing itself to pieces with little interference from outside.

[1] ACA CA leg. 582 n. 45/2, memorandum, 7 April 1662.
[2] The fate of Tomás Anglesola in 1648, ACA CA leg. 589, consulta, 15 May 1648, and later of don Ramón Sans, ARV R 542, *Elets de Contrafurs*, 22 July 1667. It should be noted that the Council of Aragon censured the Anglesola execution, reminding the viceroy that only the king could take lives without trial; leg. 589, consulta, 28 Dec. 1648.
[3] ACA CA leg. 930, viceroy to secretary Haro, 25 March 1692.

10

The loyal kingdom

If in most matters of government the kingdom was left to its own devices, in the realm of defence it was required to play a more active role in support of the Monarchy. The policy of the Union of Arms, elaborated under the Count Duke of Olivares in the 1620s, aimed to spread Spain's military burden a little more evenly instead of allowing it to fall mainly on an exhausted Castile. The scheme came spectacularly to grief, of course, in Catalonia, where it provoked the great revolt of 1640. And that fatal decade saw revolts throughout the peripheral provinces – Portugal, Naples, Sicily, even Aragon if we count the abortive conspiracy of the Duke of Híjar.[1] Standing like a rock in the tempest was Valencia.

In the Cortes of 1626 the kingdom agreed to give 1,080,000 *lliures* for the Union of Arms.[2] In 1630 and until 1642 'voluntary' levies raised and equipped by senyors and towns in reply to requests from the Crown became a new and regular feature of the Valencian scene.[3] Combined with ordinary recruiting on the open market by commissioned officers, these campaigns may have drained 12,000 or 14,000 young adult males from the kingdom by 1637.[4] From 1637, in fact, the policy took a new turn, when a form of general conscription was introduced – one man was taken from every 100 households to serve a summer campaign against the French, who were then intensifying their

---

[1] J. H. Elliott, 'Revolts in the Spanish Monarchy', in Robert Forster and Jack P. Greene, eds., *Preconditions of Revolution in Early Modern Europe* (The Johns Hopkins Press 1970), 109–30.

[2] ACA CA leg. 1372, offer of the three Braços, 19 March 1626.

[3] ACA CA legs. 555–6, 563–71, and 606, levies in Valencia; legs. 70–27, correspondence of viceroys dealing with levies, billeting and finance.

[4] ACA CA leg. 715, petition of Estament Eclesiàstic, 1637, and leg. 712, viceroy to king, 8 Aug. 1636.

223

pressure along the Pyrenees.[1] Though Olivares judged it prudent to suspend conscription in Valencia in the summer of 1640, after the Catalans had come out in revolt and in view of persistent reports from the viceroy that the Valencians would soon follow suit, by 1642 the Estates took over responsibility for defence. They had been approached unsuccessfully every year since 1634, but now, given the imminent threat of a French invasion from rebel Catalonia, they agreed to find 2,000 men to guard their own frontier on condition that all other levies were called off.[2] The effort was repeated in 1644 with 1,200 men, and in 1645 with 1,000. Eventually in the Cortes of 1645 (the last in Valencian history) the policy of cooperation was formally consecrated, when the Valencians promised 1,200 troops a year for six years to hold the key fortress of Tortosa, which guarded the Ebro crossing. Prolonging the period of observation, one notes that throughout the reign of Charles II the Valencians continued to offer – through the Estates – contingents of 400 or 500 men in critical years to ward off French attacks on Catalonia.[3] The Union of Arms appeared to have triumphed in Valencia, if not without opposition (particularly between 1634 and 1640), at least without bloodshed.

The secret of this success was partly, no doubt, that the weight of the military burden was less in Valencia than in other parts of the Monarchy. The kingdom was rarely in the front line of conflict; even after 1640 almost all the fighting took place for strategic reasons along the border between Aragon and Catalonia.[4] For this reason Valencia saw little of the billeting which played so direct a part in the Catalan revolt. Yet ultimately, one may feel, the refusal of Valencia to go the way of Catalonia can only be explained in terms of differences in political structure. 'We regard the Valencians as softer than the rest', Olivares is alleged to have blurted out on one occasion.[5] Whatever the basis for this statement in the sphere of tem-

---

[1] ACA CA leg. 564, consulta, 10 Nov. 1638; leg. 722, viceroy to king, 25 March 1642.
[2] ARV R 527–40, Deliberations of the Estament Militar 1609–50. For a more detailed discussion of the levies of the 1630s and 1640s, James Casey, 'The Spanish Province of Valencia 1609–50' (Cambridge University Ph.D. thesis 1968), 146–85.
[3] García Martínez, *Valencia bajo Carlos II, passim.*
[4] José Sanabre, *La Acción de Francia en Cataluña* (Barcelona 1956).
[5] Dormer, *Anales de Aragón,* fol. 201.

perament or psychology, it reflected an accurate perception of where the balance of power really lay in the eastern kingdom.

Valencia, according to its chronicler Escolano, was 'a commonwealth at once free and yet subject to its king and lord'[1] This mixed monarchy was governed by the traditional laws, the *furs*, which were promulgated through the parliament or Cortes, and which, as the Valencians once reminded an apathetic Charles II, 'you will find printed on our hearts no less than in books'.[2] Every king was supposed to swear to these laws at his accession. And indeed the sight of the master of two continents kneeling before his Valencian subjects, with his hand placed on a bible or missal, repeating the solemn words *yo lo juro*, was calculated to impress on all those who witnessed it the idea that the monarch was in no sense absolute.

The relationship between the king and the Valencians was conceived of as a contract: in return for respecting their liberties, their master claimed the loyalty of his subjects. As the ecclesiastical estate once put it to Philip IV: 'We have before our minds the example of Ferdinand [the Catholic]. Some advised him on becoming king of Castile and Aragon to bring the Aragonese under a firmer yoke because they enjoyed too much freedom. But he retorted that he was heir to a long tradition...and that anyway he had a rule as regards lord and vassal, which was that where there was a balance of advantage, both parties would do very well'.[3] To maintain and defend this contractual relationship Valencia had the representative institutions which characterized the other realms of the Crown of Aragon, in particular the three estates of clergy, nobles and towns, which could assemble whenever they wanted to on a summons from their elected presidents. It was on these bodies above all that the responsibility fell of checking the illegalities (*contrafurs*) perpetrated by the king and his servants.

The Ecclesiastical Estate (*Estament Eclesiàstic*) consisted of four bishops (Valencia, Orihuela, Segorbe, and Tortosa), five abbots or priors (Valldigna, Benifassar, San Miguel de los Reyes, Valdecristo, and Poblet), deputies of the four episcopal chap-

---

[1] *Décadas*, I, 545.
[2] AMV Churat 1634 vol. III n. 115, petition of the ambassador of the Estates (1690?).
[3] ACA CA leg. 715, petition of the Estament Eclesiàstic, 1637.

ters, deputies of the five Military Orders (Santiago, Calatrava, Alcántara, St John, and Montesa), and finally the head of the Mercedarian Order (whose task of ransoming Christian captives from Moorish captivity was close to the heart of all Valencians).[1] One notices the intrusion of three representatives from Catalonia – the two deputies from Tortosa and the abbot of Poblet – as well as the presence of five knights of the Orders of Chivalry. Nine out of the nineteen deputies owed their position to royal favour, since it was the king who appointed the bishops and the knights. Only the abbots and the canons constituted an autonomous element – though in fact the king also appointed many of the canons of the small diocese of Orihuela (erected under royal patronage in the later sixteenth century to evangelize the Moriscos of the south), so that in real terms he had an inbuilt majority of the votes in the estate.[2] In Catalonia the canons were the backbone of the clerical Estate, stubborn, fractious and immune from royal influence. In Valencia the chapter of Orihuela was emasculated, that of Segorbe was too desperately poor and backward to pull any political weight, and all real power lay with the extremely wealthy canons of the metropolis.[3] But the latter were already important enough to be candidates for bishoprics, like don Francisco López de Mendoza, deputy of the Valencian chapter in the Cortes of 1626, president *ex officio* of the Ecclesiastical Estate and one of Philip IV's most loyal servants, who was rewarded for his services in 1626 with the bishopric of Elna.[4] Perhaps typically, the only dissentient voice in these Cortes came from the Catalan representative, Canon Pere Jaume Bru of the chapter of Tortosa, who refused any subsidy from his Church to the Crown.[5]

The Estament Real or Third Estate was also very weak. In the first place, outside the time of a Cortes, no town but the city of Valencia was allowed to be represented. After the Cortes of 1585 the Crown took steps to dissolve a union of these towns for fear it would strengthen the popular Estate; and after those

[1] Mateu, *Cortes Generales*, 77–8.
[2] Gonzalo Vidal Tur, *Un obispado español: el de Orihuela-Alicante*, II, 127–8.
[3] Segorbe was also created a bishopric under Philip II; see Mateu, *De Regimine*, 190. For its inadequate financing, ARV R 521, chapter 4 of Estament Eclesiàstic, 1645.
[4] *Coses evengudes*, II, chapter 2872.
[5] ACA CA leg. 1353, offer, of 5 March 1626. Cf. Elliott, *Revolt of the Catalans*, 243–4.

of 1645 the Council of Aragon warned the king of the 'disadvantages of allowing any deputy from the towns to sit with those of the city of Valencia' in administering the subsidy just granted.[1] This long-standing aim of royal policy was motivated by the fact that the government of the metropolis was more firmly controlled by the Crown than that of any other community. Even after the *insaculació* of 1633, the king could prevent undesirable candidates from being voted into the lists from which city officials were drawn; before 1633 the proud *jurats*, *racional* and *síndic*, the eight men who constituted the Estament Real, were little better than royal nominees. The hegemony of the city, of course, was reinforced by her economic superiority – though this did not prevent rivalry and disputes breaking out between her and the other towns of the kingdom whenever they met together in the Cortes. In 1626 the city's demand for half the votes in parliament was opposed by the smaller fry 'with very angry debate', and in 1645 the exclusion of the Valencian deputies by the king because they had not come with plenipotentiary powers was approved with indecent haste by a majority of their colleagues.[2] The struggle for power between the capital and her satellites was a weakening factor in the Estament Real, which played straight into the hands of the Crown.

The real force behind the 'free commonwealth' of Valencia was the Noble Estate, which contained the more than 500 individuals in the kingdom (excluding the knights of the Military Orders) who could lay claim to gentility. Unlike the other two Estates, in which were was a carefully graded order of speaking and voting according to traditional rules of seniority, the Estament Militar was a chaotic jumble of individuals whose meetings were liable to end in riot, 'for almost all its members come with a sword...and if one draws his, then friends and kinsmen place themselves by his side'.[3] In such a body there was no question of majority voting: to have any chance of success resolutions had to be unanimous, *nemine discrepante*. This famous privilege (which one royal minister

[1] ACA CA leg. 725, consulta, 1 Sept. 1646.
[2] AMV Cortes 30 fol. 4, 31 Jan. 1626; 31, 13 Nov. 1645.
[3] Mateu, *Cortes Generales*, 135.

lampooned as a sixteenth-century innovation and 'contrary to the ordinary rule of law which allows majorities the right to speak for all'[1]) could cause enormous problems for the king when he sought a subsidy. On the other hand it had its uses for the authorities, making it difficult for the Estament to agree on opposing royal policy. The classic instance of this was the expulsion of the Moriscos, when the Noble Estate was so hamstrung by its internal divisions that it could do nothing until it was too late. Even on 14 September 1609, when there was general agreement on sending an embassy of protest to Madrid, the opposition of just one man, don Jerónimo Rebolledo (perhaps a stooge of the viceroy) held up a final resolution for another couple of days.[2]

And yet the Estament Militar was 'the sinews of this kingdom', the body to which the other two estates invariably deferred on every matter of public importance. No assembly could have held the centre of the political stage for so long without some form of discipline. Bringing order out of chaos was the president, *Síndic*, of the estate, an influential figure drawn by lot every two years from a list of ten candidates.[3] These ten in turn were chosen for life by a complicated process of indirect election designed to guard against the influence of factions. First, a panel of *examinadors* was elected by secret ballot to scrutinize the claims of all members, and then, from the list of names they approved, a lucky draw determined the successful candidate.[4] It was up to the Síndic to call meetings, propose business, regulate the order of speaking, and generally by his 'prestige and wisdom' to neutralize the factions. The theoretical rigidity of the rule of unanimity, meanwhile, could be circumvented in practice – as in 1609 when Rebolledo was eventually thrown out of the room, or on the famous occasion quoted by one authority: 'I once witnessed a youthful knight obstinately opposing a good decision, till a sage elder called out – "let this motion be carried and I will see to it that our friend agrees" – to which the abashed youth had no reply.'[5] Inevitably, political experience, age, and the prestige of family all determined a certain hier-

---

[1] *Ibid.*, 91–2.   [2] Fonseca, *Justa expulsión*, 28–9.
[3] ARV R 528 fol. 70, 25 Aug. 1612; 529 fol. 362v., 28 Oct. 1619, etc.
[4] ARV R 538 fol. 268, 7 May 1640.   [5] Mateu, *Cortes Generales*, 134–5.

archy, and made the Estament Militar less anarchic than one might suppose.

Yet it remained a cumbersome, slow-moving machine. Often enough agreement could only be reached on the general outlines of a problem, and then it was left to a small elected committee, meeting with the Síndic, to decide by a majority vote on the details of execution. These committees of *Elets* were chosen, like the president, in a very roundabout way, characteristic of the age – by lot from a list of names approved by *examinadors*, the latter being either elected directly, or sometimes (in very controversial matters) nominated by a panel of so-called *electors*, who were themselves drawn by lot from the body of the Estament.[1] Despite all these elaborate precautions, it was still sometimes possible for one faction to dominate the committee. Thus on 21 July 1622 the Estament Militar agreed that the kingdom was passing through a grave economic crisis; on 26 October 1623 the small panel of *Elets* set up to remedy the problem resolved that it was all due to the failure of the senyors to pay the *censals*, and they despatched an embassy of protest to Madrid, despite the outraged protests of the senyors.[2]

The events of 1622–3 – and indeed those of 1609 – highlight one very important point: the Estament Militar could never be the representative of all the nobility because the latter were too numerous, too scattered, and too divided in their interests. The meetings, which were always held in the city of Valencia, only needed a quorum of 25; the most controversial issues of the age, such as the resolution of 16 September 1609 against the expulsion of the Moriscos or the presentation of the Union of Arms on 20 December 1625, attracted 70 and 168 participants respectively.[3] Perhaps surprisingly, only eight lords of Moriscos were actually present at the earlier date, but then September was in the summer season when the senyors had scattered from the metropolis to their country seats.[4] Inevitably, power within the Estament Militar passed to a clique of politically active individuals, resident in the city of Valencia, whose names recur time after time, both in the records of debates and in the social

[1] ARV R 528, fol. 69v., 27 July 1612; 527 fol. 396, 17 Sept. 1609, etc.
[2] AHN Osuna leg. 899 n. 1, 'las razones que ay para que no sea casso de embaxada el que aora se offrece' (1623?).   [3] ARV R 527 fol. 399; 530 fol. 492v.
[4] At least their womenfolk were there; see Escolano, *Décadas*, II, 785.

chronicles of the time. In Philip III's reign, the outstanding figures were the Counts of Anna, Buñol, Castellar, and perhaps Alacuás as well – a handful of men whose habits of residence and styles of life gave them a preponderant influence on political life, whose epicentre was always the city of Valencia. The eight magnate families – the Dukes of Gandía and the rest – played no active role in the Estates. They were mostly not resident in the city of Valencia anyway, but even those who were (like the Marquis of Guadalest in the 1640s) were too close to the throne and too conscious of their own superior status to participate freely in a deliberation of equals. Of course, behind the scenes they pulled the strings: the Count of Anna, who played a critical role in getting the Estament Militar to agree to the expulsion of the Moriscos on 22 September 1609, and who presented the formal reply to the Union of Arms in 1625, was a kinsman of the Duke of Gandía and deeply in the latter's debt.[1]

Intermarrying among themselves and with the Castilian aristocracy, the great families had become fewer and more powerful with time, serving as a vital link between the kingdom and the court. Undoubtedly their influence was crucial in maintaining the general loyalty of the Valencian nobility to the monarchy, through ties of friendship and patronage. The ease with which the expulsion of the Moriscos was carried through is partly attributable to this Mafia network of blood ties stretching from the throne to the Estates. As we have already noted, the Duke of Lerma, the favourite of Philip III and the guiding hand behind the expulsion, was a cousin through his Borja mother of the Duke of Gandía, while his second son was married to the heiress of that other Valencian magnate, the Duke of Infantado. Infantado, meanwhile, himself a leading member of the Council of State, was kinsman to the Marquis of Guadalest, and first cousin to the Duke of Mandas.[2] Thus the family connections of two prominent members of the government covered at least five of the eight Valencian magnates, and 165,000 of the 974,565 *lliures* of seigneurial rent at stake in the eastern kingdom.

---

[1] AHN Osuna leg. 1041, Duke of Gandía to Count of Anna, 1626.
[2] On the Mendoza connection generally, F. Layna Serrano, *Historia de Guadalajara y sus Mendozas en los siglos XV y XVI* (4 vols., Madrid 1942).

The autonomous institutions of Valencia were somewhat overshadowed, therefore, by this strong courtier interest. Nevertheless, the Estates had a certain sense of their own corporate identity. The defence of the *furs* was the great rallying cry which could to some extent override sectional interests. Also, though the king was sacrosanct, the king's ministers were an easy and popular target, even among some of the grandees, and opposition to unpopular measures could often be seen as a way of undermining their authority. Basically the Estates saw their role in very conservative terms, as that of defending the traditional liberties and privileges of their members against attack.

According to the theory of the age, the king was the father of his people and only required to be informed of grievances to set them right. Hence the passionate attachment which the estates displayed to the practice of sending embassies to court. The instructions for don Cristóbal Crespí in 1626 bade him 'get into the presence of the king himself, and choose for this purpose the best and most opportune moment which presents itself, even though he should have to wait for the king and catch him while he is taking a stroll'.[1] But the Valencians were not so politically naive as to suppose that informing the king was enough. Embassies had a great nuisance value, and they persistently pursued one issue after another year after year. The Count of Gestalgar was told in 1636 not to leave court until he had got satisfaction on the conscription of vagrants for the army. If he was ordered out by the government, he was to stay in hiding near Madrid unless he was threatened with pain of death.[2]

Essentially in these circumstances the Crown had to play for time, and rely on the willingness of the Valencians not to push matters too far. For underneath all the bluster, the representative institutions of the little kingdom were not perhaps geared to sustaining a full scale conflict with the king. Though the ambassador was appointed by a small committee of *Elets*, the latter were an ad hoc junta with no long-term authority: in a crisis the ambassador would really have to refer back to the full meeting of the Estaments, with all the consequent risks of delay and division. Thus, on 1 July 1640 the *Elets* for the suspension of conscription told their ambassador in Madrid,

[1] ARV R 530 fol. 506.   [2] ARV R 538 fol. 92v.

don Jerónimo Ferrer, to express their grief at the revolt in Catalonia, but on 7 August 1640 the presidents of the Estaments rebuked Ferrer and the *Elets* for offering Valencian support against the Catalans.[1] Clearly the whole impact of the Catalan revolt on Valencia goes far beyond the manoeuvring of a handful of men, however important. But the lack of any steering committee with the capacity to speak for the kingdom as a whole was a fatal weakness in a time of crisis. Valencia lacked the instruments of defence which Catalonia and Aragon had enjoyed for centuries through the medium of the standing committee of the Estates, the *Diputació*.[2]

The great political difference between Valencia and her sister states of the Crown of Aragon – and perhaps much of the explanation of Valencia's legendary 'softness' – lies in the role of this body. The Diputació of Valencia, like the others, had originated in the fourteenth century to administer the subsidies granted by the Cortes to the Crown.[3] But unlike the others it remained to the end of its days a revenue-collecting machine without any political function beyond that of ceremonially representing the kingdom (in competition with the *jurats* of the city of Valencia) in formal expressions of grief or joy at royal marriages, births and deaths. As the Valencian Diputats had to point out time after time to ignorant outsiders, 'we do not enjoy the plenitude of power held by our colleagues of Catalonia or Aragon'.[4]

The body consisted of six titular Diputats, six accountants, three treasurers, and three general managers, all holding office for three years, and employing a staff of 76, not including workmen and musicians. The big triennial offices were shared out equally among the three estates. All the members of the Estament Eclesiàstic took it in turns to serve, or to elect representatives in the case of a cathedral chapter. In the

[1] *Ibid.*, fols. 288, 294v and 304.
[2] Cf. Elliott, *Revolt of the Catalans*, 46. The Cortes of 1626 and 1645 both asked for a small committee which could deal expeditiously with illegalities perpetrated by the government. It was eventually set up in 1645 as the *Junta de Contrafurs*, ARV R 521, cap. 4 of Braç Militar, 1645.
[3] José Martínez Aloy, *La Diputación de la Generalidad del Reino de Valencia* (Valencia 1930).
[4] ARV G 1957 fol. 85, Diputats to Prior General of San Juan, 29 Nov. 1624. Cf. ACA CA leg. 1352, governor of Valencia to king, 17 Aug. 1627.

Table 21. *Expenditure of the Valencian Diputació 1599–1626*

	lliures
Interest on debts	871,025
Embassies to court	780,782
Defence	716,779
Festivities	397,665
Salaries (including ⅔ Audiencia)	364,959
Building and furnishing	244,766
General administrative	112,051
Miscellaneous	97,059
Total expenditure	3,585,086
Total income over the period	2,357,850

SOURCE: ACA CA legs. 869 and 1353, ordinary and extraordinary expenditure.

Estament Real the four 'cities' (Valencia, Orihuela, Alicante and Játiva) and the six oldest towns took it in turns to nominate one of the oligarchy as Diputat, while another thirteen towns were allowed to join the rota for the posts of accountant. Only in the cases of the Estament Militar was there any element of competition. Here names had to be drawn by lot every three years from a list or *matrícula* of candidates holding their position for life, rather as in Catalonia.[1] But unlike the Catalan, the Valencian list was very much under the thumb of the royal authorities. For though the Estament Militar chose the people in the first instance, the names had to be forwarded to Madrid for approval. In 1608 the Council of Aragon struck off many names, 'some because they are not nobles at all, others because they are too young, and yet others because they are very poor, lawless, and not well disposed to Your Majesty's service'; in 1644 it postponed any resolution on the new *matrícula* of that year in order to see how the candidates performed in the forth-coming Cortes.[2] Rather exceptionally, Philip IV actually appointed someone to the list in 1643 entirely on his own initiative.[3] Given this degree of royal control it is hardly surprising that the Diputació remained a political cipher.

But what finished it off as a force to be reckoned with in the seventeenth century (as with so many other Valencian institutions) was financial bankruptcy (see table 21). From the customs

[1] Mateu, *Cortes Generales*, 142–4.
[2] ACA CA legs. 653 and 1355, consultas, 15 March 1608, and 9 April 1646.
[3] ACA CA leg. 884, petition of Vicente Yrles, 4 Dec. 1643.

dues voted by the Cortes over the ages for the defence of the realm and which it had been created to administer, it had an income of 92,400 *lliures* a year in the 1620s. This was roughly equivalent to the revenue of the Crown itself, and contrasts interestingly with the situation in Catalonia where the Diputació was four times as wealthy as the king.[1] In any case the original purpose for which the funds had been voted had long since been lost sight of in both countries.

Money, it has been said often enough, is the sinews of war. One might add that money is the sinews of political combativeness. Already on 14 September 1609 it had been one of the grounds of don Jerónimo Rebolledo's opposition to an embassy on the expulsion of the Moriscos that the kingdom simply could not afford it. The financial collapse of the Valencian Diputació seems to have been more serious than the embarrassments of its Catalan counterpart, where the trouble was lack of reserves for new commitments rather than an inability to meet existing ones.[2] In any case the political weakness of the eastern body invited growing interference by Philip III and Philip IV, who, from about 1606, began inspecting the books, dismissing corrupt officials, limiting salaries, vetoing expenditure, and in general conducting themselves as masters of the old parliamentary funds.[3] Without financial independence the political independence of Valencia was sabotaged from the start.

The most striking demonstration of this fact over the early seventeenth century was the way in which the kings began to legislate by decree, ignoring the traditional mechanism of the Cortes. The *asientos* of 1614 which settled the legacy of the expulsion of the Moriscos, and the reductions of interest rates to help bankrupt nobles, were all made specifically in virtue of the sovereign's 'absolute power' – though Philip III promised to seek approval for his actions in an eventual Cortes (which was never held). Protesting against the twisting of the law to help the Duke of Gandía, his creditors warned: 'any rescript or royal letter which is against the *furs* need not be obeyed,

---

[1] Elliott, *Revolt of the Catalans*, 134–5.

[2] *Ibid.*, 135–6.

[3] ARV G 1956 and 1958, king to Diputats, 13 Jan. 1614, and Diputats to king, 21 Sept. 1638; ACA CA leg. 654, consultas, 12 March 1609 and 15 Oct. 1624.

even if it is issued a second time'.[1] Such brave talk could not conceal the fact that the Cortes had been losing ground for some time in the face of the growing legislative power of the Crown. Though they were supposed to be held every three years, there had in fact been six sessions of the Cortes under Charles V, two under Philip II, and one under Philip III. A royal minister at Monzón in 1626 jotted down the reasons for this decay: 'because of the costs of the royal journey, because they take too much time, because of the importunate demands of those who attend'.[2] It is true that from the point of view of Madrid convening the Cortes was hardly worthwhile. Traditionally the Cortes voted a subsidy of 100,000 *lliures* plus 10,000 *lliures* to cover costs, the money being raised by direct taxation – 21½ parts each by the Estaments Militar and Real (with the former able to recoup half by taxing its vassals) and 7 by the clergy.[3] One-third of the subsidy went customarily in indemnifying individuals who presented grievances alleging maltreatment at the hands of royal officials. The rest would easily have been eaten up by the costs of travel, or offset against the pensions which had to be loaded onto the royal treasury in order to secure the subsidy in the first place. It is true that the Cortes of 1604 increased the grant to the popular Philip III to 400,000 *lliures* – but the concessions needed to extract it bankrupted the treasury, and to add insult to injury the full subsidy was never paid.[4]

For the Valencians, parliament was essentially a place for making 'a reciprocal and mutual contract between Your Majesty and this kingdom'.[5] In return for a subsidy the king conceded favours, privileges and new laws, which then had the binding force of a contract on both parties: such was the theory of how the Cortes worked in both Valencia and Catalonia. But some royalists took a different view, approximating the Valencian body much more to the Cortes of Castile. 'The force of law',

[1] AHN Osuna leg. 899 n. 1, petition of don Baltasar Mercader (1622?).
[2] ACA CA leg. 1353, 'tres puntos que propuse sobre Cortes'.
[3] ARV R 533 fo. 384; AMV Churat 1634 vol. III n. 129, 'recopilación de lo que importan los servicios hechos por la ciudad y reyno de Valencia desde el año 1510 hasta él de 1665'.
[4] ACA CA leg. 1352, 'minuta sobre el alcance que ay en el dinero de 1604', 28 Feb. 1628.
[5] ACA CA leg. 1357, petition of ambassador don Josef Sanz, 1647.

236 *The kingdom of Valencia in the seventeenth century*

declared one native son, 'lies in the power of the king and what he decides to promulgate, not in the petitions [of parliament].'[1] The issue had become more acute in the seventeenth century with the growing volume of legislation, which in itself reflected the breakdown of an autonomous Valencia and the increasing interference of the Crown, which the Cortes found it necessary to combat. Under Charles V there had been less than 100 items of business in any session; under Philip III and Philip IV there were between 450 and 700.[2] The sheer volume of petitions coming up from the Cortes in the seventeenth century made it very difficult for the king to give final answers (as he was supposed to do) at the formal closure of parliament. Though the junta of ministers resolved to work all night in order to finish business when the king left Valencia in 1645, they found it impossible to achieve their aim. It was not until the summer of 1647 – a year and a half after the end of the Cortes – that final decisions were taken on crucial petitions.[3] This meant that the king enjoyed the subsidy while retaining the right to modify or amend or even refuse the petitions on which that subsidy had been conditional.

Thus the Cortes were in some danger of becoming during the seventeenth century simply a device for extracting money. This change put a premium on the arts of parliamentary management on the royal side, on the technique of winning votes through fear or favour. Certainly to understand the legendary docility of the Valencian Cortes in the face of royal demands, one has to begin with the resources of patronage, far more vast than those in either Aragon or Catalonia. Money was perhaps the least important. True, Philip III gave away 33,400 *lliures* in pensions and subsidies to individuals at the Cortes of 1604 and came nearer than any other king actually to 'buying' votes. But even his purse was not limitless, and the Duke of Gandía at first refused his pension of 5,000 *lliures* as

---

[1] Mateu, *Cortes Generales*, 227–8.
[2] Dámaso de Lario, *Cortes del Reinado de Felipe IV* (Valencia 1973), xiv.
[3] ACA CA leg. 1357, consulta, 5 June 1647. Cf. leg. 1372, Tratadores to Olivares, 16 Feb. 1626, reminding him that 'by right the Cortes are not concluded nor the subsidy ratified until His Majesty and the kingdom are in agreement and the *fueros* proclaimed'. This was a constitutional theory which was being seriously eroded in practice.

being too small.[1] After his day a complete stop was put to cash grants in view of the exhaustion of the treasury. In 1626 the junta of ministers in charge of the Cortes 'refused to admit or discuss' any claims for pensions; their successors in 1645 'have very much in mind Your Majesty's orders not to forward petitions for rents'.[2] Paradoxically, therefore, Philip IV was demanding greater subsidies than any of his predecessors but without disbursing a single *sou* of his own.

Nor did the king have a great deal to offer in terms of office or employment. On 16 March 1626 the Braç Militar (as it was called in a time of Cortes) made a major demand for half the posts in the royal household to be reserved for natives of the Crown of Aragon, as well as half those in the Councils of Inquisition and Cruzada, and four in those of State and War. But Philip IV could give them little satisfaction on the issue: 'he will take care to favour the kingdom in this matter as far as possible, as he has always done in the past, as anyone can see from the examples of those who are alive today'.[3]

Though some of the bigger families did carry off spectacular prizes – the Duke of Gandía, his uncle Cardinal Gaspar de Borja, and don Cristóbal Coloma, son of the Count of Elda were appointed to the Council of State in 1630 – the mass of the ordinary nobility had to confine their ambitions within the kingdom of Valencia. Valencia remained cut off from the mainstream of Castilian political life, which was a serious obstacle when it came to providing jobs. Don Pedro Franqueza had foreseen the problem when, at a time when he was busy buying up fiefs in the eastern kingdom, he determined to establish his main household in Madrid for his descedants, 'for if they come here they can expect promotion from their kings, which would not be the case if they retired to Valencia, for the king is king of Castile and of nowhere else'.[4]

It was for this reason that the Valencians jealously guarded their own preserve. Apart from the few offices of dignity

[1] ACA CA leg. 1357, *mercedes*, 1604; Luis Cabrera de Córdova, *Relaciones de las cosas sucedidas en la corte de España* (Madrid 1857), 217–18.
[2] ACA CA leg. 1357, consulta, 12 April 1626, and leg. 1353, consulta, 14 Jan. 1646.
[3] ARV R 518 fols. 97–9, Braç Militar, 16 March 1626; *furs* 171 and 174 of 1626.
[4] Quoted in Julián Juderías, 'Los favoritos de Felipe III: don Pedro Franqueza', *Revista de Archivos, Bibliotecas y Museos*, XIX–XX (1908–9), XX, 19–20.

reserved for the sword nobility, they had one asset which was denied to their colleagues in Aragon or Catalonia – a Military Order of their own. The Order of Our Lady of Montesa was a purely Valencian institution, created in the Middle Ages out of the spoils of the Knights Templars, who played an important role in defending this frontier kingdom against the infidel. By the seventeenth century it had become a purely honorary fraternity, an exclusive club for the elite – although in principle the knights were still supposed to fulfil vows of chastity and obedience, and live a communal, monastic life in the great castle of Montesa near Játiva. Since Philip II took over the mastership of the Order, the Crown had the sole right to create knights. In addition, it distributed the thirteen *encomiendas* or benefices attached to it. Together with the three benefices of the Order of Santiago, the two of Calatrava and the one of St John of Jerusalem which were located in Valencian territory and usually allocated to Valencians, the Crown had at its disposal some 26,565 *lliures* worth of patronage before the expulsion of the Moriscos – a sum equivalent to the income of a Marquis of Guadalest or a Count of Cocentaina.

Resisting the attempt of Charles II to give the biggest *encomienda* of Montesa to the son of the Princess of Squillace, the viceroy pointed out: 'this is a very small kingdom, and its people have no chance for promotion outside it, while at home they can count on little but this sort of benefice'.[1] The *encomiendas* as such were too few in number to make much difference. But the knighthoods of the Military Orders undoubtedly provided an abundant source of cheap patronage. 'Cheap' is perhaps the key word. Juan Cascant de García turned down the offer of a knighthood of Montesa for his son, because the youth 'lives near the border with Castile, where the other Military Orders are better known and held in higher esteem'.[2] In any case, according to a list of 1642, some 62 Valencian nobles were knights of Montesa, another 18 of Santiago, 8 of Calatrava, 6 of Alcántara, and 5 of St John of Jerusalem – a grand total of 99, or roughly one in six or seven of all the nobles in the kingdom.[3] So many of the Valencian nobility, in fact, wore a

[1] ACA CA leg. 671 n. 31/2, consulta, 1 Feb. 1694.
[2] ACA CA leg. 1353, consulta, 3 May 1646.
[3] ARV R 535 fol. 321. The contrast with starved and rebellious Catalonia is staggering; cf. Elliott, *Revolt of the Catalans*, 74.

knight's tunic, emblazoned with its red cross, that Philip III
could jokingly tell mossèn Bleda after the expulsion of the
Moriscos: 'at last we have wrested the cross from the hands
of the infidel'.[1] The cross had become a chain, tying the nobles
to the throne. Philip IV gave away forty of them in the Cortes
of 1626: it was the single most numerous type of reward for
those who voted the right way in the Braç Militar.

Second to it in importance were the other dignities – the
so-called *noblezas*, or right to put 'don' before one's name,
awarded to forty members of the Braç Militar in 1604 and to
nineteen in 1626, and the precious *títulos* of count, marquis or
duke, of which six were given in 1604, eight in 1626 and four
in 1645.[2] Though there was an inflation of honours in the
seventeenth century it tended to take place mostly at the lower
end of the scale – and then usually through purchase. With
regard to titles, Philip IV always played his cards close to his
chest. In 1645 there had been seventeen claimants for the title
of count, but all but four of these were refused, avowedly so
as not to cheapen the dignity.[3] Had it not been for Montesa,
one is tempted to feel, the rewards for the Valencian nobility
would have been pretty small.

They would certainly have been too small to control the 500
members of the Braç Militar.[4] Inevitably the government
concentrated on winning the more important nobles, who could
be trusted to bring with them the support of their kinsmen and
clients for the Crown. The Count of Real came to the Cortes
of 1626, 'bringing with him several comrades who had a vote,
and they all voted for Your Majesty's subsidy'; the Count of
Alacuás meanwhile exerted his influence with 'his kinsmen and
many other persons' on behalf of the Crown.[5] Among the
private papers of the seventh Duke of Gandía are a bundle of
26 letters written to ministers and fellow nobles on the eve of
the Cortes of 1626, soliciting their support. There was a little
present of jewels for the Count of Anna to help pay the cost

[1] Bleda, *Crónica*, 980–1:
[2] ACA CA legs. 1357, 1372 and 1354, *mercedes* of 1604, 1626 and 1645.
[3] ACA CA leg. 1354, consulta, 2 Dec. 1645.
[4] There were 508 individuals listed in 1626, 550 in 1645; ARV R 518 and 521, *Habilitacions*. Another 100 or so nobles, knights of the Military Orders, were ineligible to sit.
[5] ACA CA leg. 874, petition ofReal, 14 July 1631; leg. 655, consulta (for Alacuás), 6 March 1627.

of his journey to Monzón where the Cortes were being held, with an apology that the Duke could not afford more, 'given the tightness of our family finances'; there was a note to don Jaime Sapena, reminding him of 'the bonds which have always linked your family with mine'.[1] It was by these means that a sort of party following was built up in the Braç Militar. By negotiating with the leaders the Crown could hope to hold their clients in obedience.

Yet, as the ministers reminded Olivares, 'if even one noble opposes us, we cannot settle'.[2] Ultimately there were limits to what the arts of parliamentary management could achieve. The government had to control the nobility, as well as woo them. No noble, Mateu reminds us, in his work on the Valencian Cortes, would have liked to be seen in outright opposition to a subsidy. In Catalonia they could take refuge behind the *dissentiments*, the vetos which brought the whole Cortes to a standstill. But such a safeguard did not exist in Valencia. Hence fractious nobles had to go on talking about the king's money, glancing over their shoulders at the king's ministers who were watching and listening.[3] 'I find no one who is directly opposed to making a very good subsidy to Your Majesty', wrote the Duke of Gandía in 1642, 'because on that point all are in agreement. Some have different approaches, one man seeing things one way, someone else another, but nobody is definitely opposed'.[4] The danger of 'definite opposition' was only too clear in people's minds. After the Cortes of 1626 two nobles, Guillén Ramón Anglesola and don Vicente Vallterra, opposed the introduction of the new taxes on wine and imported goods. Sealed letters were despatched from Madrid ordering them to be deposed from the junta handling the matter (to which they had been elected by the Braç Militar) and to be held at the king's pleasure in separate parts of Castile. The new taxes went ahead without their consent; within a couple of months they were broken men, pleading to be allowed to return to Valencia.[5] In

---

[1] AHN Osuna leg. 1041, copies of correspondence concerning the Cortes of 1626.
[2] ACA CA leg. 1372, Tratadores to Olivares, 16 Feb. 1626.
[3] Mateu, *Cortes Generales*, 95–6; cf. Elliott, *Revolt of the Catalans*, 220–1.
[4] ACA CA leg. 722, Gandía to king, 23 July 1642.
[5] ACA CA leg. 1352, viceroy to king, 18 July 1626, and petitions of Vallterra and Anglesola, 29 Dec. 1626.

1653 a demand for a subsidy to the Estament Militar met with the resolute opposition of the Count of Real and don Cristóbal Zanoguera. Immediately the government swung into action with the *poder económico*, ordering Real into detention in Ocaña and confining Zanoguera in the fortress of Cullera (of which he was warden), where he contracted malaria and died.[1] In the Cortes of 1645 don Juan Sanz, the ruined senyor of Alboy, had the audacity to oppose the subsidy (which he for one coud hardly afford to pay). But he was simply browbeaten into withdrawing his veto. When he tried to claim a knighthood of Montesa afterwards for his son, the Junta of ministers in charge of the Cortes commented: 'we do not think he should get it in view of his behaviour'.[2] What the Duke of Gandía called 'definite opposition' led nowhere in Habsburg Valencia.

It is against this background that one has to see the crumbling of the Braç Militar in 1626 and 1645. In both Cortes, deliberations were cut short after about a month by peremptory orders to vote the subsidy immediately. On 9 March 1626 the king told the Braç Militar he expected 'blind obedience' to his demands, as though to 'a father and a tutor, for such I am'. On the same day the Braç Militar unanimously agreed on a subsidy, 'considering...that His Majesty expressly orders them to lay aside their own judgement and opinion in the matter and serve him with blind obedience'.[3] This rather gives the lie to Escolano's notions of the free commonwealth. It was the same story in 1645. Philip IV prosaically told the Cortes that he was leaving that afternoon, 9 December 1645: 'I was waiting for your decision until midnight, and now all this morning, and still nothing has come from you – something which I would never have believed of vassals who bear me so much love'.[4] Again it was this ultimatum which did the trick.

In real terms the weakness of the nobles in the face of royal demands stemmed from their isolation. In 1645 as in 1626 they were left alone at the end of the day, face to face with the king,

[1] ACA CA leg. 580 n. 44/3, copy of deliberations of Estament Militar, 21–2 Aug. 1653, and no. 6, consulta, 3 Dec. 1653.
[2] ACA CA leg. 1354, consulta, 2 Dec. 1645. For his desperate financial circumstances, cf. leg. 885, petition, 1643.
[3] ACA CA leg. 1353, king to Braç Militar and reply, 9 March 1626.
[4] ACA CA leg. 1357, king to Braços, 9 Dec. 1645.

for the other two estates had already surrendered. Invariably the tactics of the Crown were to strike the first blows at the soft underbelly of the kingdom, its clergy and towns. As Archbishop Aliaga perceptively observed in 1642: 'the most powerful lever to use on the nobility is the agreement of the other two estates to our demands'.[1]

The Braç Eclesiàstic was always the first to yield. Mercenary considerations were not perhaps uppermost in this small body of nineteen men. In 1645 the deputy of the Orihuela chapter asked for a knighthood of Alcántara for his nephew, and the delighted junta of ministers noted on the petition: 'tell His Majesty that the Ecclesiastical Estate have not sent in a single petition to date, though they have served with the utmost satisfaction'.[2]

More of a problem was the Braç Real, augmented for the Cortes by deputies from 32 royal towns besides the city of Valencia (which however held 5 of the 37 votes). It was axiomatic in government circles that the popular assemblies of the towns would resist a subsidy, and the only problem was how to neutralize or ignore their influence. Although the assemblies approved the instructions for the deputies or *síndics*, it is not clear that they had much of a voice in electing them. In the city of Valencia the magistrates for the year were *ex officio* deputies. In Orihuela the popular assembly elected their representative, but since the assembly itself was drawn from the *insaculats* this made little difference to the type of man chosen.[3] All or most of the *síndics* in fact came from the urban oligarchies. Gaspar Pujalt, deputy for Alcira, was also senyor of the neighbouring village of Montortal; Constantino Descals of Alcoy was senyor of La Sarga; Antonio Almunia of Beniganim was senyor of Ráfol (and his descendants became Marquises of Ráfol under Charles II); Rafael Torremocha was the biggest landowner in Corbera, which town he represented in the Cortes of 1626.[4] They came with orders from their towns to procure local privileges and redress local grievances. The instructions

[1]   ACA CA leg. 721, archbishop to protonotario, 14 June 1642.
[2]   ACA CA leg. 1356, petition and endorsement, 1645.
[3]   AMO II/5/32, IIB/2/48, and III/1/4, elections of 1604, 1626 and 1645.
[4]   AMA 03/137 (Pujalt); ACA CA leg. 887, petition of Descals, 1645; ARV MR 5669 (Torremocha); ARV MR 5522 (Almunia).

from the city of Valencia in 1626 make no reference to general issues: the deputies were to look after the supply of wheat to the city from Sicily free of duty, to protect the jurisdiction of the urban magistrates against the encroachment of the Audiencia, and above all to secure an *insaculació* for the government of the city.[1] The instructions of Orihuela in 1604 have almost an isolationist tone: the city was unfairly crippled by the silk tax while other parts of the kingdom got off too lightly, and something was to be done either to give native sons a monopoly of local royal offices or a fairer chance at competition for the big ones in the city of Valencia.[2] Inevitably the oligarchies of the Valencian towns and their representatives were too closely dependent on the Crown, and too much at odds with their local assemblies to take a clear stand on the issue of a subsidy. When the Valencian *síndics* in 1626 asked their principals for further instructions on whether to accept the king's demands, they were told: 'measured against our resource, it seems too much. We would remind you, Sirs, of the trust which has been reposed in you, which you have justified so far by your upright conduct. You know what you must do; the good or ill you do your country will be laid at your door; and so whether you say yes or no may the Lord guide your judgement and your conscience'.[3] This surrender of responsibility reflects the dilemma in which the oligarchy found itself – they were dependent for their position on the king's favour.

Such opposition as did materialize came when the popular assemblies seized the initiative. This happened in the city of Valencia in 1645, when, in view of the deteriorating financial situation, the assembly refused to give the *síndics* powers of voting a subsidy. But generally it was the smaller towns, where the influence of the assemblies was greater, which showed their strength. The *síndic* of Villarreal came in 1626 with rigorous orders from his town not to agree to more than the traditional subsidy of 100,000 *lliures*. The problem was that these little communities really could not provide the leadership for a united opposition to the Crown. Villarreal (with under 500 families) was only too well aware that 'His Majesty may order by his

[1] AMV MC 152, 22 Jan. 1626.   [2] AMO 11/5/32.
[3] AMV CM 59, *jurats* to *síndics*, 4 March 1626.

absolute power that the Union of Arms be accepted', and agreed that if its deputy 'sees that so much pressure is being brought to bear that he cannot hold out, he should agree to the subsidy to be offered to His Majesty'.[1]

The first task of the Crown, in fact, was to see that the deputies came as plenipotentiaries, 'because the towns can act more independently of Your Majesty than can their deputies when they are gathered here in the Cortes'.[2] And the next step was to make sure that they could be coerced as individuals by the rewards and penalties that awaited them – personal honour or disgrace. Do not worry about what your principals think, don Luis de Haro told the Braç Real in 1626: we will 'safeguard you from any retribution'.[3]

The problem was that the *síndics* were fearfully isolated in the awesome surroundings of the church of Santa María at Monzón in 1626 or the Dominican convent in Valencia in 1645, in the midst of the court and the proud nobility of the realm. In 1626 they failed to get the Militar or Eclesiàstic to agree with them on a joint approach to the king about the question of plenipotentiary powers.[4] Left to make their own way in an unfamiliar world, they could not stand up to the relentless pressure aimed at them by the royal ministers. In 1645 they made one effort – their first and last – to combine against the browbeating tactics of the Crown. 'If any minister of His Majesty or any other person', ran one of their resolutions that year, 'tries to take any of the *síndics* out of the meeting of the Estament Real, the said Estament will not dissolve and will not take any resolution whatever until the absentee returns'.[5] This was an unusual display of unity for a body so deeply divided in its own ranks, for the characteristic feature of the Braç Real was the bitter rivalry of its members. They saw themselves not as a community, but as a chance collection of individuals, thrown together for a couple of weeks once in a generation. Their chief ambition was to catch the eye of the king, with a view to getting favours for their own little *patria* back in the sierras (and perhaps something for themselves into the bargain). In 1626

[1] AMV Cortes 30 fol. 64v, 18 March 1626.
[2] ACA CA leg. 1355, consulta, 12 Nov. 1645.
[3] AMV Cortes 30 fols. 42–3, 14 March 1626.   [4] *Ibid.*, fols. 38v, 3 March 1626.
[5] AMV Cortes 31, 14 Nov. 1645.

Játiva and Orihuela were at loggerheads over which of them should have second place in the Braç; Morella disputed third place with both; and Alcira then chipped in with a protest against them and 'anyone she can or ought to protest against'.[1] Such a fragmented assembly never presented great problems of management to the Crown.

Votes could be bought here more cheaply than in the Braç Militar. The deputy for Biar – a notary who had lost an arm in a bandit attack – was happy to get an army commission for one of his seven burdensome children.[2] True, greater efforts had to be made with troublemakers. The *síndics* of Castellón, Alcoy and Jijona, who had stood out against a subsidy in 1626, had to be bought off with patents of nobility.[3] By the time of the Cortes of 1645 the practice of selling nobility had anyway become so common that virtually all the deputies of that year were given them. To the persistent black sheep – but there were few enough of these – the Crown showed no mercy. The ex-deputy of Castellón, who held out to the end against a subsidy in 1645, was arrested in 1647 on a fire-arms charge, and his dossier carried the note: 'an inveterate opponent of Your Majesty's service'.[4] In general such strong medicine was not required. The Braç Real did not need a taste of the *poder económico* to convince it that political disobedience led nowhere.

No doubt Valencia had always been less well protected against the arbitrary power of the Crown than her Aragonese or Catalan neighbours; this was perhaps the legacy of having been called into existence by the will of a king. A land of powerful senyors and servile vassals, it had only a hazy concept of its own unity. At the time of the expulsion of the Moriscos, the only reply the Estament Militar could make was to ask Philip III 'where there was another kingdom to be conquered, so that they might live according to their station or die fighting'.[5] The leaders of this society had never really shaken off the image of themselves as a band of camp-followers round the Crusader King, Jaime the Conqueror. Racially and socially divided for

---

[1] AMV Cortes 30 fol. 4, 31 Jan. 1626.
[2] ACA CA leg. 1357, consulta, 2 May 1626.
[3] ACA CA leg. 1372, *mercedes* of 1626.
[4] ACA CA leg. 725, governor of Castellón to king, 25 May 1647.
[5] Escolano, *Décadas*, II, 786.

much of its history, Valencia had signally failed to develop a strong sense of its own identity.

To control the Valencian Estates the Crown had perhaps more in the way of patronage than was usual in the Crown of Aragon. But patronage by itself would never have been enough, even supposing that the treasury had not been bare and that the king had been more willing to give away 'toys' (titles, knighthoods and the like) than in fact he was. Nor ultimately would fear of punishment have sufficed to discipline the 500 men of the Braç Militar. Don Gerardo de Cervellón had distinguished himself in the Cortes of 1645 by his initial opposition to a subsidy, conduct which the Vice-chancellor and Treasurer of the Crown of Aragon thought merited rustication. But the majority of their colleagues on the Council disagreed: 'though he may have spoken a bit strongly on some occasions, we think this is probably because he followed his conscience, for he is a very right-living and god-fearing man, and by nature inclined to Your Majesty's service, and it would never be right that voting should not be free in the councils, meetings and the like, so long as people behave in good faith and with a clear conscience, and if Your Majesty made an example in these cases it would be very bad indeed'.[1] Officially, then, the 'free commonwealth' still survived, but on the terms laid down by Madrid. Of course the Cervellón case illustrates more than anything else that by and large the Valencian elite shared the assumptions of the king's servants. Only a little crack of the whip was needed every now and then to make them move a little faster along the chosen path.

[1]   ACA CA leg. 623, consulta, 12 March 1649.

Conclusion

'The Valencians are a kingdom in name alone and quite happy to be so': such was the opinion of a Catalan bishop in 1640, when he advised his compatriots against counting on the support of their brothers south of the Cenia.[1] Undoubtedly there were very powerful forces counteracting any centrifugal tendency in Valencia throughout the Habsburg period. The region was too closely tied to Castile by the bonds of economic self-interest to get involved in a separatist movement. After all, the Valencians could not live without the meat from the *meseta* and the bread from La Mancha (but more particularly the bread from Sicily, controlled by Castile). The coins which bought that bread also came from the Castilians, for Madrid and Toledo were always the best customers for Valencian silk. Apart from material considerations, there was a less easily definable cultural transition, best symbolized, perhaps, in the decay of the native language and the adoption of standard Spanish. The secretary of the Estament Militar noted in 1639: 'there was once a time – and not so long ago that I cannot remember it myself – when the Valencian tongue was held in such esteem that if someone began using Castilian in debates. . .he would be shouted down and told to speak his own language. But now things have changed to such an extent that Castilian is used at almost every meeting'.[2] No official pressure was ever brought to bear to produce this state of affairs: rather the demand came from below. When in 1635 the bishop of Tortosa ordered that his Valencian priests must preach in the local tongue, the *jurats*

[1] The bishop of Seu d'Urgell, quoted in F. M. de Melo, *Guerra de Cataluña* (Seix Barral edn, Barcelona 1969), 98.
[2] Marcos Antonio Ortí, *Siglo Quarto de la Conquista de Valencia* (1640), fol. 2v.

247

of Castellón appealed to the Council of Aragon. The bishop's insinuation that the people did not understand Spanish was a slur on the town's good name, 'for this is a populous place, with a lot of distinguished people living here'. Cautiously the government merely endorsed the petition: 'write to the bishop. . . .telling him to do what he thinks best in the interests of convenience and the consolation of souls'.[1]

Valencian patriotism seemed to be dead, no doubt because this was such an exceedingly fragmented society – a land of exclusive urban oligarchies and powerful feudal lords who looked to the Monarchy to safeguard their hegemony within the little kingdom. The great conflicts in Valencian history, after all, have been social: the First Germania, right at the beginning of the Habsburg era in 1519–22, when the populace overthrew for a time the clique of nobles and rentiers who governed them, and the Second Germania, right at the end of our period in 1693, when one of the most 'cowed and submissive' peasantries in all Spain (to quote the words of the Audiencia) rose up in arms against their masters. We could lengthen the list by including the attacks of the assembly on the *jurats* in Valencia city, a period of unrest bounded by the first and third bankruptcies of the Taula (1614–49) and rising to a crescendo (encouraged, however, by the viceroy) in 1646. The historical parallels here are quite clear. The Valencia of Luis Feliperia and Francisco García (two leading rebels of 1646 and 1693) resembles, not the Catalonia of Pau Claris, but the Naples of Masaniello or the Sicily of Alessi.[2] In both Valencia and the south Italian provinces there appear to have been marked social divisions, bad oligarchic government, considerable popular unrest, and a consequent tightening of the bonds of dependence of the local elites on the Spanish Crown.

A central feature of the situation in the three regions was the backing which the monarchy gave the feudal aristocracy in the matter of their debts. Examining the possibility of selling off the estates of the bankrupt Duke of Gandía, the Council of Aragon concluded that to alienate any one piece would be financially futile and that to break up the whole lot would be

---

[1] ACA CA leg. 878, petition of Castellón, 21 Jan. 1636.
[2] Cf. H. G. Koenigsberger, 'The Revolt of Palermo in 1647', *Cambridge Historical Journal*, 8 (1946); Villari, *La rivolta antispagnola a Napoli, passim.*

undesirable on political grounds.[1] As the threatened magnate put it himself in his submission to the Council, 'the holders of this title have ever been eager to lay their life and their all at Your Majesty's feet when the need arose, and it behoves Your Majesty as an affair of state to preserve this house in all its dignity and prestige'.[2] In the event Philip III and Philip IV, in varying ways and at varying times, gave the required support, not only to the Borjas but to about half the seigneurial families in the kingdom, including most of the bigger ones.

One is justified in asking what return the Crown got for its benevolence, and the answer must be: not very much. If there was ever a period when the king could have used the 'lives and the all' of his trusty fief-holders it was during the epic struggles of the 1630s and 1640s against France. Alas, as the wads upon wads of papers in the Council of Aragon make clear, the pillars of monarchy turned out in the end to be weak and ineffectual. The Countess of Cocentaina, asked to raise 100 men in 1634 to accompany the Cardenal-Infante on his march to Flanders, replied (truthfully enough) that 'she finds herself beset by so much hardship, litigation and poverty that no words of hers could adequately describe her suffering'.[3] She had to be excused. There were many variations on the pretext: some stressed that they were too old, too sick, or that they lived out of town – this was a favourite excuse in a society where living in the country was the surest proof of abject poverty. My losses in the expulsion, claimed the Count of Sinarcas (who was approached for troops in 1630) 'have made it absolutely neces-sary for me to withdraw into village life'; the baron of Bélgida, asked to serve at the front in 1640, was so poor that he 'has no option but to live in one of the villages he owns'.[4] Of course there was some special pleading here, and the Count of Sinarcas, like others, did eventually find all or part of his quota of troops. As the viceroy put it, the senyors might be poor, but they would 'attempt the impossible'.[5] The point is simply that the Crown retained a very effective lever to prise open seigneurial coffers

---

[1] ACA CA leg. 1357, consulta, 5 Nov. 1621.
[2] ACA CA leg. 1352, petition of the Duke of Gandía (1614?).
[3] ACA CA leg. 567 n. 8/11, consulta, 7 April 1634.
[4] ACA CA leg. 566 n. 7/3, Count of Sinarcas to king, 22 Sept. 1630; ARV R 534 fols. 33 ff., reply of the six knights of Alcántara, 11 March 1640.
[5] ACA CA leg. 566 n. 7/7, viceroy to king, in consulta of 27 Sept. 1630.

– the threat that the courts would be instructed to review the question of a family's debts. This was what happened to the eighth Duke of Gandía. He had been refusing to levy men in 1635 and 1636. On 29 January 1636 the cathedral chapter of Valencia conveniently reminded the Council of Aragon that a reinvestigation of the circumstances in which the Borjas had obtained their favourable *concordia* with their creditors was long overdue. The Council resolved to hold the enquiry, the Duke gave way and raised 153 men during 1637, and the enquiry was called off.[1] Financial protection was not a once-for-all gift which the monarchy had given the senyors; it was a political weapon which it could use to keep them under its influence.

Certainly the cooperation between the great feudatories and the Crown was far from perfect. There was an undercurrent of resentment in noble circles against the court – or rather against a dominant faction at court – of the kind which provoked the revolts of the Duke of Híjar in Aragon, or the Duke of Medina Sidonia in Andalusia.[2] The eighth Duke of Gandía was incensed, for example, at the imprisonment of his uncle don Melchor de Borja in 1645, and in 1651 he ostentatiously refused to greet the Queen when she came to Gandía, when he learned that he would not be treated as a grandee of the first order.[3] His more robust and spirited grandson, the tenth Duke, actually dabbled in palace revolts in the chaotic age of Charles II; he participated in the *coup d'état* of Juan José of Austria in 1677, and joined the Castilian grandees in their assumption of power in 1691. But on the fundamental issues the Borjas, like the other Valencian senyors, remained thoroughly loyal to the Crown. Separatism of the Catalan or Portuguese variety seems to have been far from their minds in the critical 1640s. In the end this was perhaps the greatest

[1] I have pieced together the story from ACA CA leg. 878, petition of chapter, 1636 and leg. 715, petition of Duke of Gandía (requesting permission for his son to marry the daughter of the Duke of Arcos), 22 June 1637, and, *ibid.*, viceroy to king, 22 June 1637.

[2] One still knows too little about these obscure affairs, but see R. Ezquerra Abadía, *La Conspiración del duque de Híjar* (Madrid 1934) and A. Domínguez Ortiz, 'La conjuración del duque de Medina Sidonia', *Crisis y decadencia de la España de los Austrias* (Barcelona 1969).

[3] AHN Osuna leg. 9 n. 11, Duke of Gandía to Duke of Arcos, 11 July 1645; leg. 745 n. 126, Duke to don Melchor de Borja, 19 June 1651.

service which they could render the Monarchy. The majority of the nobles were too poor to provide active military support on any considerable scale – in this sense all the talk of preserving the *mayorazgos* as the firmest buttress of the throne had been of little consequence. Yet their general loyalty to the king in the face of harassment, threats and even (between 1637 and 1640) the conscription of their vassals contrasts markedly with, for example, the behaviour of the nobility of the peripheral provinces of France who encouraged their peasants to resist Richelieu's tax-collectors.[1] In answer to criticism of his refusal to raise a company in 1636, the Duke of Gandía reminded the viceroy that he had allowed recruiting captains from Castile into his estates in the past, 'and if I had not given the word, no one could have recruited a man'.[2] At least here, one feels, the government was getting some return for its investment in the *mayorazgos*.

On the other hand, all the reductions of debt and sequestrations may have been counterproductive. For ultimately it was the Estaments, not the senyors, who controlled politics and the purse (such as it was) in Valencia. This was perhaps hard for a Castilian to understand. The eighth Duke of Gandía, while viceroy of Valencia for a few months in 1642, had to point out to an increasingly frantic Olivares that in a parliamentary system men had to be cajoled: 'there are so many varying kinds of person, some who do not get the point of the discussion, others who do not heed their duty to the king'. The matter would be so much simpler 'if we were dealing with persons of breeding and family'.[3] As it was, the 500 members of the Estament Militar included some pretty obscure backwoodsmen, any one of whom was capable of throwing a spanner in the works. There is no need to repeat here the way in which the cumbersome machine was made to function. But if we tended to emphasize the subservience of the Estates on earlier pages, it is perhaps time now to redress the balance a little. Certainly the Habsburgs got more out of Valencia than out of Catalonia,

---

[1] R. Mousnier, *Fureurs paysannes: les paysans dans les révoltes du XVII* siècle* (Paris 1967), 57–62.   [2] AHN Osuna leg. 1041, copy of letter to viceroy, 1636.
[3] AHN Osuna leg. 554, Gandía to Olivares, 1 June 1642; and cf. Olivares to Gandía, 6 July 1642.

but, measured against expectations, the achievements were always disappointing.

The original draft for the Union of Arms assigned 6,000 men to Valencia. On the basis of mortality rates in Pedralba as applied to the total population in the kingdom at the time, there may have been 65,103 able-bodied young men available for conscription.[1] If this figure can be trusted, Olivares' demand of 1626 would have been equivalent to putting one in eleven male adults under arms – a high proportion, which reflects not so much militarism run amok as a faulty calculation of what Valencia could be expected to contribute. In the 1630s the Crown stated that it was looking for one man from every 100 households, and in 1642, with a French invasion imminent, the Valencians were only asked for two men from every 100 houses.[2] On this basis the Crown might have hoped for somewhere between 650 and 1,000 men from the kingdom in 1626. In fact, after a month of discussion in the Cortes, the government reduced its demands very drastically to bring them into line with this reality: on 7 March don Luis de Haro in the king's name told the Braç Real that 1,666 men would be acceptable. In the end, after another couple of weeks' haggling, the Crown settled for cash – 1,080,000 *lliures*, which were reckoned sufficient to pay for 1,000 soldiers for 15 years. The sum appeared enormous to the Valencians themselves; but for the government it was disappointingly little, and had to be explained away by reference to Valencia's peculiar history of economic distress as the province most affected by the expulsion of the Moriscos.[3]

The disappointments continued. Olivares was shocked at what he called the 'paltry showing' (*corta demostración*) of the Valencians in 1642, with a French army in Catalonia hammering on their door (or so it then seemed).[4] Philip IV came to the Cortes of 1645 looking for 3,000 men a year, 'paid as long as the war lasts in Catalonia'. He had to accept a final offer of 1,200 conscripts, serving six campaigns of eight months each. Much later, in the reign of Charles II, even the spokesmen of the Estaments themselves were somewhat apologetic about 'the

[1] See above, chapter 1.
[2] ACA CA leg. 564, consulta, 10 Nov. 1638; leg. 722, viceroy to king, 25 March 1642.
[3] ACA CA leg. 1353, draft consulta, 20 March 1626.
[4] AHN Osuna leg. 554, Olivares to Gandía, 29 May 1642.

paltry little tercio' of 500 men which the kingdom gave in 1691 to defend Catalonia against the French.[1] Not unexpectedly, when the Bourbons came, they were scathing about Valencian cooperation, and spoke of Valencia as a territory which 'for all its opulence did not give a penny to the king's treasury'.[2] The comment was unfair, but it explains why Philip V took the opportunity of his victory at Almansa in 1707 to abolish Valencian autonomy.

Yet, within certain clearly defined limits, royal power was perhaps greater in Valencia than in other parts of the old Crown of Aragon. Long before Almansa, a Habsburg viceroy could write home: 'Your Majesty is master of this entire territory, conquered, as it was, by your glorious progenitors'.[3] This remark – it is unthinkable that it could have been made in Catalonia or Portugal – reminds us that Valencia owed its very existence to the will of a king, whose descendants continued to enjoy a special measure of prestige and authority. One may feel that the robe of majesty had been worn rather threadbare by the seventeenth century, as successive alienations of the royal demesne (especially during the later Middle Ages) increased the power of the feudal nobility and diminished that of the king. A man who had an income of around 90,000 *lliures* a year (counting all three royal receipts of Valencia, Alicante and Montesa) was perhaps in no position to give orders to 157 others who had 878,000. Nevertheless, I believe that the seventeenth century – paradoxically the age of Spain's decline as a great power – saw a quiet consolidation of royal authority in all the ways that really mattered, and above all in the day-to-day running of the country.

Government in Valencia was never allowed to fall, through financial weakness, out of the hands of the monarch and into those of the barons, as seems to have happened in seventeenth-century Naples.[4] No doubt the lesser military burden on the Valencian treasury, combined with the sheer poverty of many of the kingdom's nobility after the expulsion of the Moriscos, accounts for much of the difference. The balance of financial

<hr>

[1] García Martínez, *Valencia bajo Carlos II*, II, 181.
[2] Macanaz, *Relación del antiguo gobierno*, fol. 4.
[3] ARV R 593, viceroy to king, 6 Dec. 1689.
[4] Villari, *La rivolta antispagnola a Napoli*, 165–6.

strength lay with the Crown rather than the barons in seventeenth-century Valencia – exactly the reverse of the situation in Naples. By talking about 'the rule of the judges' I have tried to suggest what strikes me as the immensely ordered and immensely conservative political life which the kingdom enjoyed during this period. Policy withered away in a web of routine – a big, sticky, very strong web which caught up all the seigneurial gadflies who might have been tempted to strike out on their own. Of course, the consequence of this central position which government – or perhaps we should simply say the bureaucrats – occupied in Valencian society, was that it came to reflect the failings, divisions and shortcomings within that society. Judges and ministers succeeded admirably in taming the overmighty subject, but in doing so they created something of a power vacuum. Nobody 'ruled' in Valencia any more. The king's government remained too small in terms of personnel to take on that role very effectively. But the 'indirect' sphere of action of the bureaucrats was vast. Through their families they were in touch with the struggles for money, office and influence which occupied most of the time of the small elites in communities up and down the land, and through their official positions and their access to the ear of the king, they held enormous resources of power and patronage, which became, of course, prizes to be captured at all costs. In this very oligarchic society – 157 lay senyors, perhaps 500 nobles without fiefs and another 1,000 *ciutadans*, who concentrated economic and political power in themselves – factionalism became a disease. The king's government risked nothing, for the factions were basically working within the loose, ramshackle framework of that government and thereby paying an indirect compliment to its strength. *Mafioso* judges and ministers were as typical a feature of seventeenth-century Valencia as they have been of twentieth-century Sicily. They grow out of conditions which are roughly comparable across the ages – the breakdown of an old, feudal order of society, its incomplete replacement by a more centralised system. Habsburg Valencia was a half-finished product in transition between the medieval world and the modern.

Of course, the Mafia has also grown historically out of an

incompletely urbanized and underdeveloped economy. Valencia, potentially, with its silk, a rich agricultural area, was also one of the most violent in Spain. The patrons of the outlaws were not dirt farmers but in many cases men with commercial interests, who found it more profitable to intimidate than to invest, and easier to steal silk than to grow it themselves. The economic troubles of Valencia have, indeed, certain parallels with those in the rest of Spain – the scarcity of wage-labour as population fell, the decline of production in agriculture and the decay of native manufactures in the face of foreign competition (though the sheer severity of the demographic collapse in Valencia after the expulsion of the Moriscos tends to magnify the scale of the problems). Do they, in the end, cast any light on that old and much debated question, the decline of Spain?

The Valencian economy appears, like the Castilian, to have been overwhelmingly a subsistence economy. This simple fact no doubt lies at the root of the trouble which was beginning to afflict both of them from the end of the sixteenth century; an expanding population could not go on expanding indefinitely with traditional methods of cultivation, for the land itself was finite. The stagnation in the tithe yields from about 1580 marked the end of a cycle. Stating this Malthusian proposition so baldly, of course, tells us nothing. Was the worsening ratio of land to manpower the only factor involved? It is interesting to note the result of the cut in population, of between a quarter and a third, which occurred in 1609. Contrary to expectation it is not at all clear that the condition of the ordinary people was much improved by this (I leave aside for the moment the question of the economic damage done by the expulsion itself). The fertility of couples in the newly occupied lands of Pedralba seems surprisingly low and their mortality rather high for a pioneering community. What the Valencian evidence seems to demonstrate is that the social structure was so top-heavy, what with the exactions of senyors, *censalistas*, and perhaps above all aristocrats, clerics and lawyers who grabbed land but did not cultivate it, that little advantage could be taken of the post-expulsion opportunities. When one allows for the other exogenous factors – the weather, the plague and conscription – is not the poor state of the post-expulsion economy in large part attributable to this collection of parasites? There is, of course, the damage caused by the expulsion itself. Production and rents both fell; at least 4,000,000 ducats worth of urban investments in the rural economy were lost. All this is now beyond question. But the more interesting point, perhaps, is why Valencia proved so slow in recovering. Here it seems to me that the problems of analysis are extremely complex and force us to look at the whole structure of society. The poverty-stricken senyor, the down-at-heel *censalista*, and the man of violence dominate the history of seventeenth-century Valencia. They are no doubt themselves the product of an economy in decline; but their monopoly of power, and the way in which they abused that power, intensified the decline. Economic backwardness, an oppressive social structure and a stiflingly conservative political framework are all interlocking pieces in this puzzle.

Appendix 1

Fluctuations in the tithes 1500–1700: ACV libros de arriendo de diezmos 4388–4397

Years	(A) *Tithes of 'bread and wine'* Value of tithes	Deflated index
1501–4	14,945	28.7
1521–4	19,679	32.7
1525–8	20,312	33.3
1539–43	22,505	37.9
1553–6	43,448	57.6
1565–8	61,904	65.4
1569–72	75,745	66.7
1573–6	84,905	66.8
1577–80	93,042	62.8
1581–4	91,862	52.3
1585–8	98,422	57.5
1587–92	100,778	63.4
1593–6	104,107	59.7
1597–1600	112,620	65.4
1601–4	116,145	68.1
1605–8	114,769	67.8
1609–12	86,700	52.3
1613–16	90,033	56.4
1617–20	89,669	54.6
1621–4	86,238	53.3
1625–8	83,398	48.7
1629–32	96,027	46.4
1633–6	82,284	37.4
1637–40	85,965	41.0
1641–4	77,863	39.7
1645–8	81,745	36.9
1649–52	88,935	38.5
1653–6	90,789	44.2
1657–60	81,804	43.0
1661–4	83,931	46.1
1665–8	82,682	47.6
1669–72	82,807	47.6
1673–6	78,568	49.1
1677–80	79,053	43.9
1681–4	82,104	44.8
1685–8	84,581	54.2
1688–92	79,398	56.0
1693–6	84,755	56.7
1697–1700	100,768	61.8

(B) *Tithes of cattle*

Years	Value of tithes	Deflated index
1501–4	1,701	134.9
1521–4	2,361	163.1
1525–8	2,215	144.4
1539–42	2,437	167.8
1553–6	5,110	194.2
1565–8	4,812	176.6
1569–72	6,308	189.5
1573–6	5,586	157.4
1577–80	5,768	172.7
1581–4	4,581	147.7
1585–8	4,978	142.3
1589–92	5,591	155.0
1593–6	5,652	165.1
1597–1600	5,807	164.1
1601–4	5,848	129.5
1605–8	5,666	127.8
1609–12	3,275	83.8
1613–16	4,704	110.9
1617–20	4,489	111.1
1621–4	4,523	114.8
1625–8	4,574	103.0
1629–32	5,037	104.9
1633–6	3,711	77.6
1637–40	3,470	68.8
1641–4	3,315	67.7
1645–8	3,519	73.3
1649–52	3,461	62.4
1653–6	3,129	25.8
1657–60	3,663	31.5
1661–4	3,452	31.5
1665–8	3,179	29.9
1669–72	3,095	29.1
1673–6	3,126	31.6
1677–80	3,107	30.7
1681–4	3,322	34.3
1685–8	3,136	34.7
1689–92	2,821	31.2
1693–6	2,956	31.2
1697–1700	4,173	40.4

Quotations for mutton end at 1652. Figures for the period 1653–1700 are deflated by the General Index of Commodity Prices.

(C) *Tithes of fruits (paner)*

Years	Value of the tithes	Deflated value
1553–6	2,336	5.26
1565–8	2,884	6.35
1569–72	3,354	6.58
1573–6	4,023	7.29
1577–80	4,054	8.12
1581–4	4,506	6.57
1585–8	4,943	7.43
1589–92	5,076	9.07
1593–6	4,890	5.91
1597–1600	4,626	4.81
1601–4	5,026	6.50
1605–8	5,417	7.00
1609–12	4,841	5.89
1613–16	4,674	6.22
1617–20	4,445	5.15
1621–4	3,895	4.68
1625–8	3,912	5.38
1629–32	4,534	5.96
1633–6	4,966	6.63
1637–40	4,613	8.10
1641–4	4,141	7.03
1645–8	3,932	6.45
1649–52	4,112	6.10
1653–6	4,557	6.59
1657–60	3,853	5.44
1661–4	4,272	6.26
1665–8	4,106	6.02
1669–72	4,090	6.84
1673–6	3,987	6.16
1677–80	3,987	7.07
1681–4	4,223	8.00
1685–8	4,238	8.03
1689–92	4,216	6.84
1693–6	4,778	7.76
1697–1700	5,619	9.12

Appendix 2

The exploitation of a Valencian senyoriu: the marquesate of Lombay 1559–1700 (Figures in *lliures*, to the nearest unit)

	1559	1587	1609	1641	1700
Monopolies					
Flour mills	260	500	570	246	450
Bread ovens	84	159	234	62	224
Butcheries	70	100	100	69	160
Hostel/tavern	45	120	120	53	50
Shops	58	128	95	107	166
Gypsum mill	100	200	120	58	40
Knife grinder	2	—	—	—	—
Potter's oven	2	3	2	—	—
Fuller's earth	2	2	2	—	—
Wax mill	—	2	2	—	—
Oil press	132	19	625	336*	1,531*
Mulberry weights	—	34	—	—	34
Total monopolies	755	1,267	1,870	931	2,655
Tolls and poll taxes					
Transit toll	3	2	—	—	—
Peyta	356	430	431	55	—
Morabatí	9	—	—	—	—
Tribute (hens, Christmas present, etc.)	29	6†	28	—	—
Total tolls	397	438	459	55	—
Share-cropping					
Wheat	519	1,273	1,023‡	529	1,095
Millet and maize	554	627	716	83	178
Barley	1	7	6	1	1
Rice	18	7	—	—	—
Wine	3	2	—	21	53
Raisins	142	225	312	17	226
Figs and grapes§	37	68	68	3	—
Straw§	15	73	73	—	—
Carob§	7	8	25	71	306
Flax§	4	12	6	—	—
Alfalfa and forage	37	50	24	—	—
Beans	—	—	—	21	—
Mulberry Leaf§	180	600	600	548	1,164
Peaches	—	8	5	—	—
Green vegetables	1	1	—	19	—
Total share-cropping	1,518	2,961	2,858	1,313	3,023
Miscellaneous					
Demesne	4	29	34	—	—
Labour services	34	—	—	—	—
Property-transfer tax	58	102	130	141	126
Tax on cattle and pasture	85	200	152	77	147
Tax on beehives	4	7	6	30	29

	1559	1587	1609	1641	1700
Profits of jurisdiction	15	—	—	2	1
Interest on loan to peasants	—	8	8	—	—
Total miscellaneous	200	346	330	250	303
General total	2,870	5,012	5,517	2,549	5,981

SOURCES: 1559: AHN Osuna leg. 1027 n. 8; 1587: *ibid.* 1036 n. 1; 1609: *ibid.* 1027 n. 21; 1641: *ibid.* 897 n. 16; and 1700: *ibid.* 1021 n. 28.

A blank in the table indicates that no payments were recorded that year.

* Figures include a new share for the senyor in the olive harvest as well as traditional charges for the use of the oil press.

† Some of the hens this year were consumed directly by the senyor, and did not enter the accounts.

‡ The figure excludes the wheat of Alfarp, one of the four villages of the marquesate.

§ These crops were partly compounded for fixed cash payments before 1609.

Appendix 3

Approaches to a budget for the Dukes of Gandía 1605–99

Projected outgoings	c. 1605	1636	1699
1. *Extended family*			
Annuities to			
the dowager Duchess	5,250	6,050	2,823
Borja cadets	5,400	300	1,448
the heir (when of age)	—	—	2,844
Total extended family	10,650	6,350	7,115
2. *Religious endowments*	2,187	3,004	2,830
3. *Administration*			
(a) Salaries of agents, Valencia and Madrid	1,300	847	490
(b) Salaries of bailiffs, governors and	See item (g)	1,768	1,678
police on the estates			
(c) Bonuses to tax farmers	—	320	—
(d) Building and repair	—	300	—
(e) Quit-rents for demesne	—	300	—
(f) Commutation of tithe in Cofrentes	—	1,514	1,000
(g) Costs of running the sugar mills	9,930	—	—
(h) Litigation	—	400	—
(i) Miscellaneous	—	—	49
Total administration	11,230	5,449	3,200
4. *Debts*			
(a) Repayments of capital	—	8,000*	5,000
(b) Interest on funded debts (*censals*)	35,546	3,000	3,818
(c) Interest on short-term loans	—	116	330
Total debts	35,546	11,116	9,148
5. *Household*			
(a) Salaries of palace staff	—	1,055	—
(b) 'Clothes, shoes, stables, and	—	6,944	—
extraordinary, but not counting guests'			
(c) Medicines	—	120	—
(d) Mail	—	240	—
Total household	(8,400)	8,359	(14,356)
Total projected expenditure	68,013	34,278	36,666
Projected receipts from all sources			
	68,848	34,647	36,715

SOURCES: *c.* 1605 – AHN Osuna leg. 1033 n. 38 (no date given); 1636 *ibid.* 806, 'tanteo para la casa del duque mi señor', 1699 *ibid.* 1033 n. 48 (outgoings); and 1021 n. 16 (rents). All of these are figures for projected rather than actual expenditure; all are in *lliures*. Sums in round brackets are estimates based on minimum known outgoings.
* This figure includes 1,000 *lliures* which the Duke agreed to pay his creditors on succeeding to the barony of Cofrentes in 1628.
    A blank in the table indicates that no payments were recorded that year – except for those under the final heading, which mean that no separate breakdown of these four items is available.

Appendix 4

List of viceroys 1598–1700

Juan Alfonso Pimentel de Herrera, Count of Benavente	1598–1602
Archbishop Juan de Ribera	1602–4
Juan de Sandoval y Rojas, Marquis of Villamizar	1604–6
Luis Carrillo de Toledo, Marquis of Caracena	1606–15
Gómez Suárez de Figueroa, Duke of Feria	1615–18
Antonio Pimentel y Toledo, Marquis of Tavara	1618–22
Enrique de Avila y Guzmán, Marquis of Pobar	1622–7
Luis Fajardo de Requesens y Zúñiga, Marquis of Los Vélez	1628–31
Pedro Fajardo de Zúñiga Requesens, Marquis of Los Vélez	1631–5
Fernando de Borja Aragón, Count of Mayalde	1636–40
Federico Colonna, Prince of Butera	1640–1
Luis de la Cerda, Duke of Medinaceli	1641–2
Francisco de Borja, Duke of Gandía	1642 (March-Nov.?)
Rodrigo Ponce de León, Duke of Arcos	1642–5
Duarte Fernando Alvarez de Toledo, Count of Oropesa	1645–50
Archbishop Pedro de Urbina	1650–2
Luis Guillén de Moncada, Duke of Montalto	1652–8
Manuel de los Cobos, Marquis of Camarasa	1659–63
Antonio Pedro Alvarez Osorio Gómez Dávila y Toledo, Marquis of Astorga	1664–6
Gaspar Felipe de Guzmán y Mejía, Marquis of Leganés	1666–7
Diego Felipe de Guzmán, Marquis of Leganés	1667–9
Vespasiano Manrique de Lara Gonzaga, Count of Paredes	1669–75
Francisco Idiáquez Mújica y Butrón, Duke of Ciudad Real	1675–8
Archbishop Juan Tomás de Rocabertí	1678–9
Pedro Manuel Colón de Portugal, Duke of Veragua	1679–80
Rodrigo Manuel Fernández Manrique de Lara, Count of Aguilar	1680–3
Pedro José de Silva, Count of Cifuentes	1683–7
Luis de Moscoso y Osorio, Count of Altamira	1688–90
Carlos Homo Dei Moura, Marquis of Castel Rodrigo	1691–5
Alfonso Pérez de Guzmán	1696–1700

See Josefina Mateu, *Los Virreyes de Valencia* (Valencia 1963).

Bibliographical note

The best introduction to Valencian history is the multi-volume *Història del País Valencià* (in progress), of which vol. 3, by Joan Reglà and others, *De Les Germanies a la Nova Planta* (Barcelona 1975), covers the Habsburg period. It has a good bibliography. I have limited myself, therefore, to indicating the main sources on which I have drawn for each of the chapters in the present book.

1. Population

The basis of my study has been the parish archive of Pedralba and Bugarra, supplemented by those of Algemesí, Alicante (the two old parishes of San Nicolás and Santa María), Buñol, Cocentaina (again, two seventeenth-century parishes, Santa María and San Salvador), Chelva, Denia, Domeño, Pego, Orihuela (but only one parish, Santa Justa, of the three old ones which existed in the 1600s), Teulada, Torrente and Turís. The quality of these registers and their state of conservation vary considerably from parish to parish. A fairly correct inventory exists, *Guía de la Iglesia en la diócesis de Valencia*, Delegación diocesana de información y estadística (Valencia 1963). I am grateful to Professor Nadal's seminar group in Valencia for data on the parish of Ondara.

2. Property-holding

My information here comes from four main types of cadastral survey:
(a) Terriers drawn up by the Dukes of Gandía, the Dukes of Segorbe and the Counts of Cocentaina to validate their claim to rent.
(b) Records of the *peyta* (virtually a municipal rates system) for Castellón de la Plana.
(c) Irrigation-tax registers of Alcira and Gandía.
(d) Registers of the sale and settlement of Morisco property, after the expulsion, on royal demesne.

3. Agriculture

Tithe records constitute the heart of this chapter: the *tercio diezmo*, collected and administered directly, for a view of the agrarian structure, and the *arriendos de diezmos* or tithe-farms, for an idea of fluctuations over time. Much supplementary information on agricultural practice came from the seigneurial archives of Valldigna, Gandía, Segorbe and Cocentaina.

4. Trade

I have used all the customs registers which survive for the seventeenth century for the silk producing areas of Alcira, Játiva and Carcagente, and those of the farms of the Valencian customs. Government reports (more concerned with trade than agriculture) gave substance to the statistics. The port books of the city of Valencia have been exhaustively analysed by Richard Ling, 'Long Term Movements in the Trade of Valencia, Alicante and the Western Mediterranean 1450–1700' (University of California Ph.D. thesis 1974).

5 and 6. The Senyors

The core of my study here has been the archives of four great houses: the abbey of Valldigna (whose papers were sequestrated by the state in the great liberal era of *desamortización* in the nineteenth century, and are now dispersed between Valencia and Madrid); the Dukes of Gandía (whose family died out in the eighteenth century; the title eventually went to the Dukes of Osuna, and the papers of both, in the end, to the state); and the Dukes of Segorbe and the Counts of Cocentaina (the records of both these houses, in varying ways and at varying times, passed to the Dukes of Medinaceli, who still guard their archives in Seville). Supplementary information came from a study of the government reports on aristocratic debts after the expulsion, and from dipping into the papers of the Duke of Mandas, the Duke of Villahermosa, the Marquis of La Casta (Alacuás), and the baron of Planes, all or part of whose holdings are to be found in state archives in Valencia and Madrid. A fine new study, drawing on many of the same sources as myself, and arriving at similar conclusions, is that of Eugenio Císcar, 'Tierra y señorío en una etapa crítica de la historia valenciana 1570–1620' (University of Valencia Doctoral Thesis 1976), recently published by Editorial Del Cenia al Segura (Valencia 1977).

7. The Towns

My perspective on the troubles of municipal government in seventeenth-century Valencia comes from the local archives of Valencia city, Orihuela, Castellón de la Plana, and Alcira. These are all catalogued to the extent that they are divided into sections under general category headings, and follow a chronological sequence. I worked mostly with the documentation of the treasury (*clavería*) in Orihuela and Castellón, and with the records of council meetings and correspondence (*Actes dels jurats* or *Manuals de Consells*) in Valencia, Orihuela and Alcira.

8, 9 and 10. Government

A more exhaustive bibliography for this section will be found in my doctoral thesis, 'The Spanish Province of Valencia 1609–50' (Cambridge 1968). Essentially these chapters on ministerial recruitment, outlawry, parliaments and war are based on letters from viceroys, private petitions, and reports of the Council of Aragon, together with the official registers of deliberations of the Estates. Most of this documentation is kept in the Archive of the Crown of Aragon in Barcelona (the Simancas of the Eastern Kingdoms), and in the Archive of the Kingdom of Valencia. There is an excellent new study of many of these topics, now in course of publication, by Sebastián García Martínez: *Valencia bajo Carlos II: bandolerismo, reivindicaciones agrarias, servicios a la monarquía*, of which the second volume, of appendices, has appeared to date (Valencia 1974).

Index

267